WHY DO CATHOLICS DO THAT?

WHY DO
CATHOLICS
DO THAT?

(Formerly entitled *Expressions of the Catholic Faith*)

*A Guide to the Teachings and Practices
of the Catholic Church*

Kevin Orlin Johnson, Ph.D.

BALLANTINE BOOKS • *NEW YORK*

Nihil Obstat
Rev. Robert A. Coerver
Censor Librorum

Imprimatur
✠ Most Reverend Charles Grahmann, D.D.
Bishop of Dallas

Grateful acknowledgment is made to the following for permission to reprint
previously published material:
The Liturgical Press: Excerpts from *The Faith of Early Fathers* by William A. Jurgens,
1970. Reprinted with permission of The Liturgical Press,
Collegeville, Minnesota 56321.
Ashley Montagu: Excerpt from *The Humanization of Man* by Ashley Montagu, World
Publishing, 1964. Used by permission of the author.
Vice-Postulação de Francisco e Jacinta Marto, Fátima, Portugal: Excerpt from Sr.
Lucía's memoirs, *Fátima In Lucía's Own Words*.

Quotations from the Bible follow the *New American Catholic Edition of the Holy Bible*,
Confraternity version, Benziger Brothers, New York, 1961.

www.ballantinebooks.com

Library of Congress Catalog Card Number: 95-94537

ISBN 0-345-39726-6

Cover photo © Erik Perry/Photonica

Manufactured in the United States of America

First Ballantine Books Trade Paperback Edition: November 1995

579B86

D · O · M

To
Stanley Cisler, Sr.
Best Teacher, Best Friend

THANKS

to all of the people who helped in the preparation of this book, particularly Rev. Dennis Klemash, O.F.M. Cap., Assistant Pastor, Shrine of the Sacred Heart, Washington, D.C.; James D. and Frances Lancaster, Dallas, Texas; Rev. Andrew Ciferni, O. Præm., Washington Theological Union; Rev. Robert Coerver, *Censor Librorum* of the Diocese of Dallas; Dr. James A. Coriden, Washington Theological Union; Henry Dunow, Harold Ober Associates; Craig D'Ooge, Library of Congress; Richard Gannon, Gannon's Gift Shop, Parma, Ohio; Debbie Landrigan, former editor of *The Texas Catholic*, in which some of this material appeared for the first time; Rev. Msgr. William Lori, Secretary to His Eminence the Cardinal Archbishop of Washington; Rev. Joseph Mindling, O.F.M. Cap.; Lyle Novinski, Chair, Department of Art, University of Dallas; Rev. Msgr. W. Louis Quinn, Cathedral of St. Matthew, Washington, D.C.; Rev. Charles F. Shelby, C.M., Association of the Miraculous Medal; Mary South; Rev. Peter M. J. Stravinskas, Editor, *The Catholic Answer*; and Michael Nikonchuk, F.S.C. (*ret.*).

CONTENTS

CONTENTS

CONTENTS

SUBSTANCE AND IMAGE

How to Tell Religion from Culture

I F YOU GO TO ANY of the Church's great metropolitan shrines here in the United States—or anywhere else in the world— you'll probably see the Mass celebrated in a fairly spectacular setting. You might hear sumptuous music while gorgeous vestments and clouds of incense move against a background of paintings, sculptures, mosaics, stained glass, and walls and floors of colored marble: impressive testimony to the Church's great and ancient patronage of Christian art.

But you might also go to a Mass where there's no incense, no marble, no pictorial art of any kind. If you go to a church staffed by members of the Cistercian order, for instance, or the Franciscan, you might see only the most modest setting and the simplest possible vestments. Neither of these great orders believes in putting a lot of visual art into their churches. St. Francis of Assisi, for instance, who founded the Franciscan order, noted that they "were satisfied to remain in poor and deserted little churches," and he forbade his followers to build or accept as gifts any churches "not according to that holy poverty we have promised." The 1536 *Constitution* of the strict branch of his order, the Capuchins, added that they should "be careful not to allow any costliness, rarity, or superfluity to appear in the things pertaining to divine worship."

It's a perfectly legitimate point of view; and, like many others in the Church, the Franciscans therefore build perfectly plain buildings for themselves and concentrate their creative energies on other occupations, like missionary work here and abroad. In fact, it's not that hard to find a Mass so austere that the casual observer might guess that it's a service in a Protestant church.

But it isn't. It's the same Mass, either way. You can rest assured that the words are the same, the sacrament is the same, and the priests both received their priesthood through exactly the same ceremony, from a bishop who's the direct successor of the Apostles.

So the substance of the faith is the same either way, even though the expression of that faith is different. In America today, a lot of people who seek Christ seem to be kept away from the Church on the basis of externals alone; much of the Church's liturgy—the Church's public ceremonial acts of worship—her art, and her practices must appear uncomfortably foreign to them. But, if you talk with them about religion, sometimes you'd think that they wouldn't disagree on any basic tenet of the Faith at all.

Maybe the difficulty is that style is so important to many Protestant sects. After all, a lot of Protestant denominations separated from the Church, or from previously separated sects, on precisely the grounds of external expression. That's understandable. Whenever people are confronted with foreign styles and foreign customs, it can split the world into an us-and-them situation that keeps people from ever getting to the really important part: religion itself.

In fact, your reaction to a style of worship doesn't seem to depend on what religion you hold as much as it depends on where you came from. Most Catholics in this country came here from Italy, Ireland, France, Spain, southern Germany, and Latin America. These places were all shaped by cultures that customarily express their highest and best thought visually; they paint and sculpt and build what they feel most strongly. Most Protestants, on the other hand, came here from England, northern Germany, and Scandinavia; these cultures customarily express their highest thoughts in words and in music. It's the culture of Michelangelo versus the culture of Bach.

They've never seen eye to eye, but they owe a great deal to each other. When the Church entered northern Europe after the fall of Rome, her missionaries fostered a great flowering of native literary and musical forms that brought those arts to the notice of the whole world. For one thing, they showed people how to write things down. The first written Scots text, the first written English and German texts, are all Church documents; in fact, it was early missionaries to Bulgaria who invented the Slavonic alphabet so that the literature of that language could be preserved and turned to good use. Even the Irish didn't have an alphabet before Patrick. And the missionary monks worked out musical notation, too, so the native songs of ancient Ireland and the Frankish kingdoms have echoed through the ages in the Church's liturgies all around the world.

But the early missionaries also brought with them their own rich heritage of visual art—art that was natural to these monks but foreign to these converts, incomprehensible, even. The Protestant Reformation gathered steam, in part, because the people of northern Europe were more than willing to get rid of all of the visual art that filled their churches. (The remarkable thing isn't that northern Europeans so thoroughly swept away the visual arts of the Church but that, for so many centuries before the Church arrived, there had been so much brilliant native talent just waiting to produce the things in the first place.)

Of course, when the Protestant sects rejected the Faith's expression in the visual arts, they also rejected significant parts of the Faith itself. The important thing to remember is that the faith can be the same whether it's expressed visually or verbally.

On the other hand, one system of faith can also be substantially different even though it's expressed just as another faith is. Some Anglican and Episcopalian churches use pretty much the same kinds of vestments, the same everything, as the Church, but their beliefs are profoundly different.* Greek Orthodoxy looks exactly

---

*The Church, by the way, doesn't really have a name. She doesn't need one, because Christ didn't found a lot of churches, only one; and, historically, you have to admit that she's it. Separated sects use modifiers to distinguish themselves—the Church of England, the Lutheran Church, the First Rising Mt. Zion Baptist Church, and so on—but the Church doesn't. The word *catholic* only

like the Greek-speaking Byzantine Rite of the catholic Church, as far as liturgies, architecture, and paintings go. But they don't believe the same doctrine.

The book hopes to clarify the distinction between faith and its expression, whether that expression is visual or verbal. We'll take a look at the basics of the faith itself—without that, nothing else makes sense—and at some of the ways it's manifested in worship. We'll see how that faith shapes the lives of the people who hold it, and the things that they make to express it. We'll even look at some of the more unusual manifestations that seem to center on the Church, things like pictures that weep, or reports of the appearance of Christ, Mary, or another saint, which can be the hardest of all signs of faith to understand.

In any case, if you prefer literary expressions of faith, no one will argue with you about it; on the other hand, if you prefer the wordless expression of a painting or sculpture to the black-and-white of the printed page, that's fine, too. How you say something, after all, is less important than what you say. If the idea of Christianity is to embrace the teachings of Christ, you have an infinite range of choices of how to express that faith. And the Church, throughout her history, has encouraged the expression of that faith through the best means native to peoples around the world. "Anything in their way of life that is not indissolubly bound up with superstition and error she studies with sympathy," says the 1964 *Constitution on the Sacred Liturgy*, "and, if possible, preserves intact."

And, as we'll see, that's where much of the world's art comes from.

---

means "universal"; it was first applied to the Church by St. Ignatius of Antioch by A.D. 110 as a sign that Christ came to all people, not just Jews. Or maybe, as St. Augustine thought, it's called that because she "truly embraces the whole of Christ's truth, some particles of which may be found even in the various heresies." Today the term is used to distinguish the Church from separated sects, but it isn't part of her name. She's just "the Church", with the capital *C*.

PART ONE

FAITH

CHAPTER 1

FAITH OF OUR FATHERS

What the Church Has to Work With

THE MINUTE YOU SAY "Tradition," a lot of people think that you're talking about things like holy cards, the Mass in Latin, long-habited nuns, and fusty old priests who always said you weren't allowed to. But these are memories of culture, not faith; they're matters of *custom*, and they don't have anything to do with Tradition.

Tradition—with the capital *T*—isn't something that you do. It's something that you know. Tradition is the body of unwritten knowledge given by Christ to the Apostles and handed down by them to their successors, the Church's bishops, who teach it to everybody else. It's the first thing you have to know about the Church, because that's how it all started. After all, Christ himself

NOTE: All dates in this book are A.D., unless otherwise specified; some of the years have only three digits, while a few have only two. Also, the references to the Bible here follow the usual format: the abbreviated name of the book, the number of the chapter followed by a colon, and then the numbers of the verses. The translation followed here is the *New American Catholic Edition of the Holy Bible*, Confraternity version, Benziger Brothers, New York, 1961; it seems unsurpassed in completeness and accuracy. The chapter-and-verse references here may not match certain other translations, even approved ones, and while these others may not be exactly wrong, some strive perhaps too hard for ecumenism and may de-emphasize certain points.

never wrote a word of his teachings, and during the first couple of generations after him the Apostles converted thousands by word of mouth—by Tradition—long before the Bible was assembled (see Gal 3:2, 1 Pt 1:24–25, etc.).

The New Testament is really only one of the many products of Tradition. St. Papias, who was himself a convert of the first post-Apostolic generation, reminds us that St. Mark "was neither a hearer nor a follower of the Lord; but . . . of Peter, who had no intention of giving a connected account of sayings of the Lord. . . . Mark, then, made no mistake, but wrote things down as he remembered them; and he made it his concern to omit nothing that he had heard nor to falsify anything therein." And the so-called Muratorian Fragment, a document from the middle of the second century, notes that "Luke wrote in his own name from what he had learned when Paul associated him with himself as a companion of his journey; nor did he himself see the Lord in the flesh," which is obvious from the Bible itself. The Fragment also mentions that John's Gospel was a collaborative effort by Apostles who had heard Christ.

It's not really surprising that there would be written and unwritten parts of Christian revelation, because that's how revelation has worked ever since Genesis. The revelation to the Jews is embodied in Torah, which translates as "teaching" or "direction", and this came in two forms, too. The written part is the texts that we know as the first five books of the Bible, and then there's the oral tradition handed down among the priests and rabbis that was never written down—"the lips of the priest shall keep knowledge, and they shall seek the Law at his mouth," as Malachi put it (2:7; have a look at Is 59:21, too). Naturally, this oral deposit of faith is referred to in other Jewish writings. The Talmud, for instance, the great body of rabbinical comment on Torah, spells out more than forty definite precepts "given to Moses on Sinai" that aren't mentioned in the written Torah.

So, just as the Old Testament doesn't record every bit of God's revelation to the Jews, the New Testament doesn't embody all of Christ's revelation, either. It embodies an indispensable amount of it, of course—"ignorance of the Scriptures is ignorance of Christ," St. Jerome said, and the Church gives a resounding "Amen!" to that. But the Evangelists and the disciples who wrote Epistles made it clear that they weren't writing down *everything* (check Lk 1:1–4, 10:16; Jn 16:12–13, 21:25, Heb 13:22, 2 Jn 12, 3 Jn 13, 14, etc.). And St. Paul, Pharisee that he was, would never have conceived of Christianity as a mere book religion. He knew plenty of direct quotations from Jesus that didn't get written into the Gospels (like Acts 20:35).*

That's why the Gospels and the Epistles all assume that you're familiar with Sacred Tradition, at least in its main lines. It isn't always easy to see the relationships between the Tradition and the Bible, though; basically, the Church doesn't hold any truth on the basis of Scripture without Tradition. But then, she doesn't hold any truth on the basis of Tradition without Scripture, either.

Whichever way you look at it, you can't take one without the other because Sacred Tradition is the only source of information about fundamentally important ideas like the Trinity, which isn't explicit in the Bible. The same holds for the Old Testament, too. There are plenty of important doctrines like the immortality of the soul and the resurrection of the dead that come from Jewish oral tradition, not from the written Torah, which is why the Sadducees tried to reject those ideas (Mt 22:23, Mk 12:18, Lk 20:27). And, apart from actual articles of faith, Tradition alone sets the framework for a lot of the basics in the ways that Christians worship. The commemoration of Easter, for example, and going to church on Sundays are still part of Christian life even in the separated sects, but they come out of Tradition, not out of the Bible.

One thing about the relationship is certain, though: you need to refer to Tradition if you want an authentic interpretation of the Bible. Without reference to Tradition, you can end up taking biblical passages out of context, or, really, you can end up taking the whole Bible out of context. "This, then, you must understand first of all," as St. Peter cautioned, "that no prophecy of Scripture is made by private interpretation . . . in these Epistles, there are cer-

---

*See also Rom 10:17; 1 Thes 4:2; 2 Thes 2:14–15; 2 Tm 2:2; 2 Pt 1:20; etc., etc. Well, all of the Epistles, as well as the Gospels, tell you that the Bible doesn't contain the whole of Christ's teaching. Acts also shows the primary importance of spoken teachings (2:1–42, 8:4–6).

tain things difficult to understand, that the unlearned and the unstable distort, just as they do the rest of the Scriptures also, to their own destruction" (2 Pt 1:20).

What he means is that the Church has always relied on Sacred Tradition as the rule of faith, the touchstone that you use to test any insight, any directive, or any teaching, as well as any biblical passage (Acts 8:30–31 records an early instance). This runs along the same lines as the practices in Judaism, too, where the oral Torah served as a framework for the interpretation of the written.

(The story goes that a "heathen" came for instruction to the great rabbi Hillel, who died about the year 10, while Christ was a boy in Egypt. The heathen said, "I'll believe you about the written Torah, but not about the oral. Take me on as a convert on condition that you teach me the written Torah only." So Hillel took him on, and the first day, taught him the Hebrew alphabet. The next day, he taught him the alphabet again, but backwards. "You did it differently, yesterday!" the heathen objected. "Well," said Hillel, "if you have to depend on me to teach you the alphabet correctly, how much more must you depend on me for the interpretation of the Torah.")

There's only one Tradition, but it has a different appearance, depending on when you look at it. There's *divine* Tradition, given by God the Father before Christ's coming or by Christ himself afterward. The next phase was *apostolic* Tradition, which is the expansion of Christ's teachings given to the Apostles by the Holy Spirit (Jn 16:12–15). This is the Tradition that the Church first communicated through the Apostles' oral teaching, and it was during this phase of Tradition that the New Testament got written down. That's why we got four forms of one Gospel—the Apostles told about Christ in ways that their particular audiences would understand, and they did the same thing when they wrote down those parts of Tradition. None of the four Gospels is wrong in any way, but they sure are different. Yet they all exist against the uniform background of apostolic Tradition.

The third phase of Tradition resides in the living voice of the Church, which comes to us now through the bishops as the successors of the Apostles who are entrusted with preserving and spreading the teachings of Christ, guided by the Holy Spirit to protect them from error (Acts 13:1–12, for instance, or 2 Tm 1:6–14. Or, as St. Hilary of Poitiers put it, back in 357, "The Lord has not left this in uncertainty"). This *ecclesiastical* Tradition is embodied in preaching, in the instruction given to children and adult converts, and in other person-to-person communication. It was through ecclesiastical Tradition that the Bible was put together, and it's always been of primary importance in the life of the Church. St. Papias recalled that "when anyone came along who had been a follower of the Apostles, I would inquire about the Apostles' discourses: what was said by Andrew, or by Peter, or by Philip, Thomas, or James. . . . It did not seem to me that I could get so much profit from the contents of books as from a living and abiding voice."

Still, there's a definite change in the character of Tradition since the death of the Apostles. They had a unique relationship with Christ, and by the time the last of them died (John, in about the year 70), the revelation given by Christ was complete, and so was the revelation given by the Holy Spirit. So there's no way that anything can be added to the deposit of revelation since then. And there's no way that anything can be dropped, either. Apart from the guidance of the Holy Spirit, which is understood as guarding the Church from error, there's simply no mechanism in the Church for adding or deleting anything. The whole hierarchy of Pope, bishops, councils, and congregations is set up to do just the opposite, to keep any innovations from slipping in or any precept from slipping out, and they've always done a superhuman job of it.

But even though Tradition can't change, our knowledge of it can grow, and that's what ecclesiastical Tradition is for. It works sort of like the natural sciences, you might say. The material universe rolls along in the same way from age to age, but we can learn a lot more about it through astronomy, chemistry, physics, and the like, as we go along. In much the same way, the whole mechanism of grace and salvation, the priesthood, the Ten Commandments, and every other part of Christianity all existed from the beginning in the mind of its designer, and it never changes. But our understanding of it grows steadily because Tradition unfolds as the Church faces new situations.

Or you might compare it to the way chemicals crystallize. You start out with a given amount of certain elements mixed in solution, but, as time goes by, one atom after another takes its place in the larger pattern of a crystal. Over time, although no more elements are added to the solution, and although it isn't diluted, the cloud of elements in the solution gradually takes on a more definite, more orderly, and clearer form that catches more of the light.

That's why you can't just write Tradition down and be done with it. Tradition is the living presence of the Holy Spirit in the living Church, and you can't capture that on paper. Situations change, cultures change, empires rise and fall; you need the constant presence of the institutional Church to touch base with, a rock against the constant ebb and flow of human affairs. You need a reliable mechanism to articulate Tradition when you have questions about good and bad, about truth and heresy, about right and wrong. The Church does this for you, and she's done it consistently since apostolic times.

You can see the consistency in the Church's transmission of Tradition right from the start. "What they found in the Church, they kept," St. Augustine said. "What they learned, they taught; what they received from the Fathers, they handed down to the sons." And they wrote about it, too, just as before, so there's plenty of documentary evidence. There's *patristic* writing, for instance, the work of the Fathers of the Church, that ranges from the writings of the first-century pope St. Clement of Rome to those of St. Isidore of Seville six hundred years later, from the *Letter of Barnabas* to the eighth-century homilies of St. John Damascene. These writings come to us from different countries, different cultures, different centuries. Their authors were some of the most intelligent people who have ever lived, and they had some of the most definite personalities—however saintly they were, there were curmudgeons among them. They disputed, they squabbled, and they practically brawled with each other, sometimes. Some of them (St. Jerome, for one, and, yes, even St. Augustine himself) weren't above insult, and they usually got insulted right back.

Now, it's not that the Fathers legislated; the Church isn't bound to follow what any of them wrote just because a recognized Father wrote it. Instead, the Fathers derive their authority by conveying revealed Tradition intact, and they incidentally supply plenty of documentary evidence that the Church has always done so. It's also true that, as private teachers, the Fathers can make mistakes. That's what makes it so exciting to read through collections of their writings, like the series put out by Father Jacques-Paul Migne during the last century. You can watch Tertullian slip gradually into the heresy of Montanism, for instance—the Montanists thought themselves a spiritual elite directed by the Holy Spirit, charged with the purification of the Church and supercharged with all kinds of spurious spiritual gifts, full of new revelation. But you can also watch the other Fathers, Jerome, Origen, Clement of Alexandria, Epiphanius, and the rest, all rallying to set the record straight, and in no uncertain terms. "What more perverted notion could be expressed?" snorted Augustine. "But it's not surprising that Tertullian could dream up such an idea."

Yet, on matters of faith and morals, the Fathers speak with an almost miraculous unanimity, bearing witness to the same Sacred Tradition. They had to be tough about it, sometimes, because it was up to them to refute all of the heresies that cropped up during the early centuries of the Church's life.

(In fact, they've already taken care of the things taught today by separated sects, which are all *neo*-something, the repetition of some old heresy that goes officially by a tongue-twisting name. Some of the knockers at your gates say that Christ came as a visible spirit to teach humans the difference between the kingdom of the light and that of the dark, which is nothing other than Neo-Manicheanism, the original form of which was annihilated by Augustine after his own conversion. You may also run into Neo-Arianism, which asserts that Christ was not truly God but only a creature. Or Neo-Nestorianism, which teaches that Christ had two separate personalities, the divine joining the human after his birth. Or just the opposite, Neo-Monophysism, which holds that Christ had only one nature. There's also a great deal of Neo-Antinomianism, teaching that salvation is by faith alone; Neo-Gnosticism, believing in a secret "underground church" that keeps Christ's "real" teachings; and Neo-Albigensianism, denying the sacraments and the hierarchy—both of these last are especially prevalent today in the southern United States. You'll also find outcroppings of Neo-Catharism, a kind of Albigensianism that takes particular exception to infant baptism, Neo-Pelagianism, which says that grace doesn't initiate a good work but only perfects it, and plenty more. Even Neo-Montanism shows up these days, and where you'd least expect it. And of course they all interpret the selfsame Bible as proof of their creed.*)

Well, things have quieted down considerably, since patristic times, but Tradition still speaks in some ways that may surprise you. It comes through in the Mass because that's where Scripture is interpreted in its original setting, read and explained to the faithful at large, assembled in community worship. Through the Eucharist—the sacrament of communion that is the centerpiece of the Mass—the liturgy embodies Christ's life, death, and resurrection, no less than his teachings; the Mass is where Christ speaks and acts among us today, reaffirming the New Covenant for each of us.

But this communal property of the Mass means that Tradition also works through the laity, through the ordinary people who respond to the Church's teaching and pass on the Faith generation upon generation. Individually, we might not be particularly aware of our role as transmitters of Sacred Tradition, but collectively we actually focus it and make it a lot clearer. "As their consciousness of a Christian truth develops, they express this awareness with a living practice," said Vatican II, and the Church always keeps a sharp eye on what the laity's up to, as a whole. For example, some important aspects of the Marian mysteries were first articulated by the laity, just by the consistent strength and coherent development of Marian devotions around the world, and these expressions of faith ended up guiding the Church as a whole.

Of course, it's not a matter of voting, or of our own little

---

*Heresy is the willful denial of any of the truths of Christianity, but it's got to be willful. It probably can't be counted willful if a person's sincerely seeking Christ but is misled by well-meaning friends. Or, as St. Augustine said, those who received an heretical creed from their parents "are by no means to be counted among the heretics". Vatican II reaffirmed the definition: "one cannot charge with the sin of separation those who at present are born into these communities and in them were brought up in the faith of Christ, and the catholic Church accepts them with respect and affection as brothers".

bunches of Pharisees and Sadducees espousing a cause, rejecting a teaching, or—God forbid—coming up with an innovation. The evidence from the laity at large has to be examined to see if it has any substance, and it has to be focused and defined by constituted authority. Again, that's where the institutional Church comes in, as the guardian of Tradition.

But the Church doesn't stand between Tradition and the rest of the human race like a filter, letting only some of Christ's teachings through. She works more like a lens, focusing here or there as needed, to illuminate shadows wherever they fall. The light that shines through her is always the same. After all, that's the nature of Tradition. It isn't a matter of your own opinion that you stubbornly stick to no matter what anybody says. Tradition is the teachings of Christ that you stubbornly stick to, no matter what anybody says.

CHAPTER 2

FEED MY SHEEP

How the Church Makes Laws

ELEVISION REPORTER recently asked a Vatican official about the Church's stand on birth control. "If the Church is going to have a place in America today," she asked, "why don't you just change your ruling on birth control? You changed your ruling about taking interest on money."

It's a faulty analogy, on more than one level. For one thing, the Church has never objected to the principle of interest (no pun intended). There are some biblical warnings against taking payment for a loan, but they refer to an entirely different matter. In the ancient world, there were banks (see Mt 25:27), but the idea of debt was abhorrent. You borrowed money because you had to, because your crops had failed, maybe, and you needed the money to keep yourself and your family alive.

But nowadays, you usually borrow money because you want to buy a new car or start a business or something. The lender offers you the use of his money—his property—and has every right to expect payment for it. He's renting you his money, you might say. If the lender asks too much for it, you can go to someone else who asks a lower rate. As long as you have choices at every stage of the transaction, there's no moral objection to interest *per se*. Still, if you need money to live because of some catastrophe, and somebody takes advantage of your emergency by forcing you to pay for a loan instead of offering outright charity, or charges unfair interest in any circumstances, that's *usury*, which is and always has been morally offensive to Christians. And the Church's regulations on usury have never changed.

The reporter's analogy doesn't hold in a larger sense, either, in the broad view of how the Church formulates and maintains her teachings. It's not generally realized in this country that the Church *can't* change her rulings on birth control, nor those on usury. In fact, the Church has never changed her ruling on *anything* pertaining to faith and morals.

That's hard for an American to understand. We're used to running things with a Congress that can make or repeal any laws it wants, and a Supreme Court that can interpret those laws any way it likes, regardless of precedent. We even see some religious denominations meeting in convocation to vote on what they're going to believe about Christ and what they aren't. But the Church doesn't run like that.* And her unique character is reflected in her laws and customs.

To understand this character, you have to step back and look at religion as whole. Some religions are assembled piece by piece over the years by people who observe the workings of nature. Hinduism is one such religion, as are the animal-based or spirit-based religions of North American native cultures or those of Africa and the Pacific Islands. These *developed* religions continue to evolve and change, sometimes adding new gods to their pantheon

---

*The mistaken idea that the Church can change doctrine as Protestant denominations do is widespread, but it isn't new. Back in 1850, an Anglican canon of Durham, one George Townsend, D.D., was deeply frustrated by the scandalous division of Christianity and couldn't see why the Pope didn't just repeal all of the Church's teachings that differed from the Anglican—just as, the Canon said, the English Parliament would change any law that was no longer convenient. Obviously, he figured, that would reunite the denominations instantly. Townsend bustled off to Rome to explain this clearly to the Pontiff, and he was attentively received by Pius IX (who thought him "an excellent and a good man" and gave him a forty-minute private audience), but for the rest of his life he could never understand why his "sensible" proposal wasn't acted upon. Townsend's account of the adventure, *Journal of a Tour in Italy in 1850*, is endearing and incredible at the same time.

or even absorbing whole other religions when new tribes move into the region.

Some other religions are based on the ideas of a single teacher, as Buddhism is, or Confucianism. As times goes on, and as the religion moves into new territories, other teachers add to the original body of doctrine or change it to accommodate different beliefs. Or, more usually, they produce new writings under the teacher's name but adapted to a new social situation. After a few hundred years, usually, nobody can tell with any certainty exactly what the teacher said in the first place.*

But Christianity is a *revealed* religion. So are Judaism and Islam. They claim to have been designed in the mind of God, as a whole, and given to humans one way or another. Mohammed said that the angel Gabriel came to him and dictated Al-Koran to him word for word. Moses, Abraham, and the other fathers of Judaism received the Old Covenant from God, often by speaking with him directly. And, through the prophets of the Old Testament, God revealed his plan of salvation to people and then came as Christ to reveal the culmination of that plan. But the plan itself, in a revealed religion, doesn't change. Once you get a body of divine revelation, human beings can't add to it or take anything out, or the rest of it doesn't make any sense. A revealed religion is a sort of package deal. You have to take the whole thing or leave it.

You can see this in what Christ said when the time came for him to ascend to Heaven again. He gave his Church a unique mission: "Go, therefore, and make disciples of all nations . . . teaching them to observe all that I have commanded you" (Mt 28:19–20). That's a very specific order: he didn't say, "tell people about me in any way you think right" but *teach them to observe all that I have com-*

---

*Just a few years ago, for instance, archæologists in China unearthed a silk manuscript of the *Tao Te Ching* by Lao-tzu, the centerpiece of Chinese religion and thought. This unique discovery let scholars reconstruct something closer to the original text, which lots of different sects and cults had "improved" out of existence during the past two thousand years to make it fit their own predetermined beliefs better. But no comparable early version of the teachings of Confucius or the Buddha has come to light, so we're left with all the various "improvements" in those cases. Each sect still has its own version of these teachers' doctrine, and they're all different.

manded you. It means that the Church has to stick with precisely what was revealed, never to alter it—which no human has the power or authority to do, if you believe that Christ is the Messiah.

Keeping a body of teachings intact is evidently beyond the power of human beings by themselves. It's never happened for very long, except in Judaism and Christianity. But the preservation of the teachings has always been of paramount importance to the Judeo-Christian tradition: "This is my covenant with them, said the Lord: My Spirit that is upon you, and the words that I have put in your mouth, shall not depart out of your mouth, nor out of the mouths of your children, nor out of the mouths of your children's children, says the Lord, from now until forever" (Is 59:21). Christ reiterated the promise, too—see Jn 14:25—another guarantee that the Church wouldn't lose the revelation that he suffered and died for.

So, in the Church today, you have an unchanged body of teachings, the deposit of revelation, to start with. Principles of conduct are either consistent with this revelation or they're not. Once the Church has stated a ruling based on that revelation, that's it; the teaching can't change later, no matter what the social pressures might be.

(And, when you think about it, to which society should the universal Church bend? Twelfth-century Armenia? First-century Rome, during the persecutions of Nero? Twentieth-century America? Eighteenth-century France? Third-century Syria? No. The universal Church would never have been able to preserve Christ's teachings had she changed whenever her ideals didn't match those of a particular secular culture.)

This means that the Church makes regulations about faith and morals just the opposite from the ways that secular governments make laws. Our congresses and parliaments react to new situations by making new kinds of law, but the Church reacts to a new situation by articulating the Gospel in light of that situation. The Church never innovates or invents; she just articulates. Her pronouncements about faith and morals are not just arbitrary matters of "Thou shalt not", still less matters of personal opinion of the hierarchy; they're simply logical statements that certain ideas and acts are incompatible with Christianity.

And the more you know about Christianity, the more reasonable the rulings seem. After all, the hierarchy doesn't sit around making up nit-picky rules like the one about whether idly chewing a blade of grass violates the Eucharistic fast. These rulings happen because somebody asks about the matter, and the hierarchy is obliged to give an answer consistent with the Deposit of Faith, no matter how silly they may feel about the case in question. Usually, they express general principles in response to specific questions, as Christ did (Lk 12:13–15). So you need to study any ruling that's hard to understand at first, but in the long run this clears up a lot of things, because you learn the principle.

And the principle remains the same through many articulations, even though each pronouncement is couched in language that people in that particular time and place will understand. This continuing process of clarification—not change—has always been the Church's way. The Epistles were written like that, in response to some specific difficulty that had arisen; people started misinterpreting a point of doctrine (or whole lots of doctrine, as they were doing in Corinth before the ink was dry on the New Testament), and they needed a direct and clear statement of faith and morals as relevant to their case.

You can see this same kind of crystallization in canon law. (*Canon* is from the Greek word meaning a ruler, like the ones that nuns use to keep your attention in grade school. It means a standard, either a law or a definitive list of parts of something, like items in a code of law or the books of the Bible.)

Canon law gives guidelines for actions, not for beliefs. It has to do with the management of the institutional Church, not with faith and morals, which are embodied in the Bible and dogmatic documents of the great councils and the popes. For the mechanics and rationales of public worship and the sacraments, there are liturgical books (*ordines*) that give participants proper words to say and direct their actions, and that give full explanations of liturgical rules.

For the basic regulations, there are the Six Commandments of the Church (those are easy: assistance at Mass and rest from servile labor on Sundays and holy days of obligation, fasting and abstinence as directed—but note that the details of this are left open to change—confession at least once a year if your sins are serious, reception of the Eucharist at least once a year during Easter season, adherence to the Church's rules on marriage, and support of the Church according to your means—no one shall come before me empty-handed, as it says in Ex 34:20).

All of these kinds of regulation are closely interwoven, but canon law as such confines itself to what you call the *discipline* of the community of the faithful in its public life. It doesn't try to judge or compel anyone's personal conscience.

Canon law is as old as the Church. The disciplinary decrees of the popes (the *decretals*) are one important source of canon law, and they came about much as the Epistles had, prompted by specific questions or problems but understood as binding expressions of the universal Church's uniform practice—again, they deal with the application of principles. There are also local written records of custom, and these too were set down, beginning very early in the Church's life, to establish usages against innovations and improprieties. And, also very early on, bishops of a certain region or province began having more or less regular meetings, getting together to address general crises or just to keep things running smoothly in general. The first ecumenical council (one that included all Christian bishops) was held at Nicæa in 325. It established the Nicene Creed, a standard statement of Christian faith that was needed to distinguish the Faith from certain heresies that had arisen, but it also set forth matters of discipline: things like clerical celibacy and the rules about the ordination of bishops that have remained the same until today.

Over the next thousand years, the Church made collections of decretals, but it was hard to keep up. In 1500 six previous collections were published together in a collection of collections, the *Corpus Iuris Canonici*—literally, the *Body of Canon Law*. This was the main source of Church regulations for the next four hundred years, but it was unwieldy, to say the least. A good percentage of the questions that it answered had come up once upon a time and never again, and it addressed perennial questions in little pieces scattered throughout the volumes. The great jurists of Christendom indexed it six ways till Sunday, but you still couldn't easily find all of the regulations on whatever question you had. And even if you did track down all of the references to a topic, they could seem ambiguous or contradictory. Of course, the jurists themselves knew the material forward and backward, and they knew how to get behind the items to the principles, but a browse through the old *Corpus* really gives you a healthy respect for their scholarly stamina.

Fortunately, one of the world's great reformers became Pope in 1903—St. Pius X Sarto. He had pretty well had it with the impenetrable tangle of the old *Corpus*, and the first thing he did when elected was order the "collecting of the laws of the universal Church, in a clear and concise order, and adapting them to the conditions of our time." Keep in mind that they could be adapted to the times because they don't directly touch unchangeable faith and morals, and that he meant by that phrase that they should address twentieth-century questions uniformly.

So St. Pius X and his canonists sorted through two millennia of incredibly complicated material. They threw away a lot of obsolete laws, brought other partial laws together into single canons, and smoothed out ambiguities, rewriting the canons in a subtle and precise style that sets a high standard for anybody's legislation. They extracted overall guidelines and grouped the laws by subject. That way, the law could anticipate questions that would arise in the future. They got the job done in only about ten years—you get the impression that they'd all been chomping at the bit for some time—and, in 1917, the Pope promulgated the new *Codex Iuris Canonici*, the *Code of Canon Law*.

Old habits die hard, though, and in just a few years the *Code* had picked up all kinds of additions. They were necessary, but they were contrary to the whole point of having things codified. John XXIII Roncalli saw that things were on their way to confusion again, and he ordered a renovation of the *Code* in 1959. This update took longer than the first codification, from then until 1983, because it was part of the overall reforms of the Second Vatican Council, but it got all necessary regulations down to 1,752 individual canons. It sets the precedent that you need to update the *Code* every fifty years or so, and it sets the standard for future renovations; it's concise, clear, and consistent, and it's very easy to use.

You can carry the whole thing in your pocket, yet it governs a church of eight hundred million.

All of these sources together—canon law, liturgical books, and the rest—give you a fair perspective on anything that looks like a change in the Church's way of doing business. The next time you have a question, look it up. And next time you hear a reporter ask one of those ill-informed questions, call the station.

CHAPTER 3

CHAPTER AND VERSE

The Hard-Fought Genesis of the
New Testament

T HE FIRST THING you might notice about the Mass is that it has such a biblical ring to it. The readings from the Epistles and Gospels, the Lord's Prayer, and the greatest prayer of all, the consecration of the Eucharist, are all familiar passages from the New Testament. But it's surprising to remember that the Church was saying those words for nearly four hundred years before there was anything like a Bible at all.

Of course, Christ himself never wrote a word of Scripture, and he never told his Apostles to write anything. But he was just about the only great religious teacher of the time who didn't. All of the other religions of the time had their sacred scrolls or books of secrets, and people in the Roman Empire generally took it for granted that a religion would be encapsulated in an official holy book.

So, as Christianity exploded out of the Holy Land, dozens of writers rushed to cash in on the immense market for books about Christ. Suddenly there were scores of books of the best-selling type, novels and apocalypses and the like; a few of these resonated with genuine Christian doctrine, but none taught it properly. There were also stacks of less-than-reliable books like the *Acts of Paul* or the *Acts of Pilate*. And there were any number of books by misguided or hostile writers, forgeries and fabrications that included pagan fables disguised as Christian doctrine, outlandish miracles attributed to Christ (some of which reported him exterminating bad little children with a glance), and other wholly objectionable material, often mixed in with scraps of genuine Christian teachings.

None of these books was ever taken seriously by the early Church, and the really bad ones were condemned officially by the bishops.* But at least these bad books prompted the creation of good ones to reinforce the Church's oral teaching of Sacred Tradition. "Inasmuch as many have undertaken to draw up a narrative concerning the things that have been fulfilled among us," as St. Luke says, "I also have determined . . . to write for you, Theophilus, an orderly account, that you may understand the certainty of the words in which you have been instructed."

Still, only five Apostles (Matthew, John, James, Peter, and Jude) wrote any part of the Bible; and, like Mark, Luke, and Paul, they wrote whenever problems came up, either to assist people's memories or to address specific questions, just as the Church pronounces doctrine today.** None of them ever intended to produce a complete written account of Christ's teachings; such a thing is not possible, given the nature of living Sacred Tradition and the extent of what Christ did and said during his ministry (Jn 21:25).

*Even today, a few of these truly bizarre books survive, and some academic-sounding authors still try to use them to "expose" Christianity as a garble of everybody else's old myths. Somehow they always fail to mention that the Church has insisted from the first that these spurious texts have nothing to do with Christianity.

**Lk 1:1; see also Rom 15:15; 1 Cor 5:1–5; 2 Cor 2:3–11; Gal 1:6–20 (and 3:1); Col 2:4–23; 1 Thes 4:1–12; 2 Thes 2:5; 1 Tm 1:6; 2 Tm 2:14; etc.; other Epistles, like Ephesians, Philippians, Titus, and Philemon, as well as those of Peter, John, and Jude, clearly imply what the problems were. It's also interesting that the Apostles claim divine authority when they speak (Acts 2:14–18, 4:19–20, etc.), but they don't when they write. The living Church, as Paul wrote (1 Tm 3:15), is the "pillar and mainstay of the Truth", not anything written.

Beginning just after they were written,* these books were read in the assembly of the Eucharist, just as they're read at Mass today. Writings from around 100 show that the unsurpassed quality of the fourfold Gospel was already recognized, but any number of other books were also read at Mass, different ones in different places, at the discretion of the local bishop. There was evidently some standard of doctrinal purity imposed, but nobody saw much need to work up an official "canon" or exclusive list of books acceptable for reading at Mass.

But then, in about 140, a man named Marcion started teaching that the Apostles had misunderstood Christ completely and that only Paul (sometimes) and he himself (always) got it right. To support his heresy, he told his followers to use only ten of the Epistles of Paul—to each of which he added his own "prologue"—and St. Luke's Gospel, which he considered the only genuine one, for some reason. Marcion "moreover mutilated the Gospel according to Luke," St. Irenæus says, "removing all that is written about the generation of the Lord; and he removed much of the teaching of the Lord. . . . He convinced his followers that he himself was more truthful than the Apostles who have handed down the Gospel; and he furnished them not with the Gospel but with a small part of the Gospel."

This naturally upset a lot of people—St. Polycarp of Smyrna so far forgot himself as to call Marcion "the first-born of Satan", to his face, because he had chopped up the holy books that way. To clarify things, the Church fathers put out a universal canon of the New Testament, including twenty-two or twenty-three of the twenty-seven books now in the New Testament. (The Muratorian Fragment, a text recovered in Rome in 1740, is a copy of this canon; it lists the books and gives a little explanation of where and how each book was written.)

There was still a considerable gray area, though. In some parts

---

*It's easy to get a heated debate going about the exact dates, but Matthew, the first of the really good books, dates from about ten or twelve years after the Resurrection. Mark dates from about 60. St. Luke's Gospel and his Acts of the Apostles from before 63; St. Paul's Epistles date from about 52 to about 68. St. John's Gospel was written only a little later, and his Apocalypse was apparently around 70.

of the Christian world, books like the Epistles of St. James and St. Jude, 2 Peter, and 2 and 3 John were accepted as Scripture, but in others they weren't. There were still questions about the epistles to the Hebrews and to Philemon, too. And there were bishops who thought that, genuine or not, some of these writings just weren't vitally important. Besides, there were still no fewer than fifty other "gospels", lots of other apostolic epistles, and hundreds of apocalypses, including the one by St. John: they had never received an official approval, but was it all right to use them liturgically or not?

Again, it was a crisis that prompted the definitive answer: in 303, the Emperor Diocletian decided to stamp out Christianity. Assuming that anybody who founded a new religion would write down everything that he had to say, Diocletian went about it by destroying Christian books, and he used torture or execution to get them. Christians had an advantage because the police weren't completely sure which books—if any—were really important to Christianity; but then Christians couldn't tell where to draw the line, either. Which books could you give up with no great loss, and which were worth dying for?

As soon as the persecutions died down, the Church began to settle the canon once and for all. All of her great scholars concentrated on the question as never before, and by 367 St. Athanasius of Alexandria published for the first time the definitive list, including all twenty-seven books that we know today. These are the ones, he said; "let no one add to them or take anything away from them." Athanasius's canon was widely accepted almost immediately (although 3 Corinthians kept showing up for a surprisingly long time). It was adopted by Pope St. Damasus I in the "Decretal of Gelasius" in 382, and it was confirmed by every subsequent council that took up the question. Finally, in 419, the Second Council of Carthage again confirmed the canon, and this time Pope Boniface promulgated it officially. The New Testament as we know it today was born.

Meanwhile, in the deserts around Bethlehem, St. Jerome was doing a standard Latin edition of the books in this canon. His version, the *Vulgate*, is still the Church's standard Latin Bible; it was this version that the Church took into northern and eastern Europe during the great age of monastic missions. After that, the story of the Bible is a story of language. The first things written in many modern languages was often the Bible, or at least the Gospels—that's where written Slavonic, Gælic, and even German came from.* The first Bible in an English language (Saxon) seems to be a seventh-century translation by a monk named Cædmus, and a hundred years later the Venerable Bede started another but died before he finished it. King Alfred the Great may have planned a contemporary English Bible; he started a translation of Psalms, but he too died before he got it done. Fortunately, other translators were more durable, and there were plenty of English-language Bibles available in every century.** Through all of these vernacular Bibles, you can see our modern languages taking shape. Even things like putting a space between words, making capital and lower-case letters, and using punctuation got their start in the making of Bibles.

In fact, nearly all of the books of the Middle Ages were Gospels or complete Bibles (the word itself, after all, is from the medieval Latin *Biblia*, which means simply "the books"). Every church had to have at least one Bible for the Mass readings, and most had an extra or two in the public space of the church, chained down the way we chain down directories at public telephones now, and for

---

*The oldest German document of any kind is a translation of the Bible done in 381 by a monk named Ulfilas; he translated it into Gothic, which is what German was back then. You often hear that Martin Luther was the first to liberate the Bible from the Church's grasp and give it to a Scripture-starved people, but that's obviously nonsense. Since Ulfilas, there had been more than a thousand years of manuscript German-language Bibles, and at least twenty-one *printed* German editions (by Cardinal Gibbons's count) before Luther. And, as we'll see, Luther had other reasons for doing his own version. For more on the Vulgate, see the following chapter; for more on early European missions, see chapter 17.

**There were too many others to cite here; in fact, the preface of the first King James Version gives an almost exhaustive list. But early Protestant versions in England weren't so much translations of the Bible as wildly inaccurate variations, like the "Wicked" Bible that commanded "Thou shalt commit adultery" and the "Murderer's" Bible that gave Mk 7:27 as "But Jesus said unto her, let the children first be killed." The one by William Tyndale was so bad that even Henry VIII called it "crafty, false, and untrue" and ordered that it be "utterly expelled, rejected, and put away out of the hands of the people." Then, of course, Henry had his own innovative version written.

similar reasons: so that anybody could use it and nobody could steal it.*

And evidently everybody really did use it. The Bible was the whole context of daily life, back then. Besides the readings at Mass, the Bible was—is—read aloud every day at other public devotions; homilies at Mass and sermons in the marketplaces were full of references to Scripture, and everybody understood and even enjoyed them. People embroidered Bible stories on their festival banners and wove them into their tapestries; they worked Scripture into stained glass and acted it out in their Mystery Plays. It even shows up in people's letters, in treaties and deeds, and in all kinds of legal documents. You really can't find a single artifact from the Age of Faith that doesn't make some literal or symbolic reference to Holy Scripture.

Things went along smoothly this way for a thousand years, with no more questions about the contents of the New Testament. But in 1546, the Council of Trent, prompted by another serious outbreak of heresy, had to remind everybody very clearly what was Bible and what wasn't. Like Marcion before him, Martin Luther had decided that only he and Paul really understood Christ and, like Marcion, he frequently thought that he knew better than Paul.** Luther translated the Bible himself, altering it substantially to suit his own views, and published it in parts between 1523 and

---

*Remember that a new Bible would cost a community about as much as a new church building, and the finished book was easily worth a manor. Books in the Middle Ages were done on parchment or on vellum (made from the skins of young sheep or cattle) and lettered, gilded, and illuminated by hand. A whole Bible took maybe four hundred animals and years of work by a score of scribes and artists. Then as now, there were plenty of unscrupulous collectors, so a stolen Bible could always be converted into an immense sum of cash. Plus there were the customary "garnitures", the covers and bindings that could run to twenty pounds of gold, decorated with jewels and enamels (when Henry VIII burned all of the Bibles in England, he was careful to keep the bindings for himself). The miracle is that so many still survive.

**He based his evaluation of the New Testament entirely on Paul, putting even the Gospels in second place. But then he strongly disparaged Hebrews, and he deleted or added things wherever he thought he knew better than Paul. He put in the word *only*, for instance, after the phrase "we are justified by faith", which makes it into a completely new doctrine.

1534. After that, various incompatible translations came thick and fast all over northern Europe.

Henry VIII and Elizabeth I, for instance, each commissioned heavily revised Bibles to support their claim to be supreme head of the Church in England. Elizabeth told her commission to "note such chapters and places as contain matters of genealogies, or other places not edifying; that all such words as sound to any offence of lightness or obscenity be expressed with more convenient terms and phrases."

It's surprising that they'd judge any part of the Bible "not edifying" or "obscene", but note that these instructions tell them to change whatever they don't like—to make it "more convenient", which is just the opposite of reliable. Still, even these "revised" versions didn't suit the government, so Elizabeth's successor James I convened a conference at Hampton Court Palace in January 1604; they produced the King James or Authorized Version, which also changed a number of crucial passages in both testaments. The original salutation of the angels to the shepherds at the Nativity, for instance, reads, "Peace on Earth *to people of good will*"; that agrees with the rest of Scripture, which is based on the idea of covenants between God and Man, each party contributing something through a free-will choice. But the Anglicans taught that salvation is a free gift that you get simply by believing in Christ; so the commission changed this verse to "Peace on Earth, good will to Men".*

Today, some of these unreliable versions have done a little backtracking, fixing up verses that were changed during the Reformation. The Church, for her part, continues to update her own translations, but she never strays from the original texts that she has

---

*The commissioners also changed Joseph's coat to one "of many colors" because they figured that nobody would know that his original "long-sleeved" coat was the distinctive garb of a Middle-Eastern prince. Specific, deliberate changes like these obscure the King James Version, but even in general its archaic language is no more understandable than Shakespeare's; the "firkins" that the commission put into Jn 2:6 may have clarified things at first, but they're unintelligible now. People who still use the King James probably have to rely on what they're told it means rather than understanding it directly. Some modern Protestant Bibles are translated from the King James Version rather than directly from the original texts, which, again, would still contradict Protestant tenets.

so carefully kept since they were written—"not because," in the words of the First Vatican Council, "having been composed by human industry, they were afterwards approved by her authority; nor only because they contain revelation without error; but because, having been written under the inspiration of the Holy Spirit, they have God as their author."

CHAPTER 4

THAT OLD-TIME RELIGION

Why the Church Still Guards
the Old Testament

T HEY THOUGHT IT WAS A revolution. After that First Pentecost, the High Priests and rabbis saw thousands and thousands of Jews acknowledging Christ as the promised savior
and flocking to join the Church. The Book of Acts shows that
they did all they could to suppress the movement, but Christianity
kept growing, with unparalleled speed. Conversions, alarming
enough during Jesus's lifetime (Jn 7:13, 9:22, 10:19), so completely outnumbered the Jewish hierarchy that it could hardly begin to prosecute—or persecute—Christians without help from the
Roman army.

Even that didn't work. Roman military personnel converted,
like the centurion (Lk 7:1–10). Some of the priests themselves
confessed that Jesus of Nazareth had, indeed, come as the Messiah
(possibly a majority of them; Jn 12:19, Acts 6:7). Within only a
few months, Christianity came bursting out of Palestine and flood-
ing into every corner of the Empire.

Of course, the Apostles taught people to render unto Cæsar
(Heb 13:17; 1 Pt 2:13–17; etc.), as had Christ (Mt 22:15–22), but
the imperial government had seen plenty of others who claimed to
be the Messiah, men like Theodas and Judas the Galilean, who

stirred their fanatic followers to riots or even battle against Roman rule. So even before the Apostles died, the state was executing thousands of Christians all over the known world. And these thousands were only a small percentage of the whole Church.

What could convert so many so quickly, even the Jewish priests themselves? What could convince so many pagans to die for a new religion so radically different from their own? Of course, there was the direct work of the Holy Spirit; the speed and scope of the early conversions have no parallel in purely human endeavors. But inspiration had been working already, quietly, long before this, to give Christianity one thing that no other religion ever had, before or since: more than a thousand years of consistent prophecy, written in the holy books of the Jews.

Evidently, the first of Judaism's sacred books (Genesis, Exodus, Leviticus, Numbers, and Deuteronomy) were written down about 1250 B.C. These five books together constitute the written Torah, the basic scripture of the Israelites. The Torah was kept intact, generation upon generation, but as the Jews' national identity crystallized, as God revealed more and more of his nature and their mission, they wrote more and more books to explain these developments. That's how we got Joshua, Judges, the Books of Kings, and the Chronicles (which used to be called Paralipomenon, the Greek for "things left out" of Kings). And that's why the prophecies of Ezra, Nehemiah, and the others were written down.

These books kept pace with the continuous unfolding of God's plan of salvation, but the Israelites wrote lots of other books, too. They wrote the *Words of the Days of the Kings of Israel* and the parallel books for Juda mentioned in Kings. They wrote commentaries on every tiny little point of every Law of Moses that there was. They recorded the opinions and sayings of the great teachers, and they wrote educational books with the literary technique of using the name of a long-dead prophet who might have said (or *ought* to have said) such things. By about 200 B.C. it got hard to tell where the basic books left off and the commentaries began.

Help came from a very unexpected quarter: the Pharaoh of

Egypt, Ptolemy Philadelphus, the Greek-speaking successor of Alexander the Great. Ptolemy wanted his great library of Alexandria to have at least one copy of every book in the world, all arranged in order. But—like many of the Jews themselves—Ptolemy couldn't make much sense out of the mountain of Jewish writing about God and the Covenant. So he commissioned seventy Jewish scholars to come up with a standard canon of Jewish scripture and a standard version of each book in that canon. The collection of forty-six books that the seventy men on this committee established is called the Septuagint, because the Latin word for "seventy" is *septuagintus*. It's often abbreviated LXX.

The Septuagint was used universally by Jews right up to the time of Christ. It's the only scripture that he and the Apostles used (in Hebrew or Aramaic translations, because the original Septuagint was in Greek). When Christ read from prophecy in the synagogue, it was the Septuagint's Isaiah that he read from (Lk 4:16–21); when he said "search through Scripture" (Jn 5:39), he meant the Septuagint.* These were the books that let his disciples recognize him (Jn 1:45), and reading them makes it very hard to deny that Christ is the Messiah. Everything in these books points to that conclusion: not just the prophecies, but also the laws, the poems, and even the histories, which center around that one remarkable family from which he was born.

The things recorded in the books of the Septuagint, things "that were observed and celebrated in obedience to the Law," St. Augustine explained, "were by the way of prior announcement of Christ who was to come." The Church naturally adopted the Septuagint as the only inspired Testament to Christ's nature and mission as promised by the Old Covenant. And just as the Septuagint convinced so many Jews that Jesus is the Messiah, it laid out the same message for Gentiles, a message that had been preserved intact for twelve centuries—a record far beyond purely human

---

*There are those who figure that he meant our modern Bible, parts of which weren't written for another century; the whole Bible wasn't put together until nearly four hundred years later. See the chapter on the New Testament.

means.* To this day, the Septuagint is the sole and official canon of the Church's Old Testament.

But outside the Church, these books have had their share of tribulation. The details are still subject to intensive study, but it all started in the year 70, with another devastating blow to Judaism as it had been before Christ: the Roman Emperor Titus, leading his armies into Jerusalem to put down a rebellion, completely destroyed the Temple of Jerusalem. The Ark of the Covenant and all of the other necessary Temple furnishings were carried off in triumph to Rome, where you can still see them represented in the sculptures of the Arch of Titus.

(The permanent loss of that wonderful Temple is tragic, of course, but—while God's revelations to the Jews are still true—the Temple wasn't needed after the Old Covenant had been fulfilled, and the New Covenant doesn't need that kind of Temple. Its destruction just after the death of the last Apostle has been seen as a material proof of the truth of Christianity. Certainly no one has ever been able to rebuild the Temple, although many have tried. The Emperor Julian the Apostate gave orders to rebuild it in 383, just to disprove Christianity, and Jews from all over the Empire rushed to help. But Julian's contemporaries St. Ambrose, St. John Crysostom, and St. Gregory of Nanzianz, and his pagan court historian Ammianus Marcellinus, tell us that an earthquake and a series of explosions, possibly from old underground storage vaults, overturned the unfinished foundations. Julian himself died within six months, and the work was promptly abandoned. The Wailing Wall is the only part of the old Temple's foundation left; the site itself is covered by the seventh-century mosque of the Khalif Omar. Nor did God smite the Roman looters with hemorrhoids, as he had done to the Philistines before, and rescue the Ark—see

---

*Then as now, the preservation of revelation for so long was a powerful point in favor of Christianity. The other major religions of the day were not nearly that old. The Romans dated their state religion to the time of King Numa (715 to 673 B.C.); the cults of Mithra, Isis, and Hercules had roots in older creeds but were then known in new forms that had been patched together between 200 and 300 B.C. None of these pagan religions was backed up with anything as consistent and as clear as the revelation to the Jews, and the fact wasn't lost on potential converts.

1 Kgs 5. Roman records show that the Ark was displayed in Rome for a while with the rest of the Temple furnishings and then melted down for the gold.)

With no Temple, the hard core of rabbis who still denied Christ could no longer perform the liturgies required by the Torah, but they undoubtedly thought that the Ark would be brought back and the Temple rebuilt, as had happened time and again in the past. Their leader, Jochanan ben Zakkai, took them out of the ruined city to the village of Jamnia, where they settled down to assess the situation. More than a million Jews had been killed by the Romans in the rebellion; those that survived kept pouring away in a new flood of converts to Christianity, while the others split into all kinds of sects fighting with each other and with the Romans. But the rabbis of Jamnia were determined to preserve the sacred trust as they understood it.

They needed to develop a new form of Judaism that would unite all Jews, at least until the Temple could be rebuilt, and to somehow undercut Christian claims of the divinity of Jesus and his identity as the Christ. To do this, they assembled a completely new version of Jewish scripture, omitting some books entirely and rewriting the others. The result, which you call the Jamnian or Palestinian canon, changed Judaism forever.

This reconstruction of latter-day Judaism at Jamnia was heavily influenced by rabbis who were Sadducees, members of the literal-fundamentalist party of the day. Politically, they tended to favor the Romans, but doctrinally they were really rather heretical, refusing to believe in the teachings of the oral Torah such as the resurrection of the dead and life everlasting. So they took out a lot of the books in the Septuagint that point to these beliefs. They had always been particularly zealous enemies of Christianity, too (Acts 5:17–19), so they also rewrote the prophetic texts. One of them, for instance, a translator by the name of Aquila, removed the word *parthenos*—"virgin"—from Isaiah 7:14 and rendered the passage "a young woman (*neanis*) shall conceive". That way, they could assert that the prophecy didn't match what the Christians were teaching about the very nature of Christ.

So, while the Jamnian canon may have been undertaken in good faith, you could say that it's really a fabrication, in the sense of being a set of texts purposefully changed but presented as if it were the genuine ancient version. It is profoundly different from the original text of the Septuagint, which, again, is still the Old Testament of the Church.

The only problem that the early Church had with the Septuagint was keeping up with demand for copies. First, the whole thing had to be translated into Latin for use in the Mass and in teaching. And as the Church exploded out of Palestine, the scribes just didn't have the leisure enjoyed by their Hebrew predecessors. As a result, a lot of what you might call typographical errors crept into the manuscripts by the late fourth century. "I am not so ignorant as to suppose that any of the Lord's words are . . . in need of correction," complained St. Jerome, "but the Latin books are proved to be faulty by the discrepancies that they all exhibit among themselves".

So, at the urging of Pope St. Damasus, St. Jerome moved out into the desert near Bethlehem. There, free from distractions, he set about making a complete standard Latin translation, corrected from beginning to end and compared carefully against the surviving Hebrew and Aramaic texts as well as against the original Greek. He finished it in only thirty-five years, by about 426. It's called the Vulgate,* and its Old Testament is the most complete and accurate record of the scripture that Christ himself used. For more than a thousand years it was the only Old Testament that Christians used. Then, starting with the Protestant Reformation, the story of the variant versions of the Old Testament outside the Church took another fairly illogical twist.

It happened like this. Reformers like Luther, Wycliffe, Huss, and Calvin rejected certain tenets of Christianity.** Of course, de-

---

*It's called that because it's written in the "vulgar" language, the non-classical Latin that everybody spoke, not in the high-toned Greek of the Septuagint and not in classical poetic Latin. Jerome, the first trilingual scholar on record, knew more about Hebrew scriptures than anyone else alive. The Jewish hierarchy used to visit him in the desert when they had questions, and he's still regarded as an authority among Hebrew scholars because he alone preserved many pre-Jamnian texts that Judaism had destroyed.

**Just by definition, that's what makes them Protestant. The assumption here, though, is that people who oppose the Church on basic tenets of faith do so

letions or innovations are prevented by Sacred Tradition (which
the Reformers therefore rejected entirely) and by the New Testament (which they rephrased freely). But Christian teachings are
also supported and clarified by the Old Testament. If the Reformers wanted to deny the importance of works in the Cycle of Redemption, they'd have to get rid of whole books like Tobit; to
deny the existence of Purgatory, they'd have to dispose of Macca-
bees. And even then, they'd have to rephrase all of the remaining
verses that echoed these teachings. That's why the Jamnian version
of Jewish scripture appealed to them—the rabbis of Jamnia had
written it, after all, to remove the basis for a lot of the Christian
teachings that the Protestants themselves were rejecting. So the
Reformers took the Septuagint out of their Bibles and substituted
their own translations of the Jamnian canon.

That's why the Old Testament of a Protestant Bible is so different from that of the Church's Bible; whole books have been taken
out of the Protestant versions, and the texts that remain have been
thoroughly rewritten. The Protestant Reformers claimed that the
books taken out of the Jamnian canon aren't directly quoted in
the New Testament, but they knew that whenever Christ and the
Apostles do quote the Old Testament, their phrases come only
from the Septuagint. The rephrasing that you find in the Jamnian
canon wasn't done, of course, until they had all passed from this
Earth.*

---

honestly believing themselves to be correct; people wouldn't stick with a creed
that they didn't believe. So, while a book like this has to draw the distinction between the doctrines of the Church and the doctrines of those who have left her,
that doesn't mean that any specific person is evil—or good, for that matter. Accurate or inaccurate in teaching, yes; but not personally trying to do anything
wrong, necessarily. After all, the enormous damage of heresy is specifically that
it misleads good people who actively seek Christ and genuinely want to know
him and do his will. Heresy never teaches the fullness of Christ's teachings, and
it usually teaches things that are contrary to what Christ taught. Or, worse, it
makes such well-meaning people indifferent, convincing them that specific articles of faith don't matter "as long as you're Christian," which can keep them
from giving the matter any further thought. It gives people the idea that religion
doesn't have to be logically consistent or make any sense.

*It's impossible to justify the substitution on historic or scholarly grounds, and
the Protestant co-option of the Jamnian canon has caused all kinds of problems
for good people trying to figure out Christianity. Apart from introducing

As for the Church, as you might expect, she has updated the language of her Old Testament occasionally but has never changed its substance. Her texts are materially the same as they were when Christ read them himself; her attitude toward them is the same as that stated by Pope St. Leo the Great fifteen centuries ago: "in the area of moral precepts, no decrees of the earlier Testament are rejected; rather, in the Gospel teaching many of them are augmented, so that the things that give salvation might be more perfect and more lucid than those that promise a Savior."

---

specific confusions like Aquila's *parthenos/neanis* ploy, it has provoked all of the incompatible ideas about the Cycle of Redemption found among American sects that center on things like "the Rapture" and the "End Time". It keeps people from reading passages like Sirach 5:1–7, which is why so many separated brethren ask bewildering questions like, "Have you been saved?" It's even led some mainline Protestant sects to declare that there's no such thing as a human soul. Protestant scholars are aware of the historical status of the two versions; some acknowledge the situation indirectly by referring to the Septuagint as "the Greek original" and the Jamnian as "the received version".

CHAPTER 5

THE CHURCH'S
FAMILY ALBUMS
Other Good Books Besides the Bible

W HEN PEOPLE OUTSIDE the Church see some religious images and customs, they might say, "It's not in the Bible!" Well, no, not all of the Church's images are found in the Bible. But that doesn't mean that they aren't good Christian images—the Bible only contains a tiny portion of the ancient writings about the Faith, and there are plenty of other perfectly good sources for a Christian artist to use.

In fact, when the Church fathers started to sort out early Christian writings for the New Testament, they had stacks of books to choose from, some of them attributed to Apostles. They condemned the obvious fakes and the ones that contained error, but they didn't throw away anything of real value. A lot of books that didn't make the grade for the Bible are still valuable reading, even if they don't exactly correspond to our modern ideas of objective history.

After all, people in former ages didn't just relate the facts for their own sake; they composed epics and chronicles of the past to make some truth more accessible and memorable, or to make its meaning and implications clearer. Naturally, these accounts accomplish this by pointing to older legends and other historical events, too, or by repeating their form with different particulars. Over the course of the centuries, you can see which parts were added to the original version, and, if you understand the old strategies of historiography, it's not too hard to figure out why.

The Christian authors of these not-quite-biblical accounts were following popular instructional customs at the time. They particularly favored the ancient and respectable traditions of Judaism, where you find literary forms like the *haggadah*—a story that brings out the moral lesson of some set of facts—and the *midrash*, a biblical investigation in which you search through scripture and history to find specific guidance for a novel situation, or to find prophetic signs of what will be accomplished later. Both of these story-forms contain plenty of facts, but they're facts purposefully arranged to teach you something about the way the world works. The Book of Daniel and even the Gospel according to St. Mark are structured this way, rather than chronologically as we'd probably do today.

So these early Christian writings, even those that are structured in a highly artificial way, are consistent with the Bible, and there's no doubt that they include a good deal of oral history that we wouldn't have, otherwise—Mary, Joseph, the Apostles, and their families were certainly prominent in the region, and people knew lots about them that wasn't really relevant for the Bible itself. You might say that these books are the Church's family albums, full of literary portraits of people we know and love from long ago.

For example, everyone knows that Ann is Mary's mother, and that Joachim is her father, the grandparents of Jesus. But "they aren't in the Bible!" No, they're not; the genealogies of Jesus in Matthew and Luke run on Joseph's side of the family, because Christ's legal paternity was of the House of David, and that's more important for the points that these Evangelists need to make. These ancestor lists follow the Jewish practice, of course—the genealogies of the Tribes of Israel were memorized as part of each child's education, which is why those long lists of exotic names and "begats" show up in books like Ruth and Chronicles, as well as in the Gospels.

So the early Christians, knowing that the Old Covenant was fulfilled and that there would soon be no more Tribes of Israel, thought that they should make a written record of Mary's family—

which was also part of Jewish tradition, because when previously obscure people become prominent in the Bible, their family histories got written down, as with Samuel and Saul and David. That's why the story of Joachim and Ann is recorded in books like the *Gospel of the Birth of Mary* sometimes attributed to St. Matthew, and, more importantly, the *Protevangelion* attributed to St. James.

You can still get these books in modern editions. They tell the story of the pious but barren couple, their prayers and sacrifices, and the separate annunciations to each of them of the coming birth of the Virgin. "And Joachim went down [to Jerusalem], and Ann stood by the gate and saw Joachim coming. . . . And she ran, and, hanging about his neck, said, Now I know that the Lord has blessed me greatly, for behold . . . I who was barren shall conceive." This is the first of all of the supernatural events that brought about the coming of Christ, a preview of the Annunciation, and it's often shown in European art, just as the Virgin and Child with St. Ann has always been a popular type of devotional image.

In the *Protevangelion* you can also read about the presentation of the Virgin, another episode that you won't find in the Bible. It's still commemorated by the Church with a feast on November 21. Joachim and Ann, dedicating their daughter to the Lord, took her to the Temple when she was three years old so that she could live free from the corruptions of everyday life. The *Protevangelion* says that later, when Mary was of marriageable age, the priests consulted about her future. An angel told the High Priest to gather the walking-sticks of all the widowers in Israel and bring them to the Temple. Joseph's walking-stick burst into flower, just as Aaron's staff did in Num 17:16–25, signalling that he was the one. His staff topped with flowers is still the sign by which you can easily recognize images of St. Joseph.

(While we're on the subject, the *Gospel of Pseudo-Matthew*, which runs to some twenty chapters on the childhood of Christ, has something interesting to say about this. When the widower Joseph was selected by his blooming staff and the dove that "came forth and flew to his head", he said, "I am an old man and have sons; why do you entrust this young girl to me?"—which puts an interesting spin on Mt 12:46, Mk 6:3, and Jn 7:5, doesn't it?)

The so-called *Gospel of Nicodemus* is another early Christian tract that gives us at least some interesting bits of information that aren't in the Bible: information about the thieves crucified with Christ, "whose names are Dismas and Gestas." Dismas, on Christ's right, is the one who asked to be remembered in Christ's kingdom and was promised salvation (Lk 23:39–43). Accordingly, St. Dismas became patron of thieves (those who want to reform, anyway—the others are on their own) and his feast was set on March 25. Nicodemus also tells us the name of the soldier (Jn 19:34) who pierced Christ's side with a lance—Longinus—who's usually identified with the centurion who said, "Truly, this was a just man" (Lk 23:47). Naturally, nobody knows much about these men, but a body of highly instructive legends grew up around the names anyway, and their images are used even today to make certain points. You can still get holy cards with St. Dismas on them, daily reminders of the need to turn to Christ and reform. And a forty-foot statue of St. Longinus stands before one of the great piers that hold up the dome of St. Peter's in the Vatican, guarding the reliquary chapel where the point of his spear is kept.

By the thirteenth century there were so many legends about these and later figures that Jacobus da Voragine, archbishop of Genoa, wrote them all down in another "family album". His *Golden Legend* gave new popularity to these stories of the saints by including such vivid details as the eye malady from which St. Longinus supposedly suffered that was cured by the accidental touch of a drop of Christ's blood at the Crucifixion. In Da Voragine's day, the old ways of writing history still prevailed, so you can't take the *Legend* as Gospel, but it's still useful moral reading, with lots of good stories for the family. And you have to understand at least its highlights, if you want to understand Christian art—episodes from the *Legend* show up everywhere from the stained glass of the great cathedrals right down to your dashboard.

Jacobus is the one who records the legends of St. Christopher, who "was a Canaanite, a man of gigantic size and terrible aspect, and twelve cubits in height." If you check out the reference to Goliath in the First Book of Kings, you'll see that Goliath stood only six cubits and a span (17:4), so Christopher must have been pretty tall. Christopher's original name was Reprobus, a name related to the root of our word *reprobate*, which tells you something about his lifestyle.

His ambition was to serve the most powerful king on Earth, so he started with the local king, who was the best around. This worked out for a while, but then a minstrel came by and started singing a song that included a good many references to certain devils, by name. Every time the king heard one of these names, he made the Sign of the Cross. Reprobus asked him why, and the king said, "I arm myself with that sign, whenever I hear the devil named, in the fear that he might take power over me and hurt me."

Well, this was all that Reprobus needed to hear. "If thou fearest that the devil will hurt thee," he said, "then evidently he is greater and stronger than thou; therefore, I have been deceived in my hopes of serving the greatest and strongest lord of the world. But now I will make my farewells for I go forth to search out the devil himself, that he might become my lord, and I his servant." They met up a little later, as the devil was marching his army through the wilderness. They introduced themselves, the deal was struck, and Reprobus joined the immense army of those who already followed the Prince of Darkness.

But the devil saw a cross by the roadside up ahead, so he turned his legions away and detoured through the wilderness to give it a wide berth. "Which seeing and wondering at, Reprobus asked him why in such fear he left the level road and deviated through such remote and rugged country." The devil hemmed and hawed until Reprobus threatened to leave his service, at which the devil said, "A man named Christ was stuck to a cross; wherefore, when I see the sign of the Cross, I am cast into a great fear, and I flee, afraid."

Reprobus, in the best nursery-tale style, repeated what he had said in his speech to the king of the Canaanites and added, "Farewell, then, for I leave thy service to seek this Christ." This quest wasn't nearly so easy as finding the devil was. Finally, Reprobus heard a hermit preaching about Christ, and he asked the monk how to go about serving him. "This king that thou desirest to serve requires of thee this service," said the hermit, "that thou shouldst fast frequently."

"Let him demand something else of me," said Reprobus, "for it is quite impossible for me to do that." Well then, said the hermit, thou must address many prayers to him. "I know not what that may be," said Reprobus, "and I cannot subject myself to that requirement." The hermit having reached the third demand (a number still obligatory in children's stories), asked if Reprobus knew of the river nearby, where so many travelers were in peril of losing their lives. Reprobus said that he did, so the hermit said, "As thou hast so great a height, and as thou are mighty strong, if thou reside near the river and carry across those who wish to go, thou wilt be doing something very agreeable to the King Jesus Christ whom thou wishest to serve, and I hope that he reveal himself to thee in that place."

Here at last was something suited to the man's talents, so he took the monk's suggestion, carrying pilgrims across on his back, steadying himself with a great pole in place of a staff. One night, Reprobus heard a child calling to him from across the river. He came out of his little house, but saw nobody. Again he heard the child, and then the requisite third time, at which he actually saw the child. Taking up the child on his shoulders, Reprobus started off. But as the river got deeper, the child got heavier, "like a great weight of lead", until the giant thought that he'd be drowned. "Child!" he cried. "Thou hast exposed me to great danger. Had I the whole world on my shoulders, it could not have burdened me more!"

The child answered, "Be not amazed, for thou hast borne not the whole world, but him who created it. For I am Christ, thy king, whom thou servest in this work!" And he called the man Christopher: in Greek, "Bearer of Christ". The child continued, "And to prove to thee that I speak the truth, when thou hast crossed over again, plant thy staff in the ground, and in the morning thou shalt see it flourishing and bearing fruit." Christopher did so, and the next morning found the pole leafy with palm fronds and heavy with dates.

Of course, there's a high symbolism in this, as in all of the *Legend*: the convert, passing through flowing water, wins the palm of everlasting life through service to Christ and so forth. And the story of a reprobate becoming a bearer of Christ is the story of everyone's conversion, in every century. That's what gives these tales their perennial value and keeps them generally interesting as time goes by. They're the folklore of Christendom, the bedtime stories of the ages. It's no wonder that the *Golden Legend* was immensely popular, circulating in hundreds of manuscripts and more than a hundred and fifty printed editions.

These books, and many, many others, don't get any official recognition from the Church, but they're still important for their religious value as well as for their literary merits. And because everybody used to know them backward and forward, you'll see lots of episodes from them in religious art. In any case, it's not a bad idea for Christians to get acquainted with those who have gone before us marked with the sign of faith. Read the Bible frequently, of course, first of all, but check out the *Gospel of the Birth of Mary* and the *Protevangelion*, too.

Then browse through the works of St. Jerome, St. Augustine, and the other Fathers of the Church, or the *Eight Books of Miracles* by St. Gregory of Tours, where a lot of ideas for icons and Renaissance paintings came from. Or look up unfamiliar saints that you see in pictures or statues in Butler's *Lives of the Saints*—first published in 1756 but updated generation upon generation. Give yourself plenty of time to do it, though. You may start out reading the entry for, say, St. Dominic, but you won't be able to stop there. You'll learn all about St. Albert the Great, St. James the Cut-to-Pieces, and St. Christina the Astonishing. And, just for the fun of it, read the *Golden Legend*.

CHAPTER 6

THE CYCLE OF REDEMPTION

Purgatory, Etc.

L IFE IS A LOT LIKE school. You're put there at a very early age, without being consulted about it. You get a lot of work assigned to you, and it helps you grow, but you're tested every time you turn around. Then there's the big test, and you find out whether you graduate or flunk. You see this pattern of life reflected everywhere you look, not just in your own career but also in literature like the *Odyssey*, in the Hindu and Buddhist scriptures, in the Koran, and even in our fairy tales and popular literature, like *The Wizard of Oz*. And you find the same view of the universe revealed in the Bible.

It's the major theme of the Church's art and ceremonies, too. From the Church's point of view, this journey through life is governed by God's plan of creation, sanctification, and salvation: what you might call the "Cycle of Redemption".

But although this cycle is mirrored in our secular art and culture, you hear all kinds of inaccurate accounts of it. It's not very well understood by the press or the broadcast media, and of course separated Christians don't see it this way. So we'll just run quickly through some of the basics here, with references to a few of the relevant Bible passages (but remember, the Church doesn't teach these points because they're in the Bible; they're in the Bible because the Church has always taught them). And we'll sample a few of the uncounted millions of words that the Church has written about the cycle during the past nineteen centuries. That should be enough to clarify the Church's art and liturgies a little, and to aim you in the right direction if you want to read more about it.*

For each of us, the Cycle of Redemption can be summed up as birth, sin, reconciliation, death, judgement, and verdict—and grace, which pervades all of these.

Birth and the Beginning of the Cycle

We're all born into a flesh that's affected by the original sin of Adam and Eve (Gn 3). God created Adam and Eve good, in his own image and likeness (Gn 1:26). And, out of love, he gave them certain gifts that they had no right to expect, being human as they were. They got integrity, which means that their emotions (and even their passions) were controlled by their intellect—they didn't have any psychological problems, no compulsions, no shame, and no guilt. Well, they didn't have any sin yet, so they didn't have anything to be guilty about.

They also got an intimate union with God, who lived with them visibly and on terms of friendship. And God gave them the promise of immortality, so that they could enjoy this way of life forever. But to get this, they had to obey one simple little commandment: don't eat the fruit of that particular tree. God gave them everything else, but not that.

He also gave them free will. They didn't have to sin (Gn 4:7), but the devil got to them, and they decided to go ahead with it anyway. Since their supernatural gifts were conditional on their obedience, their sin was a rejection of their innocence, wisdom, and bodily immortality. "Man too was created without corruption," as St. Methodius of Philippi wrote in about 300, "but when . . . he transgressed the commandment, he suffered a terrible and destructive fall and was reduced to a state of death."

*Remember, too, that this book isn't a catechism—this outline of the cycle is accurate as far as it goes, but there's a *whole* lot more to it than this. For the rest of the story, check the sources listed at the end of the book.

Sin, Original and Inventive

So now we're all born in original sin: not that we're punished for what Adam and Eve did, because God is not cruel, but just that we're born without those supernatural gifts that we'd otherwise have had. And this original sin also opened the gates for all subsequent sins, all of the times when people choose their own wills as opposed to God's (Rom 5:12–14). These are called *actual* sins, and they cut a person off from God (Is 59:1–2, for instance). And you can't save yourself on your own, so, as you remove yourself from God step by step, sin by sin, things get worse and worse for you.

But that's not all; when you bring sin into being, you distort the whole world that much more. The story of Noah, for instance, says that "the Earth was corrupt; for all men lived corruptly on Earth," and God himself put the blame where it lies: "the Earth is full of violence because of them" (Gn 6:11–13). So, when one person sins, everybody else has to put up with the consequences, too—sin is sort of like air pollution: you can't hide it, and it ruins the quality of life everywhere, even far from its source (as in Is 24:5). We're all tied together in the great scheme of things, which explains why bad things happen to good people. If we were all the way Adam and Eve were before the Fall, there wouldn't be any death or taxes or crime or traffic jams or anything. God made the world, but we spoiled it.

But note that original sin only changed man's *state*; it didn't change human *nature*. People were made in the image and likeness of God (Gn 1:26), and created good; people can act badly, but people are by nature good.

You have to be perfectly clear about this one point, because a lot of Christians separated from the Church teach that humans are by nature depraved, sinful, and wicked—this is the point that all those fire-and-brimstone preachers have tried to make for the past three hundred years. But it isn't so; that's not part of Christian teaching, and you won't find anything in the Bible to back it up. It doesn't make sense, really. And it's interesting to hear what the notable anthropologist Ashley Montagu figured out on this point:

"Perhaps the idea before all others I would like the reader to reconsider is the notion . . . of innate depravity," he wrote in his book *The Humanization of Man*. This notion, he says,

> seems to me to have been fiendishly damaging to man's growth in self-understanding . . . it is hardly likely to occur to anyone that the age-old doctrine of innate depravity is not only open to question but is demonstrably unsound. . . . The need that is satisfied by the myth of innate depravity is the need for absolution from sin, for if sin is innately determined, then one can shift the burden of responsibility for it from oneself to one's innate heritage. Evil in this world is thus explained, and becomes easier to bear—and with a good conscience, much easier to do nothing about. My own interpretation of the evidence, strictly within the domain of science, leads me to the conclusion that man is born good, and is organized in such a manner from birth as to need to continue to grow and develop in his potentialities for goodness.

It's interesting to see a man of science coming around to the Church's teaching on the matter despite what he calls "centuries of secular, religious, and 'scientific' authority" in Protestant England teaching the contrary. But no matter how you figure it, the innate goodness of human beings is a pivotal point in the cycle, because it means that people can attain Heaven, where nothing bad is allowed (Mt 5:8, Rv 21:27). So how are you supposed to overcome all of the sin in this world and end up with God, where you belong?

Grace and the Re-Sanctification of Humans

Well, have another look at Genesis. The same book that records the original sin tells that God promised a savior (Gn 3:14–16). It doesn't go into a lot of detail, but the rest of the plan is revealed little by little through the prophets of the Old Testament, like Abraham and Moses (Gn 17, Ex). Just as he'd offered a contract—a covenant—to Adam and Eve, God offered a covenant to people after the Fall, a covenant tied directly to the way the world works, to the whole pattern of health and happiness, disease and death, and so on. You obey those Commandments, God said, and I will be your God and take care of you, and I'll receive you after you die; if you deliberately reject this offer, you're on your own, and you've got to take the consequences, here and hereafter. Finally, after people had been waiting for centuries, God incarnate, Jesus of Nazareth, was born (Lk 2). He brought the Old Covenant to its fulfillment and instituted the New Covenant, which is Christianity (Mt 5:17–19).

In only a few years of public ministry, Christ got a tremendous amount of work done. He gave us the rest of the Faith that had only been partially revealed during a thousand years of Hebrew prophecy. He established his Church to preserve his teachings intact until the end of Time and to offer them to everybody on Earth (Mt 28:18–20), he ensured that he would be sacramentally present in the Eucharist (Mt 26:26–29; Mk 14:22–25; Lk 22:14–20; Jn 6; etc., etc.), and he empowered that Church to offer that means—and the other sacraments—to keep us close to him, to give us the grace that we need to avoid sin, and to offer forgiveness, reconciliation, and a chance for atonement when we slip up (Mt 18:15–18; Jn 20:21–23).

The point of all of this is grace—getting back the closeness to God that Adam and Eve rejected. And you get it on exactly the same condition that God laid down for the first people he offered it to: obedience. You manage the necessary reconciliation primarily through the sacrament of the same name,* which is the channel for the grace that comes when you resolve to repent and you stick to your resolution, and when you ask for the help that you need

---

*To get God's forgiveness through the sacrament of Reconciliation you have to meet the same conditions as for getting forgiveness from a person. You have to acknowledge that what you did was wrong, you have to say that you're sorry, you have to resolve never to do it again, and you have to make up for it somehow. And, of course, you have to ask for forgiveness; presuming on his mercy won't cut it. So, in the Church's view, you can't figure, "Well, I'll go to confession on Saturday," and do the thing anyway. The Church also makes the important distinction—again, parallel to earthly human relations—between *imperfect* contrition (born of the fear of punishment and loss of reward) and *perfect* contrition (being sorry simply because you've offended God and not thinking of yourself). The first kind is a start, anyway. It's seen as a "beneficial sorrow", as Trent said, that prepares you for the other kind. Note, too, how important this perception of how forgiveness works is to the ideals of civilized life here and now.

to do that. (You're never tempted beyond your ability to resist, either; see 1 Cor 10:13, 2 Pt 2:9.)

Christ made this reconciliation possible by coming, teaching, and establishing his Church. Then he suffered and died, not for his own sins—he didn't have any—but to take our punishment on himself (Rom 5:15–21) and undo what Adam did (1 Cor 15:21–22). This symmetry between Christ and Adam is why you sometimes see a skull at the base of the cross in Crucifixion scenes; the legend arose that the hill called Golgotha, "place of the skull", marks the grave of Adam and, in a way, it does.

But, unlike Adam, Christ rose from the dead and ascended into Heaven, to show us what we could look forward to if we kept his commandments. In other words, Christ *redeemed* mankind from sin. But *salvation* is another matter altogether, and it's a two-way street. You see, Christ's sacrifice laid the foundation of redemption, but each of us has to build on it, working out our own salvation in fear and trembling. (Check 1 Cor 3:11–15, 10:12, Phil 2:12, Mt 24:42–51—and notice, incidentally, that nobody has any assurance of salvation, any more than you know when you're going to die; see Sir 5:5–9, 1 Cor 10:1–12, etc.)

For the Church, all of this means that this earthly life is consequential; what you do here and now influences what happens to you in the hereafter. Of course, you have to have faith—you have to believe, to know and understand, that God is God, that Jesus is Christ, and you have to hold the rest of the teachings of Christianity close to your heart. But faith alone isn't enough to get you home safely after the journey of this life.

Adam and Eve, to start with, had perfect faith. They knew God personally and talked with him, face to face, and it certainly never occurred to them to question his existence or nature. You can't get faith like that, nowadays. But their deliberate act got them (and us) thrown out of Paradise. The Jews always knew the importance of acts, too, way past Genesis. "Give alms out of your substance," the elder Tobias told his son, "for alms deliver from all sin, and from death, and will not allow a soul to go into darkness" (Tb 4:7–12). Psalms echo that same refrain, not to mention passages like Dt 30:10–14 and Lv 6:17–19. Even the stories about Satan tell how he stood next to God—again, perfect belief—but you know what happened when he willfully rebelled.

Of course, the pattern holds true in Christ's own words. There's the Sermon on the Mount, for example (Mt 7:24–27; Lk 6:46–49), and his account of the process of judgement shows that everybody facing judgement has plenty of faith (they all say, "Lord, Lord"), but the sheep who did the right things are saved while the goats who didn't aren't (Mt 25:31–46). And in the account of the Apocalypse, the returning Christ says, "Behold, I come quickly! And my reward is with me, to render unto each one according to his works" (Rv 22:12). That's why Christianity teaches that "faith without works is dead", as St. James put it (Jas 2:17, 26).

Death

Really, you could say that the major theme of the New Testament is the need to serve God faithfully, to keep up your end of the Covenant, in this life, because after you die it's too late—"after we have departed this world," explained St. Ignatius of Antioch more than eighteen hundred years ago, "it will no longer be possible to confess, nor will there be any opportunity to repent."

Now, repentance has two parts to it: forgiveness and atonement. Again, this is reflected in common sense and in daily life. When you're hauled into civil or criminal court, the people whom you've injured can forgive you, but you still have to pay the penalty of the law—restitution and punishment are both perfectly just and reasonable. In the same way, the Church teaches that you have to be forgiven for sin and, even then, you still merit punishment for your sin, and you still have to make up for it. So "repentance . . . is not conducted before the conscience alone, but is to be carried out by some external act," as Tertullian phrased it, back in 203.

You can make up for your sins, and take your licks for them, either in this life or in the next. In this life, there are sacramental penances, nowadays usually just token acts like the familiar "five Our Fathers and five Hail Marys" that may be prescribed after

Reconciliation for remission from punishment. (In the old days, the really grave sins—the ones that get you on talk shows nowadays—used to get public penance involving things like sackcloth and ashes and standing there in front of the church for a few weeks with a sign around your neck detailing your sins, or walking to the Church of the Holy Sepulchre in Jerusalem and back.)

Even today, the Church offers guidelines for optional sacrifices and penances, too. Almsgiving is as important now as it ever was, and so is fasting (which has the added advantage of) keeping the devil at bay; see Mk 9:27–28). You can turn your need for penance to good account with things like giving up a meal during Lent and sending the money that you save to foreign missions that use it to feed the truly hungry. In fact, seasons like Lent and Advent were set up to remind us of the need for acts of penance to serve as punishment for sins and acts of charity to make up for them. Basically, the idea is to do good things to balance out all of the bad, as well as avoiding more bad things.

Judgement, Personal and General

But it's a good idea to keep repenting every day, because after you die you're subject to a personal judgement (Sir 11:26–30). Then you have to face the consequences of what you've said during your life (Mt 12:36–37, Lk 12:8–10), what you've done (Eccl 12:13–14; Mt 10:42, 13:41–43, 16:27; Mk 4:24; Jn 5:29; Rom 2:6; 2 Cor 5:10; to name a few), and what you've failed to do, like the unprofitable servant (Mt 25:24–30).

Now, this judgement takes place right after you die, but then, at the end of Time, in the twinkling of an eye at the last trumpet, the dead are to be raised—souls rejoining bodies now "glorified", which is why images of Christ and the saints are so beautiful. He will come again, at that point, and then everybody has to face a general judgement (1 Cor 15:12–55, 1 Thes 4:16–18, etc.). But think about this: as soon as you die, your soul is released from your body, and it's in the dimension of the angels, outside of Time. From your point of view, then, there's no "before" and no "after", no "at the same time as", because there's no Time, period.

So, even though your friends and relatives may go on for a while putting flowers on your grave, from your point of view outside of Time, your body has already risen and there you are. You probably won't even notice any delay. Your body can be risen in Heaven while your friends are seeing it dead on Earth, but that's not being in two places at one time, because you're outside of Time. See? (Well, it's tough. Even St. Augustine, in his *Confessions*, threw up his hands on this one—"Who can comprehend this even in a thought, so as to express it in a word?" he asked. "Who can explain this?" But then he did a fair job of explaining it, himself. It's a minor point, anyway. You can figure it out when you get there.)

Well then: general judgement. Christ described it (Mt 25), and it's logically necessary because our actions affect humanity as a whole; you have to wait until everything's over to see how it all comes out. This Last Judgement stands at the end of Time, and nobody can know when that's going to hit (Mt 25:13, Mk 13:32–37, Lk 12:35–48), but that doesn't seem to stop people from guessing. In fact, whenever times get tough, a lot of people figure, well, that's it, then. Which is why, in any war or economic depression, or in years like 1000, 1666, or (already) 2000, you see so many street-corner preachers and manuscript illuminators and televangelists who come up with very creative opinions about every scary detail of the Apocalypse. That's when you get lots of people outside the Church trying desperately to figure out what's meant by The Tribulation and The Rapture and things like that.

The Verdict

So, if you die with your sins forgiven and your atonement made, for instance in full sacramental communion with the Church, then, it is hoped, you go straight to Heaven, to enjoy forever the presence of God. If you died unrepentant, with unforgiven sins so serious that they imperil your soul, there's Hell, everlasting torment. Nobody likes to think about Hell, and some separated Christians try to deny its existence, but Christ himself kept describing Hell in glowing detail (Mt 8:12, 13:41–50, 25:41–46; Mk 9:43; Lk 16:19–26, etc.), so there it is.

The Fathers of the Church have also described Hell eloquently, but one of the most moving impressions of what goes on there comes from a little girl, Lucía dos Santos, who told what the Lady of Fátima showed her:

> Our kind heavenly Mother . . . had already prepared us by promising . . . to take us to Heaven. Otherwise, I think we would have died of fear and terror. . . . Our Lady showed us a great sea of fire that seemed to be under the earth. Plunged in this fire were demons and souls in human form, like transparent burning embers, all blackened or burnished bronze, floating about in the conflagration, now raised into the air by the flames that issued from within themselves together with great clouds of smoke, now falling back on every side like sparks in a huge fire, without weight or equilibrium, and amid shrieks and groans and despair, which horrified us and made us tremble with fear. The demons could be distinguished by their terrifying and repellent likeness to unknown animals, all black and transparent.

It makes you think. But we should note at this point that the Church has never condemned anybody, never said solemnly that so-and-so is in Hell. She can't, because that would be contrary to her mission. No Christian can, in fact, because we're supposed to judge as we would be judged. The Church can *excommunicate* somebody, and always has (1 Cor 5:9–12, for instance), but that's different. It means announcing publicly that this person has acted so scandalously that he cannot receive the sacraments; this allows—even calls for—reconciliation. And even if the person dies excommunicated, the Church prays God to forgive him.

Anyway, Hell is for *mortal* sin. But there are degrees of offense. Check Dt 25:2, for instance, or 1 Jn 5:16–17, but St. Jerome summed it up: "There are venial sins," he explained, "and there are mortal sins. It is one thing to owe ten thousand talents, another to owe but a farthing. We shall have to give an accounting for an idle word no less than for adultery. But to be made to blush and to be tortured are not the same thing. . . . If we entreat for lesser sins we are granted pardon; but if for greater sins, it is difficult to obtain our request. There is a great difference between one sin and another."* If you die with some of these minor sins on your soul, or with your sins forgiven but unatoned, there's Purgatory. Purgatory is an essential part of the Cycle of Redemption, and you can't really follow the major themes of the Bible or of Christian art if you leave it out.

At judgement, St. Paul wrote, "the fire shall try every man's work. . . . If any man's work burn, he shall suffer loss; but he himself shall be saved, yet so as by fire" (1 Cor 3:13–15). Obviously, this fire isn't in Hell, because you can't be saved through hellfire, and there's no fire in Heaven. To clarify matters further, Christ himself promised that there was punishment that exacted what was due but wasn't endless: "Amen, I say to you, you shall not go out of there until you repay the last farthing" (Mt 5:26; see also Mt 18:23–35). He also pointed out that there's some place for forgiveness after death, not just acceptance into Heaven or condemnation (Mt 12:32). So Purgatory is for sins that don't deserve absolute punishment—little venial sins, done by people whose hearts are in the right places.

The souls in Purgatory suffer, all right, but they've got an advantage over us because they know that they're saved. And they're still united with us and perfectly well able to pray for us and benefit from our prayers—check 2 Mc 12:39–46, and any of the Fathers of the Church, all of whom commend the practice of praying for the repose of the dead. Those in Heaven are aware of us and of those in Purgatory, or even Hell, also (Lk 16:19–31). You can, therefore, ask your departed friends to pray for you, on the charitable assumption that they're not in Hell, just as you can ask your bodily friends to pray for you. And if you know of people

*To clarify the distinction, some catechisms point out certain criteria that a word, action, omission, thought, or desire has to meet to be a mortal sin: it has to be seriously wrong, you have to know that it is, and you have to fully consent to it. And, of course, you have to actually do it (but entertaining improper thoughts counts, too; they flash in your mind all the time, involuntarily, but you can reject them immediately). A venial sin is understood as one in which the evil wasn't seriously wrong or, even if it was, you understood it to be only slightly wrong or you didn't fully consent to it. Both kinds are willful acts that show you don't want God in your life, and the line blurs in cases like repetitive venial sins. In either case, you can't sin without knowing it or accidentally, but, here as in civil life, ignorance of the law isn't much of an excuse.

from the past (and you have reasonable assurance that they died in friendship with the Church), you can ask them to pray for you, too. After all, if bodily death separates us, then Christianity as a whole doesn't make any sense.

So, there you have it, in outline, at least. It's a view of things that doesn't let you out of any responsibility, and it doesn't cut any corners about the punishment part. But even in that, it recognizes your inherent dignity and insists upon your ability to fulfill the promise of that dignity. And it stresses—uniquely—the importance of the individual person, the innate goodness of the human being, the unity of all people with each other and with God, the need to draw nearer to our Creator, and the crucial importance of active good. From this perspective, the art and ceremonies should pretty well explain themselves, just as they are intended to do.

PART TWO

WORSHIP

CHAPTER 7

IN MEMORY OF ME

*A Short Guide to the Meaning and
Structure of the Mass*

"I AM THE BREAD OF LIFE," Jesus said one day to the crowds at Capharnaum. "I am the living bread that has come down from Heaven. If anyone eat of this bread he shall live forever; and the bread that I will give is my flesh for the life of the world."

Remember, these people had just seen him take a handful of ordinary bread and distribute it to each of them in all their thousands at Tiberias. They had seen him raise the dead, and they had heard him preach all kinds of surprising things that sounded revolutionary at first but then, when you thought about them, made sense—they fulfilled the laws of Moses, brought them into a new focus, and made their purpose clear. Still, this took them by surprise. "How can this man give us his flesh to eat?" they muttered.

So Jesus did something that he almost never did: he repeated. Then he repeated again. "Unless you eat the flesh of the Son of Man, and drink his blood, you shall not have life in you. . . . For my flesh is food indeed, and my blood is drink indeed. . . . He who eats my flesh, and drinks my blood, abides in me, and I in him. . . ." But some of his disciples still said that this was too hard to believe. They left, and he didn't call after them. But he asked the Twelve if they wanted to go, too. Peter tactfully avoided the issue—which must have been as embarrassing to the Apostles as to everybody else who heard it at that point—and said that there wasn't anybody else to go to. And that they knew that Jesus was the Christ, so they'd take what he said on faith, and stay and listen.

They stayed with him right up until the end, right through the Last Supper, when he went back to the same theme. He took the bread and said unequivocally, "This is my body," and then he took the wine and said, "This is my blood. Do this in memory of me."

Suddenly it all made sense. That was how Jesus would give us his flesh to eat and his blood to drink: sacramentally, in the Eucharist. That's how he could remain physically present among us all until the end of Time, and how he would let us fulfill his absolute requirement for salvation. From that moment on, the Church has fulfilled his command, without interruption, continuing the Last Supper in the liturgy of the Mass, perpetuating the sacrifice of Calvary in the sacrifice of the Mass.* It's an idea that's so obvious, so simple, as simple as he said it was; yet everything that the Church teaches, and everything that she does, depends on it.

The hierarchy of priests and bishops has been maintained since the Apostles chiefly to celebrate the liturgy that changes bread and wine into Body and Blood; parishes and dioceses are mapped out so that everybody has easy access to Christ in the Eucharist. The Church's buildings are designed to accommodate this liturgy, and her arts are all basically the handmaidens of the Eucharist. The music, the vestments, the metalwork of the vessels of communion, the paintings and sculpture—everything is brought into being to

---

*There isn't room here to argue the point, but it's interesting to note that, in addition to the Church's living Tradition, the documentary evidence is abundant and undivided that Christians always understood the Eucharist as the reality of Christ's presence—not just a symbol of it. The Evangelists and St. Paul, who don't usually write about the same things to the same extent, each write about the Real Presence specifically and at length, so that any one of them gets the point across unequivocally. The Fathers of the Church, too, may argue about lots of things, but on this one point they're unanimous; like Acts and the Epistles, their writings assume that you understand the fact, or they teach it explicitly. St. Ignatius of Antioch, for instance, noted by about 110 that the Gnostics were heretics specifically "because they don't confess that the Eucharist is the flesh of our Savior Jesus Christ." Even schismatics, those separated from the Church on administrative or disciplinary grounds like the Greek Orthodox or the Eutychians, still take the True Presence as the cornerstone of Christian revelation.

serve the Eucharist, or to depict it, refer to it, reflect it, or otherwise lead people to the sacramental presence of Christ.

Technically, the process by which the bread and wine become the body and blood of Christ can be described as *transubstantiation*, a word used at least since the days of St. Thomas Aquinas and officially adopted by the Council of Trent. It's sort of the opposite of transformation, in which the substance of something stays the same but its appearance changes. Transubstantiation means that the appearance of the bread and wine stays the same but their substance is changed, as Christ said at the Last Supper, the last Passover meal that he celebrated with the Apostles.

But even though the Mass got its start in the old Jewish ceremonial meal for a family, it's for a family that includes hundreds or even thousands of people. It's the main occasion for the community of the faithful to assemble, so it has a definite educational purpose, too. Most important of all, it's the way that Christ stays physically present in his Church, and the Passover service wasn't directed to that end.

So the Apostles and their immediate successors stuck firmly with the liturgy that Christ established at the Last Supper—you can't really compromise with a directive like "Do this"—and on this foundation they framed the Mass as a unique liturgy in its own right. The core of the Mass has never changed since. As time went by, though, other procedures, prayers, and symbols were attached to this basic framework, so that the Mass could do what it needs to do and be understood by everybody who attends.

The nature of these attachments was determined by the times and places in which the early Church was working—by what you might call geopolitical factors. The important liturgical centers were where the Apostles were, in the eastern Roman Empire to start with, and later in Italy and France, all of them places where it's perfectly natural for people to use outward symbols and gestures to express an inward truth. So the Church, reaching out from its Jewish heritage to embrace the known world, supplemented and supported the words of her liturgy with expressive ceremonial. She adopted many of the rituals of Roman civil procedures—ceremonies from the courts of law and the halls of the emperors, for instance—that would say the appropriate things in ways that everybody would understand.

And, as time keeps going by, some of these peripherals are taken off again when they start hiding the framework, or they're clarified so that the meaning can still show through. Most of us have seen this process for ourselves in recent years, as the stately Baroque presentation mandated by the Council of Trent was reformed by the Second Vatican Council. Now the liturgy is focused once again on the essentials, restoring its timeless simplicity and elegance and bringing the unchanging pattern of the Mass more clearly into view.

If you take a broad view of its organization, each Mass consists of an *ordinary* and a *proper.* The prayers and Bible readings that make up the proper change every day to fit one of the two major cycles of the calendar, the temporal cycle, which includes the yearly holidays like Easter and Christmas, or the sanctoral cycle that commemorates the canonized saints.* The ordinary (from the Latin word *ordinare*, meaning "to put in order"; sometimes also called the *common*) is basically always the same. It's what gives structure to the Mass; into its framework, the parts of the proper are inserted according to the date and season. Every time you go to Mass, you'll hear the same ordinary and the proper that's—well, proper to the day. That's why the ordinary is sometimes printed once at the beginning of a missal, while the texts of the propers are in another section.

Your missal will also show you that the Mass has two major divisions, too, the Liturgy of the Word and the Liturgy of the Eucharist. The Liturgy of the Word comes first, as Mass begins with an introductory rite. This consists of a prayer that varies with the

---

*The sanctoral cycle is basically universal, but a lot of the celebrations depend on which jurisdiction you're in and which religious order (if any) you belong to. So a holy day of obligation here might not be observed as an obligation in the next country over. And in addition to these regular parochial Masses, there are "votive" Masses, extra ones designed to be offered for special intentions, such as to honor Mary, to pray for help in times of public emergency, to ask the prayers of a patron saint, or to pray for the dead. These Masses aren't tied to any particular date, but in certain cases they can be substituted for regular parish Masses. See chapter 21, on the design of churches.

day, and a greeting that's always the same: the Sign of the Cross, first, and then a wish from the priest that the grace and peace of the Lord be with the congregation, to which they reply "And also with you." This exchange of greetings starts the interaction between the two major participants in the liturgy, the priest and the congregation, both active partners in the celebration of the Mass (the ministers—"altar boys"—and the choir are there as deputies of the congregation, as it were).

Then, to prepare for the sacred mysteries, there's a penitential rite performed by priest and people together, yet individually. This usually includes the *Confiteor*, named from the first word of the original Latin version, which means "I confess" (not "we" confess; each of us takes responsibility personally). This is the prayer that contains the phrase *mea culpa*, "through my fault," that you hear so much. It's customarily punctuated by a beating of the breast, which is an extremely old penitential gesture, a token of self-inflicted punishment, but people sometimes get carried away with it. St. Augustine had to caution his congregation not to do it too enthusiastically; apparently there had been injuries, or at least an unseemly level of exertion.

The confession is followed, logically, by a plea for mercy, the *Kyrie*, the only part of the Latin Mass that was in Greek. Its name, too, comes from the first word used in the prayer: *Kyrie, eleison; Christe, eleison*—Lord, have mercy; Christ have mercy. (The story runs that a prelate at Vatican II, one who didn't really want to allow Mass in the vernacular languages, objected when the Kyrie was to be put into modern tongues. "At least," he thundered, "at least keep the Kyrie. Give them at least that much Latin!" After a stunned silence, the Council broke into laughter—laughter that the prelate himself joined, to his credit, when he realized what he'd said. Now we say it in English.)

That's it for the penitential rite; from here on, the Mass takes on the character of a joyous solemnity. The *Gloria* follows, when it's called for by the liturgical books, echoing the song of triumph sung by the angels at the first Christmas. Like the Kyrie, it can be sung, or rather chanted. (In song, the words are contrived to fit a melody, but in chant the notes follow the pattern and accent of the words. The actual constituent parts of a "sung" Mass are traditionally chanted, but in between parts you can have an entrance hymn, a post-communion hymn, and a recessional, which are songs.) After the Gloria, there's an opening prayer, also part of the proper, that tells you the theme of the proper, which will be reflected in the readings from the Bible as the Mass unfolds.

Then, with the introductory rites done, the Liturgy of the Word *per se* begins. Just as in the days of the Apostles, it always consists of readings from the Bible: a passage from the Old Testament, a responsorial Psalm in which the congregation is expected to make the response, a reading called the Epistle even though it's sometimes from another kind of apostolic book like Acts or Revelation, and a reading from the Gospels.

The Gospel has pride of place in the Liturgy of the Word. The other readings can be done by readers (lectors), but the priest or an immediately delegated deacon reads the Gospel. Because the Gospels embody the words of Christ in a unique way, the book that embodies the Gospels symbolizes the presence of Christ, and the Church has always made this point visually. The book is often kissed ceremonially, and it's escorted at solemn liturgies by an acolyte carrying a censer and two others bearing lighted candles. All of these honors used to be paid to Roman imperial dignitaries—or to the code of civil law that also embodied imperial authority and was therefore given precisely the same ceremonial treatment as the living magistrate. Like its civil Roman counterpart, the book itself is bound in the richest possible covers, often with a picture of the Lord of Lords on it, and it's carried high in processions. And it's sometimes placed on a cloth that hangs over the lectern (the *ambo*), another symbol taken from Roman civil ceremonial; when the Roman judge would leave the court, he'd put the book on his seat as a sign that he'd be back and that the law was still in effect until he did. The cloth on the ambo today is the last remnant of the cushion that used to be put on imperial judicial seats.

For that matter, the ancient etiquette that surrounded the magisterial seat governs a lot of other things that still happen in religious and civil rituals. Princely thrones, the judge's bench (which really was a bench in Roman days), and the bishop's *cathedra* that makes his church a cathedral all stem from this same tradition. A chair used to be the principal sign of official status, and only the highest-ranking officials got to sit down during public ceremonies. When you stand, you acknowledge your secondary status; standing is a posture of respect, like kneeling or bowing. That's why you stand in a civil court, at least when the judge comes in, and why it's rude to remain seated when you're introduced to people—it means you're pulling rank on them. And it's why you stand at Mass when you hear the Gospel read.*

The Gospel passages, like the other readings, aren't selected at random, on the spur of the moment. They're all worked out carefully according to a process that reconciles the overlapping demands of the temporal and sanctoral cycles, the principle of thematic harmony, the goal of semicontinuous reading, and all kinds of other factors. The regulations for the selections in the *Introduction to the Lectionary for Mass* run to eighteen pages and three big concordance tables, as detailed as an astronomical ephemeris and, to the layman, about as baffling as a railroad schedule.

It all makes sense when you hear the readings themselves. If you go to Mass as often as you're supposed to, you hear just about the whole Bible in a cycle of about three years, after which it starts again. And you should hear each reading related to the other readings and explained through the homily, which is supposed to be "truly the fruit of meditation, carefully prepared, neither too long nor too short, and suited to all those present, even children and the uneducated," according to the *Lectionary*. (You can see from this that homiletics is a highly specialized field of study, demanding a deep knowledge of theology and a delicate skill in the most exacting kind of rhetoric. Great preachers can be made, probably, but you're luckier if yours was born that way.)

However it goes, the homily is followed by a statement of faith (when the liturgical books require it), the Nicene Creed, which

*Everybody but the priest used to have to stand all during Mass. People who weren't up to it sat on the floor, or brought canes to lean on, but there was no seating furnished for the congregation. Pews were invented for Protestant meeting houses, where the Mass does not occur and preaching tended to run long, but they didn't show up in the Church's buildings until a couple of hundred years ago. And in some quarters the loss of the sweeping uncluttered space of Gothic churches, and of the glorious tessellated floors of classical ones, is still acutely regretted.

was basically hammered out by the Council of Nicæa in 325 because some heretics were confusing people; it stresses those particular points that were then most in need of clarification. Of course, it still gives an accurate statement of the basic tenets of the Church, but for children's Masses and certain other occasions the Apostles' Creed, which is about a century older, can be substituted. It has a different focus, but it embodies the same creed.

Then there are general intercessions, when priest and people together ask God for what they need. Pastorally, the intercessions also work to unite the congregation, because they're often your first notice that somebody's sick or has died, and they call attention to situations that need attention, at home and abroad. So, indirectly, asking God to help with these matters is asking the congregation to pull together and do something about them, too.

The intercessions close the Liturgy of the Word. At this point, catechumens—people who have not been entirely received into the Church—are dismissed. They need to be at Mass for the instructional and communal Liturgy of the Word, but they are not yet able to participate fully in the Liturgy of the Eucharist that follows. In the early centuries, the dismissal had a practical function, too: there were still spies and persecutions, and you had to be careful about letting all and sundry approach the altar. (Besides, the early Church had to be careful about public relations: "reverence for the mysteries is best preserved by silence," said St. Basil the Great in 375, "for that which is blabbed at random is no mystery at all." Other Fathers quoted the verse about giving holy things unto dogs, but the effect was the same.) Nowadays, this dismissal is often omitted for practical reasons, except during Lent, the season during which new converts approach the end of their initial formation through the Rite of Christian Initiation of Adults.

The Liturgy of the Eucharist echoes the Passover meal, the *Seder* mandated by Moses, and it follows the mandate given by Christ at the Last Supper, "Do this in memory of me." The bread and wine are brought to the altar, usually by a lay family in the congregation, but sometimes by a group for whom that particular celebration has some special meaning—a confraternity, perhaps, or a troop of Boy Scouts, or the bride and groom who are being married at that liturgy. At this point, the baskets are passed so that the rest of the congregation can participate in the giving, too.

This is done today in the form of cash or checks, usually in neat little envelopes printed for the purpose, but it used to be much more complicated than that. People would donate all kinds of things for the support of the clergy and the poor, or simply as a kind of tribute: honey, clothes, meat, shoes, chickens, flowers, oil, songbirds, furniture, geese, everything. It must have been chaos. By 390 there was a regulation that things other than money had to be sent separately, and a lot of churches were built with a special room set apart from the liturgical space where people could deposit their gifts for distribution later. By about 1000 the hierarchy made it clear that these goods and chattels really ought to be converted into money, which is easier to handle and matches any need. Even now, in some parts of the world, certain agricultural feasts are still marked by the donation of livestock, but it's done in a little ceremony strictly separated from the liturgy itself.

The *Preparation of the Gifts* is self-explanatory, if you listen to it, but it too has lots of little symbolic acts incorporated into it. The priest pours a little wine into the chalice and adds a little water; in the Middle Ages this was said to parallel the issuance of water and blood from Christ's side, and that's an apt comparison to make, but the addition of water is much, much older than that. Wine in the Greco-Roman world was made strong, far too strong to drink unmixed unless you wanted to get drunk as quickly as possible; decent folks always cut it with water. Anyway, the requirement of adding water is why there are two cruets on the altar, not just wine alone.

The priest then puts some hosts (round pieces of unleavened bread like the bread used at Passover) onto a paten. He blesses the bread and wine, using exactly the words of the Passover service performed by the father of a Jewish family. A little prayer over the gifts recalls again the proper theme of the Mass, and then, to set off this crucial part of the liturgy, the priest once more greets the congregation, exhorts them to lift up their hearts, and invites them to give thanks to the Lord—*Eucharist*, after all, is from the Greek word meaning "thanksgiving". Then, after a short preface, he invites the people to join in the everlasting hymn of the angels and saints, the *Sanctus*: Holy, Holy, Holy, Lord God of power and might! Heaven and Earth are filled with your glory! Hosanna in the Highest! Blessed is he who comes in the Name of the Lord! Hosanna in the Highest!

The Eucharistic Prayer, which has more than one approved form, follows. While the congregation kneels,* the priest repeats the words of Christ at the Last Supper, first over the bread and then over the cup, showing each to the congregation as they become the Body and Blood of Christ. This transubstantiation is the crux of the whole liturgy; it's the "clean sacrifice" predicted by Malachi (1:11), the sacrifice of Calvary continued, now unbloody, until the end of Time. At the end of the prayer, the priest invites the people to proclaim the Mystery of the Faith: Christ's death, resurrection, and promise to come again.

Again, just as in any other imperial court, you stand at this point, out of respect for the monarch who has just come in. The Lord's Prayer follows; Christ's command to say this when we pray made it certain that this prayer would be included in the Church's basic worship. Sometimes it's recited, sometimes sung, sometimes chanted; but it's always part of the Mass. Afterward, a short doxology links the prayer to the Sign of Peace, when everyone in the congregation turns to those around and greets them, by a handshake, a bow, a kiss, a smile and a wave, or some other mark of friendship. It's a sign that everybody has put aside all grudges, forgiven everybody (Mt 5:21–24), and extended themselves to their neighbors. And it means that everybody's equal in the presence of Christ.

This is really revolutionary, if you think about it, because it dispenses with social gradations among the faithful. Lords, schoolteachers, ladies, dockworkers, senators, everybody meets at Mass on an equal footing; how would anybody have ever thought of such a thing, in the days of the Cæsars! Especially without pews,

---

*Postures during Mass are determined generally by national conferences of bishops, so kneeling, standing, and sitting might happen at different points in the Mass, depending on where you are. It's another of those practices that are well handled by St. Augustine's sensible advice: when in Rome, do as the Romans do.

when you couldn't rush in to get a seat with your social set and had to stand there where poor people, tradesmen, even your own *servants* could just walk up and hug you. It was a profound exercise in humility, but by the Middle Ages all of this equality got to be too much for some of the high and mighty. So they introduced the *pax* (from the Latin word for "peace"), a sort of mirror-shaped piece of metal, or a thing that looked like a little picture frame, with an image of the Crucifixion or the Madonna and Child on it. You kissed the pax and then passed it on, which put a whole new element of precedence to it. Well, the more this custom spread, the more pointless it seemed, so when Trent reformed the liturgy they restricted the Sign of Peace to the celebrant and ministers around the altar. But after an eclipse of only about three hundred years, the Sign of Peace was reinstituted by Vatican II. It's a good reminder of the community of all the faithful, and that you leave your rank outside.

Then the congregation's attention turns to greet Christ in the Eucharist; Lamb of God, they say in unison with the priest, you take away the sins of the world; have mercy on us, give us peace. Then the priest leaves the altar, carrying the sacred specie, usually just the hosts but often, with the help of a deacon or other minister, offering the cup also. Naturally, there are strict but simple rules about receiving communion. This supreme act of solidarity with Christ is reserved for those who have been baptized; "because the Bread is one, we, though many, are one body, all of us who partake of the One Bread" (1 Cor 10:17).

Of course, it's not enough to be a member of the Church through Baptism; you have to fully accept all of the Church's teachings, being fully aware that this *is* the Body and Blood of Christ, not merely a representation of them, and you have to profess this in your words and life. That's why First Communion is such a milestone for a child, and it's why participating in a separated sect that rejects some or all of the teachings, failing to observe the laws about marriage, or otherwise living a scandalous life in the strict sense of the word keeps you from communion. Moreover, you have to be a member in good standing—you have to observe the rules about fasting before receiving, about being sacramentally in a state of grace at the moment of reception, and the others.* If you fail to observe the relevant rules, you may not receive the Sacrament. Absolutely not. St. Paul compared the offense to murder: "Whoever eats this Bread or drinks this Cup unworthily," he said, "will be guilty of the Body and Blood of the Lord" (1 Cor 11:27). "They slaughtered his most holy body, but you," said St. John Chrysostom later to some wayward parishioners, "you receive him with a filthy soul."

Because receiving the Eucharist is so solemn and profound an experience, distribution is followed by a time for quiet prayer and reflection. But it doesn't last long. After a few minutes of meditation, the priest stands and intones the dismissal: The Mass is ended; go in peace. Some reformers at Vatican II were a little uncomfortable with this, and they proposed that the distribution of the Sacrament be placed earlier in the Mass, more centralized in the liturgy. They didn't get very far. The whole idea is that Christ comes physically to the altar, then flows outward to the congregation, who carry him immediately out into the world. Because that's where he's needed.

---

*The current rule permitting reception of the Sacrament in the hand is particularly interesting. Vatican II never discussed the idea and evidently never envisioned its introduction. Some countries had introduced the practice illicitly, though, and Paul VI surveyed the bishops of the world about it. They almost unanimously called for maintaining the customary manner, distribution on the tongue. The Pope then granted an *indult* (a concession to do something not permitted by canon law) that let those countries that already had the practice continue. Oddly enough, the bishops of the United States—where the practice had never before existed—asked permission of the Holy See to introduce it here. Even more amazingly, they got it. Still, universal Church law does not permit reception of the Sacrament in the hand, and John Paul II strongly disapproves of it.

CHAPTER 8

OUTWARD SIGNS

*Decoding Symbols of Scripture
and the Sacraments*

ALL OF THE ART THAT the Church has produced during the last twenty centuries is intended to be self-explanatory, from the catacombs right down to your missalette. If it seems like there might be something more to it than what appears on the surface, there is, but there's no secret code. It's just that the language of images can be used exactly like a language of words, with just as much subtlety, to carry a rich load of connotations in addition to its face value.

In fact, practically every scene or symbol that you see in the Church's art is part of a whole system of interrelated references that run right through both Testaments. You can follow this network of correlations in art or in the Bible itself, because that's the way scripture is organized. Episodes are very carefully placed, and very artfully constructed, to give them their fullest possible significance.

Look at St. Luke's Gospel, for example, when Christ moves toward Jerusalem for the Passover feast (starting at about verse 11 of chapter 17). He enters the city in triumph, with the crowds cheering, and crowns this journey with the institution of the Eucharist at the Last Supper. But then the journey is played through again in reverse; he moves back out through Jerusalem, this time with the crowds reviling him, and this journey of disgrace culminates in the Crucifixion. St. Luke makes masterful use of the rules of classical rhetoric here, shaping the passage according to the symmetry of Christ's movements into and out of Jerusalem. And, punctuated by the two major events of Christ's ministry, the passage underscores the equivalence between the Crucifixion and its perpetual continuation in the Eucharist.

When you see a picture of the Last Supper, it's obviously intended to remind you of the institution of the Eucharist, but it should also call to mind the whole chain of events that led up to that moment and those that followed it in good order. In a way, it's too bad that we break the Bible into chapters and verses, because it interrupts the flow and makes these rhetorical devices harder to see. But a lot of biblical passages are set up this way, standing symmetrically around certain events. Or, sometimes, passages show their relationship by recalling to mind the same images.

For instance, the miracle of the loaves and fishes comes before the institution of the Eucharist in the Gospels, so it stands as a kind of explanation in advance, using the same things in a symbolic way. That's why you might find this scene, or just the loaves and fishes themselves, worked into stained glass or ornamenting the pages of your missalette. The image isn't there just as a reminder of one of Christ's more spectacular miracles; it unfolds the meaning of the Eucharist because it refers to Christ's miraculously distributing bread to the multitude, and we all know what the bread means. (The fact that fish were also distributed is interesting, too, from a symbolic point of view, because the Greek word for fish, 'ιχθΰς, is an acronym for 'ιησοΰς χριστός θεοΰ Υιός Σωτήρ which is "Jesus Christ, Son of God, Savior".) Visually as well as scripturally, the loaves and fishes are a prefiguration of the Eucharist. Other episodes involving miraculous bread and wine show up frequently in art, too, not just as references to isolated Bible stories but as commentaries or prefigurations of the Eucharist—the Wedding at Cana, for example.

This parallel structure of themes even works on a larger scale, with passages from the New Testament reflecting passages from the Old. These recurring themes are called "types", and you need them, in Christianity, to show how Christ fulfilled the prophecies and promises of the Old Covenant. The Passover meal established at the time of the Exodus is the type of the Eucharist, for instance, although you'd have to know the Bible from stem to stern to pick up on that. It's easier if your Bible has a good system of footnotes.*

But sometimes the connections are made explicitly. Christ himself pointed out that the story of Jonah was put there to tell you what was going to happen to the Messiah (Lk 11:29–30, which is followed by mention of still another prefiguration of Christ, Solomon), and he referred to manna when he was explaining his presence in the Eucharist in the sixth chapter of John. The whole Epistle to the Hebrews is concerned with outlining these kinds of connections. That's why St. Paul draws such a strong parallel between the sacrificial lambs in the Old Testament and Christ, the Paschal sacrifice of the New Covenant. And that, in turn, is the reason for all of those figures of the lamb on an altar that you see throughout Christian art. Sometimes the lamb has Christ's four-part halo and his banner of triumph, to make the parallel clearer.

If you give the matter enough thought, just about everything in the Old Testament can be seen as a prediction of something that Christ said or did. You hear the selections from the Old Testament related to the New this way at Mass, to a degree, but basically that's what the Old Testament is for: to prefigure the New Testament. In the New Testament itself, the correspondences start even before Christ was born. Look at the account of the Visitation: Elizabeth, pregnant with the prophet St. John the Baptizer, meets Mary, bearing Christ, and, as Mary approaches, John leaps for joy in the womb, which is how Elizabeth knows who Mary's child is. A charming scene, on the face of it, but it shows its full significance when you compare it to its predecessor in the Old Testament. That's not hard to find, since prophets in the Old Testament

---

*The note to Matthew 26:27–28, for instance, about Christ's blessing the cup of his blood in the New Covenant, probably refers you forward to Hebrews 9:22 ("with blood almost everything is cleansed according to the Law, and without the shedding of blood there is no forgiveness"), and back to Leviticus 17:11 ("I have made you put [blood] on the altar, so that atonement may thereby be made for your own lives, because it is the blood, as the seat of life, that makes atonement"), and maybe to Exodus 12:7, 24:5–8, and so on.

don't jump around very often. But one of them did: David, when he danced for joy before the Ark of the Covenant as it was brought home (2 Kgs 6:12–15).

The Ark is the key to matching up the scenes. The golden Ark of the Covenant carried within it the Law, embodied on the stone tablets; it prefigures Mary, the spotless vessel who carries within her the Law embodied as Christ. David dancing for joy prefigures John the Baptizer dancing in the womb (which also shows, while we're on the subject, that the Visitation has four complete and active characters, even though two of them are still *in utero*). Here, as with the rest of these prefigurations, you can express the meaning with words or with pictures. St. Luke did it with words, but you find a lot of visual references to the connection, too, as when the old Ark is used graphically as an emblem of Mary. Even the twin tablets of the Old Law point implicitly to the Incarnation of the New Law, serving as a visual emblem of Christ, while they point explicitly to the roots of our Faith in the Old.

In much the same way, the Sacrifice of Isaac (Gn 22:1–14) is a dramatic record of absolute faith all by itself, but it also prefigures the sacrifice of Christ: in both cases, a father offers his son in place of the sacrificial lamb. The Sacrifice of Jephte (Jgs 11:30–40) makes the same prophetic point as the Isaac story, only with a daughter and a much less happy ending. Even fairly obscure episodes, puzzling if you take them by themselves, make sense once you find the correspondences. The brazen serpent on its tree, radiating healing to Israel (Nm 21:4–9), smacks of idolatry until you realize that it's a visual prediction of Christ on the Cross.

Types work backward sometimes, too, which is why pictures of the descent of Wisdom at Pentecost are sometimes paired up with pictures of the Tower of Babel. If you can step back and get a view of the Bible's continuity, looking across the artificial boundaries of chapters and books, you'll find plenty of correspondences that deepen and enrich the meaning.

(You can also look for places where the authors break the flow of a passage on purpose, to make sure you won't miss something important. Melchisedec, the king of Salem, pops into the Bible like lightning, makes his prophecy, and is gone in only three verses, Gn 14:18–20. But from that instant on, he's been one of the most important prefigurations of Christ. He was both king and priest; he offered bread and wine, a prefiguration of the Eucharist, and he came to confirm Abraham's faith with a promise of safety. St. Paul picked up on the symbolism—see Hebrews, chapters 5 through 7—as had David himself: "Thou art a priest forever," says Psalm 109 to the expected Messiah, "according to the order of Melchisedec." There's also Mark 14:51–52, where the account jumps from the dramatic events of Christ's arrest to the almost embarrassing detail of a young man sleeping naked in the garden with only a linen cloth over him. The boy wakes up and gets away when the soldiers try to capture him by leaving only the linen cloth in their grasp, which seems almost like low comedy until you find out that Christ was to do exactly the same thing, with far greater significance; see Jn 20:5–9.)

In fact, the Bible refers to itself so often that you can find a lot more prefigurations and parallels than any system of footnotes could hold. That's why it can be so misleading to just take the Bible literally, at face value, or to take verses out of context. The Bible is a whole system of images and references and symbols, all so closely stitched together that you can't pull one out without ripping the whole thing apart.

That's also why you see so many scenes from the Old Testament in association with the other sacraments, just as you see them in reference to the Eucharist. By the end of the second century, the frescoes in the catacombs like the Greek Chapel in the catacomb of Priscilla showed episodes like the healing of the cripple at Bethsaida, Moses striking the rock, and Noah's Ark as types of the sacrament of baptism. The Ark is a pretty clever symbol to put into a baptistry of that time; it has to do with water and being saved, but it also symbolizes the fact that salvation through the Church (the Ark itself) is to be open to everybody, regardless of race or nation. "Of every sort of living creature of all flesh you shall bring two into the ark, to keep them alive with you," says Gn 6:19, not just all living creatures that are kosher. Later, you'll find baptistries and fonts illustrated with just about every scriptural reference to people being saved by the agency of water: the crossing of the Jordan by Israel, maybe, or the crossing of the Red Sea. Of course, there's also the baptism of Christ; he did a good many things, like praying and being baptized, that he didn't have to do, just to show us that we're supposed to (Jn 13:15).

Because buildings are built especially for baptism and for the Eucharist (that's what churches are for), types and prefigurations like these show up frequently in the Church's public art, in the sculpture, paintings, mosaics, and such. Other sacraments, though, tend to use such references in other ways, like in the liturgical readings heard during the sacrament itself or in illuminations for liturgical books. You might see engravings of the Wedding at Cana in a printed marriage service, or the scenes of anointing in the Old Testament might be turned to good use as visual commentaries on Confirmation. They might serve to help explain the Anointing of the Sick, too.

Holy Orders doesn't show up too much in the visual arts, but there are plenty of suitable types that illustrate it when the need arises—scenes of anointing, of course, and the Last Supper as the foundation of the Eucharist, or even the charge to Peter all make important points about priesthood, as does the figure of Melchisedec. Artists don't get many opportunities to depict the sacrament of Reconciliation, either, although it's the subject of one of the most powerful types in all of Scripture. When Christ gave the Apostles the power to forgive sin, he did so by breathing on them (Jn 20:22–23). There's only one other time in the whole Bible when God breathed on Man: Genesis, when he breathed life itself into his creation. So the manner of the institution of Reconciliation is a sign that Christ gave his Church a faculty as important as that of life itself.

Well, again, the Bible is largely a matter of prophecy fulfilled, and things are designed to match up between the two Testaments.* But the human authors of the Bible also made a lot of their points

---

*That's one form of prophecy, when something happens, or God requires some action, that doesn't carry a very obvious meaning but delivers another piece of revelation that fits into the whole thing later. That kind of prophecy is over now, since the death of the last Apostle. But another form is still around: when a prophet rises up and says, essentially, that if you keep going as you are, God won't put up with it much longer (or gives some other warning). So prophecy is still active in the Church, and it occurs usually within the laity. Recognizing the gift of prophecy, the hierarchy is obliged to listen. But merely saying that

about unfamiliar heavenly things by comparing them with familiar earthly things—whether you're dealing with words or with images, this is a very common rhetorical device. It's how parables work, which is why Christ said things like "I am the light of the world"; he didn't mean that literally, either.

But you also get comparisons made through a third thing that isn't explicitly mentioned, which is what happens with images like the Vision of Ezekiel. Certainly, the Throne of God is not something that you're likely to encounter in your daily life. It's by nature unfamiliar to us. So, when Ezekiel was faced with the problem of illustrating the Throne of God, of giving his readers some idea of what it looked like and—more important—what it meant, he couched it in familiar terms. (Or you could say that God contrived the vision so that Ezekiel would be able to understand and convey it easily; the process is the same, no matter who does it.) There was a firmament, Ezekiel said; everybody would understand that, because Hebrew imagery consistently speaks of God enthroned above the firmament (Jb 22:14, 36:29; Psalms, etc.). This was reflected in the structures of the Old Covenant: the tent sanctuary of Moses, held aloft by poles or pillars, was one such model of the sky, and so were the *ephods*, ceremonial tents that represented the presence of God among Israel.

To make his point clearer, Ezekiel says that the particular firmament he saw was held up by four winged beasts rather than by poles or pillars: a man, a lion, an ox, and an eagle. Those beasts, blazing with heavenly light, are the symbols of four of the twelve signs of the Zodiac (which was simply the way that people mapped the heavens, back then; we're not discussing fortune-telling here). The man is the constellation Aquarius, the lion is Leo, the ox is Taurus, and we now call the eagle Scorpio. If you want to use the starry sky to signify the everlasting Throne of God, you have to specify these four constellations in particular because they're "fixed"; when the Sun appears to be traveling through their sectors of the sky, you're in the middle of a definite season, and the weather is steady and fairly predictable. The other

---

somebody will entertain an unexpected visitor or that some celebrity will marry in the coming year isn't prophecy. It's fortune-telling, and it doesn't count.

signs represent change of one kind or another, but with a fixed sign, the whole universe seems to be stable, definite, and unchanging (when the Sun's in Leo, you're in the middle of summer, for instance). These four astronomical signs, holding up the "firmament" in place of simple poles or pillars, tell you that Ezekiel is talking particularly about the celestial firmament of the sky.*

Well, if these four beasts symbolize the four immovable pillars that hold up the vault of heaven, the four supports of the Throne of God; if they're the beings that carry the visible splendor of God to humans—then they're also a prefiguration of Matthew, Mark, Luke, and John, aren't they! So the four beasts of Ezekiel's vision became the emblems of the Evangelists—a meaning implied in the Apocalypse (4:6–8) and explicit since at least the time of St. Irenæus. You get a three-way correspondence here, linking the Vision of Ezekiel to the Evangelists' symbols by way of the firmament of heaven supported by the immovable stars, which isn't explicitly mentioned in either biblical image.

When you see the winged man, lion, ox, and eagle surrounding the Hand of God or a figure of Christ, or if you see the four beasts displayed on the supports of a dome, you're seeing all of these meanings at once. You're also seeing, if you look through medieval eyes, the four elements that Aristotle said made up the whole totality of the universe; the man of St. Matthew is associated with the element air, the lion of St. Mark with fire, the ox of St. Luke with earth, and the eagle of St. John with water. Depending on the point you wanted to make, you might also associate them with the directions of the compass, the four times of day (dawn, noon, sunset, and midnight), the four humors of classical medical theory, the four seasons, or any other group of four things that had some appropriate significance.

After all, these interconnected symbol systems have some educational value exactly because they don't have any limits. There's no one-to-one correspondence between an item from the Old Testament and one from the New, no Periodic Table of Analogies be-

---

*The "wheels within wheels", while we're at it, are just another cosmological symbol, an image of the stars and planets beneath the sky whirling around the Earth.

tween this world and the next. In fact, you find the Fathers of the Church and their medieval successors spinning out whole sermons of this stuff, one analogy after another, dozens of them at a time. They make a fascinating study, but these parallels aren't intended to be taken as facts themselves; they're meant to point to facts. They're designed to make you think. And that's exactly what symbols are all about.

CHAPTER 9

THE SUN OF
JUSTICE

The Calendar as the Image of Christ's Life

I N THE BEGINNING, when God created the lights in the firmament to separate day from night, he gave them specific functions. "Let them serve as signs and for the fixing of seasons, days, and years," he said. Thus the heavens and the Earth were finished, and all their array.

And as long as the Earth shall last, he added, seedtime and harvest, cold and heat, summer and winter, day and night, shall not cease. Well, this divine order of things is particularly important to the Church, because she's been in charge of the calendar for nearly two thousand years. That might not seem all that difficult, but making a calendar isn't just a matter of counting off the days until you get a whole year. It's complicated because everything in the solar system runs around in ellipses, as you know, and the time that it takes each heavenly body to go around once works out to *almost* some regular fraction of how long it takes all the others.

It's the "almost" that gets you. From here on Earth, the Moon seems to go around the Earth once a day—almost; it actually takes it something like twenty-four hours and fifty minutes. And it goes around through its phases in approximately—but not quite—one-twelfth of the time it takes the Earth to go around the Sun. That makes a lunar year only 354 days long, eleven and a half days shorter than a solar year. And the days get longer toward summer, shorter toward winter, so they don't work out exactly, either. (You wonder what it was like before Adam's fall, at which instant "the blasted Starrs lookt wan," in John Milton's words, "and Planets, Planet-struck, real Eclips then suffered . . ." Maybe it really was all circular and regular before the dawn of disobedience. Sin certainly knocked everything else off kilter.)

It's hard to coordinate all of these movements into one calendar. You use the phases of the Moon to determine months, and you want a year to equal the time it takes the Earth to go around the Sun once (or *vice versa*, if you grew up when people thought that the Earth was in the middle). And you try to set it up against the background of the unchanging stars, because the Sun and the Moon seem to move across the twelve signs of the Zodiac in a year (more or less). But if you just set up a calendar and let it run, those little fractional differences build up, and before you know it you're losing whole days, or having seasons start in inappropriate months. In only three years, the lunar calendar is more than a month out of step with the solar. So somebody has to figure out how to adjust it and keep standard records about it.

The Romans gave that job to the head of the college of state priests, the *Pontifex Maximus*, because there was something sacred about the great heavenly bodies moving around in stately, almost regular, cycles. The pontifical college centered their attention on fixing the dates for public feasts, which were usually seasonal festivals related to planting and harvest, and they adjusted the calendar now and again to keep things on track. But, when the civil wars started in Rome a century before Christ, they let things slip, and the civil calendar degraded into nonsense. Finally one Pontiff, Julius Cæsar, who had to be in Alexandria on business (he was putting Cleopatra back on her throne), took advantage of the great astronomers and philosophers in Egypt to fix the Roman calendar as it had never been fixed before. This "Julian" calendar, as he modestly called it, was the standard for nearly sixteen hundred years. Still, it was structured like the old Roman calendar, and the same kinds of little discrepancies took their toll. Year after year the old Julian calendar slipped farther and farther from making any sense at all.

What does this have to do with the Church? Well, since the days of Constantine, the Bishop of Rome has held the title Pontifex Maximus, so it was up to the Pope *ex officio* to take care of the official Julian calendar (that's why we number the years from the birth of Christ). Every year, the Pope would work out a calendar and have the dates for the major feasts announced in all of the cathedrals, out loud, at Epiphany. From time to time the popes would try to correct the calendar in general, to clear up all of those little astronomical discrepancies and keep things consistent. But by the 1580s the Julian calendar was off by twelve whole days.

To straighten it out, Pope Gregory XIII Buoncompagni called together a group of eminent astronomers at the observatory in the Vatican gardens and, under his personal direction, they worked out a whole new calendar, the one that you use today. That's why they call it the Gregorian calendar. Unlike the old Julian calendar, the Gregorian is designed to correct itself whenever it needs to, which is why we have leap years, and it should be pretty well accurate for tens of thousands of years. So Gregory fulfilled that function of his ancient office better than anybody ever had before, even Julius Cæsar.

But he also redefined the other function of the old pontifical college, setting the dates for the great holidays of the year and for the commemoration of the saints. Today, these dates don't have to be figured out every year; ever since Gregory reformed the calendar, the Church's schedule for these events has been predictable and fairly uniform year after year.

The Church's calendar has two great cycles: the *sanctoral* cycle, the cycle of saints' days; and the *temporal* cycle, the "cycle of times". Everybody knows at least something about the sanctoral cycle. Even our secular culture has picked up St. Valentine's Day and St. Patrick's Day as holidays, and everybody knows St. Nicholas, one way or another. But every day has its saint—or saints. In fact, the term for being solemnly declared a saint, *canonization*, means being enrolled in the "canon" or calendar of feast days. When some of the saints were "de-canonized" back in the days just after Vatican II, there were a lot of jokes about how the Church seemed to be changing her mind about who's a saint and who isn't, but that's not what happened. "De-canonization" just means being taken off the calendar of feast days. This was done because the old sanctoral cycle was heavily weighted to Europeans, particularly Italian and French saints; ancient and worthy role models that they are, they didn't give an overall picture of the universal Church and her heroic men and women around the world, the fruits of centuries of missionary work.

So the Pontifex Maximus reviewed the sanctoral cycle and evened out the representation to give equal time to saints from Africa, Asia, and the Americas. The commemorations of some other saints had to be dropped, outside of their homelands—only so many days in a year—but, if there had been a formal or well-attested informal canonization, nobody said anything about reversing it. Once a saint, always a saint; but you might not have a universal commemoration any more.

Before you can assign feast days to saints, you still have to know which day is which, and that's what the temporal cycle does. It's the great organizer of the Church's year. The whole temporal cycle depends on the date of Easter, the greatest feast day of the year, the Solemnity of Solemnities. In the Church's view, Easter is much more noteworthy than even Christmas—everybody is born, but Christ alone rose from the dead, an act crucial to the Cycle of Redemption. So fixing the date of Easter is the starting point for any Christian calendar.

In the early Church, this was a major problem. The date of the Passover after which Christ rose from the dead had been established by the Jewish calendar. But you couldn't use the Hebrew calendar for figuring out when Easter was supposed to be, because the Hebrew calendar is lunar, not solar like the Julian calendar that everybody in the West used because of civil regulation (and its greater accuracy). It's arbitrary, too, with extra months thrown in as you need them to make it come out even—it's run by observation, not by calculation. So if you followed the Hebrew calendar, you wouldn't have Easter on Sunday, every year. It would jump around during the week. You might have Easter on a Wednesday one year and on a Tuesday the next, and you'd never know what month it would be in, either.

Obviously, the Church, spreading rapidly across the known world, had to figure out how to fix the dates of holidays so that everyone would be on the same liturgical calendar. And this was highly controversial stuff in the early years. Because Sunday was already the primary day of Christian worship, some said that Easter should be on the first Sunday after Passover, whenever Passover happened to fall, according to the Hebrew calendar. Still others said that it should be celebrated exactly at Passover.

Of course, if you took either of these strategies, Easter would fall on a different day every solar year, and that wouldn't work too well—besides, it would tie the Church's most important holiday to the decisions of another sect outside of, and often hostile to, Christianity. The minority that held this opinion were called "Quartodecimans", because they wanted Easter to always be on the *quartodecima die*, the fourteenth day, of the Jewish month of Nisan, when Passover is. They were regarded as heretics, which shows you how seriously people took this, in those days. In fact, whole segments of Christianity split with the Church over this issue.

To this day, the date of Easter is still a point of serious disagreement among Christian denominations. Protestants follow the Church's date, but even in 1964 the Second Vatican Council's *Decree on the Catholic Eastern Churches* recognized the hope that "all Christians" would "agree . . . on one day for the celebration of Easter" and urged "as a means of fostering [local] unity" that local authorities "consult all parties involved and so come to an unanimous agreement to celebrate the feast of Easter on the same Sunday."

It's better than it used to be. Although the ecumenical Council of Nicæa back in 325 didn't complete its work on the liturgical calendar, they did figure out a formula that would work for setting the date of Easter. They directed that Easter was to be celebrated on the Sunday immediately following the full moon that occurs at the vernal equinox—the day in spring when we have a twelve-hour day and a twelve-hour night. If the full moon didn't fall on that exact day, then Easter would be the first Sunday after the first full moon after the vernal equinox. This formula is still used today in the Latin Church, and, believe it or not, it simplifies matters.

The unexpected thing about our workaday Gregorian calendar is its symbolism: more than just ticking off the days until your vacation, it forms a great image of faith, showing how the order of nature corresponds to the story of redemption. "Within the cycle of the year," says Vatican II's *Constitution on the Sacred Liturgy*, the Church "unfolds the whole mystery of Christ, not only from his incarnation and birth until his ascension, but also as reflected in the day of Pentecost, and the expectation of a blessed, hoped-for return of the Lord. Recalling in this way the mysteries of redemption, the Church opens to the faithful the riches of her Lord's powers and merits, so that these are in some way made present at all times, and the faithful are enabled to lay hold of them".

The idea that all of this everyday imagery depends on, of course, is that Christ is "the way, the truth, and the light". He is the Sun of Justice, who, by rising, chases off the darkness—read Psalms 100, 103 (especially verses 20–23), and 111:4, which give you the idea. Just as sunrise makes thieves and beasts seek their dens, so does the coming of Christ make sin and evil run and hide.

Our fathers in faith were aware of what it means to have Easter near the spring equinox. After that date, the days get longer and longer, even without the Daylight Saving Time we have in our civil timekeeping. But symbolically, it means that Christ revealed himself to man ever more fully after arising from the dead, just as the Sun, weakened during the short, dark days of winter, grows stronger after the spring equinox.

This celestial symbolism fits in well with the custom of receiving new catechumens into the Church at Easter. Here, too, the language of Vatican II reflects this solar imagery: "when the sacraments of Christian initiation have freed them from the powers of darkness (cf. Col 1:13) . . . they [the catechumens] celebrate the remembrance of the Lord's death and resurrection together with the whole people of God" (*Decree on the Missionary Activity of the Church*).

The Sun reaches its fullest strength at the summer solstice, the longest day of the year and that's right around the feast of Pentecost, when the Holy Spirit descended as tongues of fire to give the Apostles the power to convert the whole world to the light of Christ.

But then there's another equinox—a day and a night of twelve hours each—that falls around the feast of St. Michael. Then the Sun's power wanes as winter approaches. As the days grow shorter and colder, as the Sun sinks lower in the sky and sends out ever-weakening rays, we mark the days until Christmas, which falls just about the time of the winter solstice, the shortest day of the year.

Why then? Well, it's the same idea, and it's very, very old. After the winter solstice, the Sun starts getting stronger, brighter, higher in the sky. In a way, the Sun "rises from the dead", restoring life and light to the winter-dead world. This is such an important astronomical event that every human society on the planet marked it somehow. It was featured in the pre-Columbian ceremonies of Native Americans, and it used to be the day that the ancient Chinese emperors appeared publicly to the foreign ambassadors, which also mirrors the idea that on this day the Son of Heaven, as they called him, shone forth in new splendor. And throughout history, the birthdays of gods who promised life after death—forgotten gods like Mithras and Hercules—were celebrated on or near the day when the Sun was reborn in strength. When the Church decided to celebrate the birth of Christ at this same time, it was following one of the oldest human traditions.

And, if you think about it, commemorating Christ's birth at that time makes sense. It also explains a lot of the Church's images and customs. Think of the things of Christmas. The evergreen (the ever-living) trees, for instance. How appropriate for a mid-winter feast that restates the promise of everlasting life when every other green thing is dead. Think of the tongues of fire we see at Pentecost—how right they are for the time when the Sun is highest and strongest in the sky.

And think of the things of Easter. The rabbits, whose regenerative powers are legendary. The eggs, symbols of new life; the Paschal candle, lighted with new fire. All of these images are ancient, pre-Christian—prehistoric—in their origins. They are all universally understood signs of springtime, of new life, of renewed life. And they are all, in their way, apt reflections of the light of Christ.

CHAPTER 10

UNTIL WE
MEET AGAIN

The Ceremonies of the Christian Funeral

A DEATH IN THE FAMILY is one of those occasions when the Church says, yes, this, right here, today, what happened to *your* Grandpa, *this* is what we've been telling you about ever since you were little; this is how life works. It's also one of those occasions, like a wedding, when your development as a Christian comes to the surface, bobbing into view along with your maturity and common sense.

You shouldn't be surprised at death, and you're supposed to know what's going on, in terms of Christianity (Jn 11). The person does not cease to exist or lose identity (immortality of the soul); death does not break the bonds between you and the deceased (communion of saints); the living Church is there to embrace and comfort you in your loss (unity of the faithful); it's not the last time you'll see the person (resurrection of the dead); and your turn will come, so get ready. Christ went through the whole cycle himself, and he took his Mother through it with dispatch, just so that you can know ahead of time how things work, and not be afraid.

Death in America throws people into a panic, though. Contrary to what the Church teaches, our secular culture encourages you to fear death, or—worse—to ignore it. So when it comes around, people are at a loss. They act angry, or insulted and surprised, carrying on as if it didn't have to happen. They take up all kinds of theories about how to handle their feelings, in an attempt to put the experience behind them and ignore it again until the next time. They may even spend every penny of the insurance benefits on a big send-off, occupying days and weeks with visitations, viewings, floral arrangements, and things that they're *supposed* to do.

You could say that American secular customs are aimed at coming to terms with the funeral, not with the death. But these frames of reference have grown up among people searching for answers outside the Cycle of Redemption. The things that Christ taught by word and example seem, somehow, to fly out of view when death happens. That's why secular funeral customs and the machinations of popular psychology tend to ring hollow for many people, and it's why these bereavement theories come and go like current best-sellers.

And then there's the funeral industry, the product of our secular culture. Nobody's going to deny that the funeral industry does fill a vital role. After all, Americans these days would rather not wash, dress, and transport their departed relatives when the time comes (although most people in the world do). Virtually no Americans, apparently, can bring themselves to learn about things like death certificates and burial permits, and it's reassuring to have professional undertakers to help out.

But it's important to note that almost all of the unquestioned funeral practices in this country were invented by the funeral industry, which deals mostly with people who subscribe to creeds that reject all or part of the Church's teachings. Many of the things that most Americans expect at a funeral actually run counter to Christian views of the universe, and you'd be surprised how recently the funeral industry came up with some of them. The "funeral home" was unknown before about 1920; ten-thousand-dollar "caskets", organized viewing of the routinely embalmed corpse, lavish "floral tributes", and all of the rest of it were unknown to our grandparents. (When these things were introduced, by the way, a lot of people found them very distasteful.)

The funeral industry, as an industry, has lobbied for a great deal of legislation in various states about the handling and disposal of human remains, but no law says that you've got to have the kind of funeral that they might say you need. Quite the contrary. The Church's law often says, or assumes, that you *mustn't* do it that way. In fact, the Church's way of dealing with death may be surprising in many ways. The new *Order of Christian Funerals* is highly flexible, full of alternatives and room for personal choice, but it keeps well within the limits of Christian sensibility.

First, of course, before anything else, you have to take care of the body. "In countries or regions where an undertaker, and not the family or community, carries out the preparation and transfer of the body," the *Order* says, "the pastor and other ministers are to ensure that the undertakers appreciate the values and beliefs of the Christian community. The family and friends of the deceased should not be excluded from . . . the preparation and laying out of the body." The body, in the Church's view, became the temple of the Holy Spirit at baptism, and it's going to rise again to everlasting life, so it has to be treated with decent respect.

But the focus of the whole funeral is the person's entry into everlasting life, not on the body that's left behind. That means that the coffin doesn't need an innerspring mattress or fifteen coats of automotive lacquer. It makes cosmetics unnecessary (are cosmetics ever necessary?). Organ donation is well within the Church's ideas on charity, and so is donation of the whole body for medical research, as long as it's respectfully disposed of afterward, which most catholic medical schools handle routinely. You can be simply (and liturgically) buried before the funeral, too. Cremation immediately after death is all right, believe it or not, "unless it is evident that cremation was chosen for anti-Christian motives", and it has the added attraction of unexpectedly low cost. The bottom line is that you don't really have to show up at your own funeral, if you don't want to.

Well, body or no, the *Order* reminds us, you've still got a family in grief, possibly in bewilderment and shock. It points out that the Church's ministry at this point consists of "gently accompanying the mourners in their initial adjustment to the fact of death and to the sorrow that this entails." Drawing on two millennia of psychological and spiritual expertise, the clergy and your fellow parishioners take over most of this ministry, but it's formalized in the *vigil*, the first of the three parts of the Christian funeral suggested by the *Order.*

The vigil can be held in a funeral parlor, of course. But it can also be held in the person's home, or someone else's home, or at church; these are eminently suitable places, and there's no rental fee on any of them. Again, you don't have to have the body there, and you certainly don't have to "view" it—that's actually contrary to the focus of the Christian funeral, and nobody we know has to lie in state, anyway. (Kings and presidents have to, because the general public has to see them dead. It makes their successors legal. So, unless you're the scion of a sovereign house, you might want to keep the lid closed.)

The vigil starts at an appointed time, and it's not too long. It includes readings and music, but chiefly prayer. Like the rest of the funeral proceedings, it may not look like you'd think. No black draperies, no lugubrious moaning organ music (unless, for some reason, you particularly specify it). Instead, the symbolism aims to recall the sacrament of baptism, the person's spiritual birthday that makes him a member of the Church on Earth and opens the way to the Church in Heaven. A pall can cover the coffin or a *catafalque* (an empty coffin used as a representation of the deceased). The old Roman Missal said that the pall could just be spread on the floor in front of the altar, if you have the vigil in the church, and that's still customary in some places. But the pall really shouldn't be black; white, the color of baptismal robes, is more suitable to the occasion.* You can put a Bible, a book of the Gospels, a cross, or a few fresh flowers on the pall, but other symbols, "for example, national flags or flags and insignia of associations," says the *Order*,

---

*It's more suitable to the symbolism of a pall, too, because a pall is a sign of life, not death. It started out as the mantle worn by monarchs to show that their offices don't die when the incumbent dies. The coronation "pallium" worn by the kings of England is made out of cloth-of-gold, to further the symbolism of immortality. The kings of France used to send such a garment from their own coronations to be laid over the tomb of Charlemagne, making the same point about the undying continuity of kingship. The Pope and metropolitan archbishops wear a vestment also called the pallium, which has been a sort of loose necktie since about the ninth century—Charlemagne's day, come to think about it—but which apparently started out as a similar royal robe. These are blessed by the Pope on the Feast of Sts. Peter and Paul and left overnight over the body of St. Peter, in the Niche of the Pallia. The square of starched linen used at Mass to cover the paten and chalice is also called a pall, and because it covers the Body and Blood of Christ it has the same symbolism of immortal life.

"have no place in the funeral liturgy." The parish's Easter candle, as a symbol of resurrection and life, can be lighted at a church vigil, just as it is at baptisms.

The second part of the rite, the funeral liturgy itself, is supposed to take place in your proper parish church (Canon 1177). Everybody in the parish should come; the only one whose physical presence can be excused is the deceased, if other arrangements have been made. You can have the funeral liturgy within the context of a Mass or without the Mass. If the body (or catafalque) is present, it's solemnly and joyously received at the church in a ceremony that also includes a number of baptismal symbols. Then there's a liturgy of the Word, with readings from the Bible and a homily. But—another surprise—"never any kind of eulogy." You're supposed to get down to principles like God's compassion and love and the promise of resurrection and everlasting life; you're supposed to console and strengthen the community in their loss, not to dwell on somebody's past accomplishments in the face of the great equalization of death.

A final commendation and farewell serves as the bridge between the funeral liturgy and the *rite of committal*, the third and last ceremony outlined in the *Order*. During the commendation, the body or its representation is sprinkled with holy water (another reminder of new birth through baptism) and maybe incensed. Then, usually, a procession forms to escort the body to the place of final deposit.

That's it. It's simple, dignified, and economical, and it's aimed in the right direction. And, all in all, you have a wide range of choices when it comes to funerals. The *Order* encourages your family and friends to take a primary part in arranging things. It almost insists on it. Or you can plan things to your own liking, within that framework and ahead of time, naturally. You can choose most of the readings and music; the *Order* allows more leeway in these things than any other liturgical book, and it offers two or more alternatives for just about every part of the funeral, all of them beautiful on a cosmic scale yet relating the whole of Christianity to this one very personal event. It also puts the ceremonial into a broad and sympathetic context, giving you the rationale for the whole thing, explaining why things are done instead of just telling you what to do.

Talk to your pastor and your funeral director about preplanning your funeral. They can help you explore all of the alternatives, plan a service in accord with your beliefs and feelings, and keep costs reasonable. Most religious-goods stores offer plenty of helpful (if sometimes appallingly cheerful) little books about it, with blank forms for you to fill in. And take a look at the *Order of Christian Funerals* itself. You just might be surprised.

CHAPTER 11

THE STATIONS OF
THE CROSS
The Logic of Their Development

WHEN WE WERE LITTLE, MANY of us used to find our pews after Communion by remembering the closest station of the Cross. Everybody knows these graphic representations of the Passion of Our Lord—every church has them. The devotion that uses these images starts on the first Good Friday, on the hill of Calvary.

When Jesus died on the Cross, Joseph of Arimathea asked Pilate for the body and laid it in a new tomb (Jn 19:38–42). This was the typical Jewish tomb of the time, cut into the rock in the side of a hill. It hadn't been used before, and, after the first Easter, the tomb was almost certainly not used again.

It may have been the site of Christian commemoration, but by the early fourth century it was completely lost, what with all of the wars and invasions that went on. Until that really awe-inspiring lady, Helena, mother of the first Christian Roman Emperor, took matters in hand in about the year 325. You may remember Helena as the one who found the True Cross; well, she went looking for the Holy Sepulchre, too. She was told in a dream that the Tomb was completely covered under accumulated earth and that it had a shrine of Aphrodite built above it.

Helena cleared away the pagan sanctuary and the rocky hill as well, leaving only the little cave-tomb and a shell of rock around it, still attached to the bedrock. Then she built a church around the whole thing.

This Church of the Holy Sepulchre is still there. All things considered, it's in pretty good shape, maintained by Roman Catholic and Greek Orthodox priests. (Protestant sects have built a shrine of their own at a nearby tomb, the so-called "Garden Tomb", but interestingly enough everyone has always known that the Garden Tomb is not the Tomb of Christ.)

People naturally started visiting the Holy Sepulchre as a pious act. And, in the Middle Ages, priests started assigning trips to the Sepulchre as a penance for certain serious sins. Penitents would usually be shown the places in Jerusalem where, according to traditional recollection, certain key episodes of the Passion took place, and their trip culminated at the Sepulchre itself, from which Christ rose from the dead. Those who could make the trip to Jerusalem and back, under the prescribed conditions, got a plenary (full) indulgence.

It's important to be clear on what an indulgence is, because those who don't understand it use the term so often in a disapproving way. An indulgence is remission of temporal punishment due to sin, provided that the sin has already been forgiven. That is, sin, even after forgiveness through the sacrament of Reconciliation, merits punishment on Earth or in Purgatory. Temporal punishment, punishment that lasts only a time, is one of the ways that the sinner makes his adjustment to God. The Church has the power to remit a person from this punishment (check, for instance, Mt 16:17–19) with an indulgence, provided, again, that the person is in the state of grace, has the intention of gaining the indulgence, and performs the required acts.

But it wasn't all that easy to gain the indulgences you could get by piously visiting the Holy Sepulchre. The Middle East has always been about as rambunctious as it is today, and travel to Jerusalem has always been dangerous, not to mention expensive. A man would have to leave his work and family for as long as two years to make the trip, and his dependents would never know whether he'd make it back. Women with children, of course, couldn't make it at all.

Well, this didn't make sense to a lot of Christians. It didn't seem fair to grant indulgences only to those rich enough or strong enough—and lucky enough—to make the trip halfway around the known world. What about those too ill, too weak, too tied to their fields and flocks? Why couldn't they get a plenary indulgence, too, if they fulfilled all of the conditions but didn't have the physical ability to travel?

So various Church organizations—confraternities, guilds, even some monastic orders—built copies of the Holy Sepulchre all over Europe. Most were simple round or octagonal churches built around a plain stone monument, or even a mark on the floor, that represented the Sepulchre, with other markers to represent events that happened on the way to Calvary. They were built in whatever style was fashionable at that place and time. After all, you didn't go to the Holy Land to appreciate the architecture; you went to get the grace of the indulgence, so these "copies" didn't have to look like the building in Jerusalem. They just had to be properly privileged and suitable as a place to meditate on the Passion and Resurrection of Our Lord.

In this way, the spiritual benefits of a trip to the Holy Land were made available to many more Christians—not just the indulgences, but a chance to walk that sad route with Christ, to meditate on his Passion and to share it in a particularly intimate way. But after a while, even this wasn't enough. Think of the thousands of peasants who couldn't make it to the next village, let alone the next principality. So the Franciscans took the next logical step to correct this situation, beginning in about the fourteenth century.

They began putting up wooden crosses in parish churches everywhere—the actual number of crosses varied, but there were usually about fourteen, each representing a "station" or episode in the Passion. As the spiritual benefits of this devotion became evident, the Franciscans obtained from the Holy See a plenary indulgence for those who undertook the Way of the Cross properly. The idea, then as now, was that you could simply go to your parish church and meditate on each of the stations, so you didn't have to go all the way to Jerusalem. The devotional Way of the Cross and its spiritual benefits were available to virtually everybody, and only a few more "copies" of the Church of the Holy Sepulchre were built.

In 1731, about four hundred years after the Way of the Cross became popular, Pope Clement XII Corsini fixed the number of stations at fourteen, as we know them today, and permitted indulgenced stations to be erected in every church, provided that they were erected by a Franciscan with the permission of the Ordinary (the bishop or other prelate who has "ordinary" jurisdiction over the diocese—from the Latin *ordinare*, "to put in order").

Now, after Vatican II, the Way of the Cross is still indulgenced. According to the new *Enchiridion of Indulgences* (*enchiridion*, by the way, means "handbook" in Greek), "a plenary indulgence is granted to the faithful who make the pious exercise of the Way of the Cross."

To gain the spiritual benefits of the Way of the Cross, you have to follow the four norms outlined in the *Enchiridion of Indulgences*. First, you have to follow the Way "before stations of the Way of the Cross legitimately erected." Well, we've already seen that erection of the necessary crosses is customarily the business of the Franciscans, but there are other legitimate means to get the crosses installed. You're probably safe in assuming that the stations in your parish church were properly installed.

Second, the fourteen crosses themselves are required, to which, adds the *Enchiridion*, "it is customary to add fourteen pictures or images representing the stations of Jerusalem." It used to be required that these be wooden crosses; they could be ornamented, but only if it was still clear that they were made of wood. The pictures and sculptures attached to these crosses have been so elaborated, sometimes, that you can hardly find the crosses.

You can still see groups of richly modeled life-sized sculptures, some of them still startling after standing silent for centuries, in European churches. And in this country, there are wonderful plaster figures, also sometimes life-sized, on the walls of older churches. Or you might see modern sculptures so abstracted that you have to think for a while before you can identify the episode that they represent. In any case, it's the crosses that matter, not the images on the wall; and the crosses are only there to help you build an image in your own heart.

Third, the *Enchiridion* notes that common practice is that "the pious exercise consists of fourteen pious readings, to which some vocal prayers are added. However, nothing more is required than a pious meditation on the Passion and Death of the Lord, which need not be a particular consideration of the individual mysteries of the stations."

Fourth, "a movement from one station to the next is required." But, if the devotion is performed publicly, then the one conducting the exercise may go from station to station, with the faithful remaining in their places. The most interesting feature of this fourth requirement, though, is the note about those who are "impeded" from making the tour of the stations or who are prevented from getting to the church at all. Such people, the *Enchiridion* says, "can gain the same indulgence, if they spend at least one half an hour in pious reading and meditation on the Passion and Death of our Lord Jesus Christ."

Think about that. What began as a death-defying trip to the Middle East has become, over the centuries, a devotion that can be followed without leaving a hospital bed.

CHAPTER 12

THE ROSARY

A Garden of Christian Images

I N OCTOBER 1571, EUROPE FACED a hopeless challenge. The Turks, raging out of their newly won empire, had already swarmed through the Middle East, conquering every land they entered, slaughtering millions and forcing the survivors to convert to Islam. Having taken the lands of the Levant, they struck out across the sea, taking the crucial islands of Crete and Cyprus. At these seafaring islands, the Turkish galleys gathered, aimed like missiles at the Christian kingdoms of the central Mediterranean, menacing Sicily, Venice, and even Rome herself.

Pope Pius V Ghislieri called upon the Christian princes of Europe to rally in a great league of defense, a new Crusade to beat back the invincible navy that threatened to overrun the continent and destroy the Church. The King of Spain, the princes and nobles of Italy, and many other monarchs responded and hastily assembled a fleet under commanders of many tongues and nations.

But the Turks had one language, one commander, and one mission. Already skilled in conquest, they far outnumbered the allied forces. There was no way that the Christian fleet looked equal to the challenge. No way on Earth.

Well, Pius V wasn't depending on earthly help alone. He was a Dominican, devoted to Our Lady, and he called upon the Rosary confraternities of Rome and all over Europe to undertake special processions and public recitations of the Rosary to ask for the prayers of the Blessed Mother.

On the first Sunday of October, the Christian fleet met the invading Turks off the coast of Greece, in the Gulf of Lepanto. As Christians all over Europe turned to Our Lady through their Rosaries, the Turks surrounded the Christian ships. But the European fleet broke through. At the end of the day's fighting, almost all of the Turks were driven to shore or drowned. Europe was saved.

Pope Pius ordered an annual commemoration in honor of Our Lady of Victory, and his successor, Gregory XIII, set aside the first Sunday in October as the feast of the Holy Rosary. From that time on, the Rosary has been encouraged, even commanded, by popes, saints, and spiritual leaders. Today, everybody can at least recognize the familiar circle of beads. But where did it all start?

The story of the Rosary is nearly as old as the Church. The Lord's Prayer, which forms a kind of framework for the Rosary, was composed by Our Lord himself (hence the name), and early Christians took seriously his command, "In this manner therefore shall you pray." Some of them prayed that way unceasingly, or as nearly as is humanly possible. One of the earliest on record to attempt it, a fourth-century hermit named Paul, was following a monastic custom already old beyond memory when he tossed a pebble into a pile each time he said one of his three hundred daily Our Fathers. So the custom of repetitive, meditative prayer had a very early start in the Church.

The Rosary as we know it today was still a long way off five hundred years later, but in Ireland some monks kept track of their prayers by counting on knotted cords. By about the year 1040, the knotted cords had been replaced with beads, usually wood or clay. Some early beads were fancier: in England at about that time, Lady Godiva (yes, *that* Lady Godiva) willed to the monastery that she'd founded a string of jewels on which she had kept track of her prayers, with the request that it be hung upon the statue of the Virgin there. All kinds of devotions took this form over the ensuing centuries—today, there are more than sixty different approved circlets of beads used to guide prayers to the Holy Spirit, for meditation on the Seven Sorrows, the Sacred Heart, or the Holy Face

of Jesus, or for praying with St. Michael, St. Anthony, or Our
Lady under one of her particular titles.* These prayer-beads are
called "chaplets" because they're like little crowns of flowers offered to Heaven.

But the Rosary, not just a little wreath of prayer-flowers but a
whole garden of roses, was to outrank them all in popularity and
in power. It got started with those same Irish monks—those who
were unable to read the one hundred and fifty Psalms of the Divine Office—who developed the custom of chanting one hundred
and fifty Our Fathers, counting on knotted cords to make sure
they didn't shortchange their devotions. During the next century,
many Christians retained the custom of saying one hundred and
fifty Our Fathers each day, but more and more people took up the
practice of saying one hundred and fifty Hail Marys.

And that requires a little explanation of where we got the Hail
Mary. There are different classes of prayer. The Our Father, for instance, is a *liturgical* prayer, and it comes straight from the Bible, so
it's always been the same as it is now. The Hail Mary, by contrast,
is a *devotional* prayer; it evolved, too, like the Rosary itself, from
the pious practices of monks, nuns, and lay Christians.

The prayer falls into two parts: a salutation and a petition. Each
of these parts, in turn, consists of two smaller parts. The first sen-
tence, "Hail, Mary, full of grace; the Lord is with thee," is of
course Gabriel's salutation to Mary at the Annunciation, right out
of Luke (1:28), although the Church added the name "Mary" as
a way to identify the one to whom the prayer is addressed. In the
very early Middle Ages, it was the custom to repeat this salutation
over and over, genuflecting or bowing to the ground each time, as
a penance, to fix the penitent's mind on the miracle of the Incarnation.

The second part of the salutation, "Blessed art thou amongst

---

*Most of these grew up, as devotions still do, from the pious practices of the
laity. To be "approved", a devotion has to pass muster as to propriety and doctrine, and then the local ordinary may encourage it in some way, in pastoral letters and sermons. Eventually, it may get encouraged by the Pope. Written
materials describing it are reviewed and approved, as a guard against abuses.
Things like burying a statue of St. Joseph and two aspirin to sell your house
aren't going to make it.

women, and blessed is the fruit of thy womb," is also straight from scripture, from St. Elizabeth's greeting to Mary at the Visitation (Lk 1:42). The Church added the name "Jesus" to this joyful call of praise—judging by archaeological remains, this was already customary by about the year 600. Again, like adding "Mary" to the angelic salutation, this is just a matter of common sense.

The first part of the petitionary section of the prayer, "Holy Mary, Mother of God," actually dates from the Council of Ephesus, in the year 431. Some scholars think that Mary lived out her earthly days in Ephesus, and there may be something to it; St. John, whom Christ charged with her care, lived there, and there's a House of the Virgin there that's old enough to have been her dwelling. Certainly, the people of that city were her staunch friends even in the fifth century.

Some heretics at the time were insisting that Mary was the mother of Christ, but not the mother of God, because, they claimed, the baby Jesus was only human until his divine nature joined his human body later—that he was not a complete person, not his complete self, from the very moment of his conception.*

The people of Ephesus weren't having any of this. They took to the streets and rioted whenever anyone tried to deny the title "Mother of God" because if Jesus is true man and true God, and Mary is his mother, then Mary is the Mother of God. And when the Council of Ephesus broke the news that they had decided that the title had always been proper for the Blessed Mother, the Ephesians took to the streets again, with torches, shouting, "Holy Mary! Mother of God! Pray for us sinners!"—giving us the other half of the petition.

Well, by the eleventh century, something very like the current form of the Hail Mary had begun replacing most of the Our Fathers that still framed the devotion, punctuating the prayers into decades (groups of ten). As the centuries passed, the association of the Christian prayer-beads and the Virgin Mary became ever

---

*This complicated opinion centered on the patriarch of Constantinople, Nestorius. The Nestorian heresy still has about thirty-five thousand adherents in the Middle East, and it comes up here, too, as when people opine that a fetus isn't fully human from the instant of conception.

closer. By about 1400, the familiar circlet of fifteen decades of Hail Marys separated by fifteen Our Fathers had become standard.

By the end of the fifteenth century, another customary feature of the holy beads crystallized. People had always known that simply repeating standardized prayers over and over again may be a worthy act, but it can turn into an automatic act that doesn't bring the fullest possible spiritual benefits.

So Christians very early took advantage of this very fact: while we recite the prayers over and over again automatically, we're supposed to meditate upon an episode in the life of Jesus and Mary, as recorded in the Bible. A book from 1489 gives a list of these episodes or "Mysteries" that is almost exactly the one most used today.

There are fifteen Mysteries: five are Joyous (the Annunciation, the Visitation, the Nativity, the Presentation, and the Finding of Jesus in the Temple), five are Sorrowful (the Agony in the Garden, the Scourging, the Crowning with Thorns, Carrying the Cross, and the Crucifixion), and five are Glorious (the Resurrection, the Ascension, Pentecost, the Assumption, and the Coronation of Mary as Queen of Heaven). All together, they sum up the life and mission of Christ and of Mary.

You can start with the Bible verses that record the episodes (the Assumption and Coronation of Mary come out of Sacred Tradition, but there are Bible verses customarily assigned to them, by courtesy). Meditation on these Mysteries is the heart of the Rosary, not the mechanical repetition of the prayers and clicking of the beads. St. Alphonsus Liguori, in his *Glories of Mary*, records that Our Lady told St. Eulalia that she was "more pleased with five decades said slowly and devoutly than with fifteen said in a hurry and with little devotion."

All of this might make the Rosary sound like just another devotional custom, sort of like the practices of many Eastern religions, in which a single phrase or word is repeated (often with beads, too) until the devotee reaches a calm state of clear meditation. But there are important differences: chiefly, the oriental meditational exercises are aimed inward, to enhance the spiritual state of the person himself, but the Rosary also has an outward thrust, aimed at making the world better as well as the person. And certainly the promises, the benefits, the sheer power of this humble devotion make it unique.

As your fingers count off the beads, you don't think about work or bills or school. You spend time with Christ and his mother—you keep them company, you might say—contemplating the great events of their lives, the turning points in the Cycle of Redemption. You feel the happiness of the Joyful Mysteries, the pain of the Sorrowful, and the triumph of the Glorious. And when your fingers reach the end of the decade, the larger bead gently recalls you from your meditations and transfers your attention to the next Mystery. It's very relaxing, reassuring, deep, immense, and transcendent. As prayer, the Rosary gives you a reliable technique that lets you lift up your heart. As a spiritual exercise, it draws you closer to God, and grace is a matter of your drawing closer to God.

And this drawing closer to God is the grace that you need to handle work or bills or school, and everything that comes with them. You find, curiously enough, that you've learned something after every decade. So the Rosary helps you to grow in grace, with all of the effects of that gift. Our Lady herself made a series of extraordinary promises to St. Dominic and the Blessed Alan de Rupe—among them, that regular practice of the Rosary "will cause virtue and good works to flourish; it will obtain for souls the abundant mercy of God. . . . You shall obtain all you ask of me by recitation of the Rosary." And, most intriguing of all, she said that "the Rosary shall be a powerful armor against Hell; it will destroy vice, decrease sin, and defeat heresies."

Similar promises of the devotion's power abound in Marian literature. Padre Pio, the Italian mystic who died in 1968, called his Rosary "that weapon". When Our Lady appeared at Fátima in 1917, she introduced herself as the Lady of the Rosary, carried her own Rosary, and caused the heavenly smell of roses to permeate the area. And she told the children, "Say the Rosary every day, to obtain peace for the world and an end to the war."

Powerful words. Powerful promises. But notice that the Rosary has always been the devotion of the little people of Christianity—

hermits, illiterate monks, the wives and children of the sailors of Lepanto, three little shepherds at Fátima. Have another look at the Rosary. If these prayers can turn back the Turkish fleet, think what they might do for you.

PART THREE

CULTURE

CHAPTER 13

THE RITE STUFF

The Many Faces of the
Universal Church

I N ANY GATHERING OF PEOPLE who remember the liturgy before
the Second Vatican Council, you'll likely hear some nostalgic
remarks about the Latin Mass, with the priest facing the same
way as the congregation. Some may miss the dignity they found in
the glorious Latin phrases, thrice repeated in stately Baroque ca-
dences. A few have gone so far as to separate themselves from the
Church and attend no liturgy but the former kind of Mass—an
extreme example of taking faith's expression for faith itself.

But those who long for the sense of timelessness of the Latin
Mass, and its feeling of universality, might do well to put the liturgical changes of Vatican II in perspective. It's important to remember that the "old" Mass that we all knew and loved was only about
three hundred years old. It followed forms established by the
Council of Trent that were made definitive in the Roman Missal
finally issued by Urban VIII Barberini, who reigned from 1623 to
1644. In fact, the Mass we see today is a lot more like it was in
early Christian times than the Mass of Trent was.

And we shouldn't forget that the liturgy most Americans knew
before Vatican II was never the one and only way to do it. Even
in the "old days", when the Latin Mass predominated in this
country, it was perfectly legitimate, for instance, to say the Mass in

Greek, or Syriac, or several other languages even farther removed from Latin. It's all a matter of the Rite that you belong to.

The universal Church embraces a number of Rites, many different ways to celebrate the Eucharist and the other sacraments. A Rite (capital R) is the sum total of these different ways of doing things, the forms and ceremonies of liturgical worship and the whole expression of the theological, spiritual, and disciplinary heritage of particular churches and communities of churches. And to find out where the many different Rites of the Church came from, we have to go back to the very earliest years.

When the Apostles and their companions went forth after the Ascension to spread the Gospel, they all went to separate places. St. Jude went to Edessa in Syria; St. John to Ephesus in Asia Minor; St. Matthew to Ethiopia, which had already heard the Gospel from St. Philip (Acts 8:26–40). St. Thomas, according to ancient tradition, went as far as Mylapore in India, where he was martyred. St. Peter didn't go directly to Rome; he set up his first episcopal seat in Antioch. St. Mark, evidently, went to Alexandria in Egypt.

So there are a good many areas in the world that received the Faith directly from an Apostle. This gives them a tremendous and respectable tradition in their own right (no pun intended). In addition, there are other places that were converted to Christianity very, very early in the Church's history. France, for instance, came to the Church through the efforts of St. Denis, who is thought to be the same man as Dionysius the Areopagite mentioned in Acts, and by Clovis, king of the Franks in the fifth century, which is why the King of France was always called the "eldest son of the Church." These roots, too, are venerable in age and pedigree.

Each of these sections of the Church developed its own customs and its own methods of doing things. As these areas became more consistent and more cohesive in their practices, their ways of doing things came to be treasured and encouraged. Each became a *Rite*, from the Latin *ritus*, "usage".

The amazing thing is that all of these different regions, expressing the Faith along their own lines, preserved the fullness and clarity of the Gospel message, and they all stayed in close union with the Bishop of Rome, whom they recognized as supreme head of the Church. And these many Rites have preserved and developed their customs to this day, giving the Church as a whole a richness and a variety we sometimes overlook.

In the West, the Roman Rite follows the forms that developed around the city of Rome after St. Peter settled there. The Pope lives in Rome, and he's Patriarch of Rome, but there's no rule that he has to be of the Roman Rite.* The Roman Rite is the major Rite of the United States; the familiar bishops and cardinals belong to this Rite, as do the large religious orders like the Franciscans and the Cistercians. All of the devotional practices that we know, the Stations of the Cross, the First Fridays, and the like, are developments of the Roman Rite, and they're pretty much restricted to it. The Roman Rite's customs and styles of religious painting, sculpture, architecture, and liturgy are also distinctive and not the universal practice of the Church.

As a matter of fact, the western part of the Church also includes the Ambrosian Rite, developed by St. Ambrose in and around Milan in the fourth century. There's also the Mozarabic, which is today centered on Toledo in Spain. It developed in the sixth century, and it picked up features from northern African Christian churches and, in its music and art, even some Arabic influence. Before the French Revolution, there was a Gallican Rite, which has now been reabsorbed into the Roman. And the English had their own customs and rituals, too; before the Anglican Church separated from Rome, it was already something like an Anglican Rite, although it never reached that status officially because it developed too late.

Liturgies celebrated by these Rites, even here in the United States, would look almost completely foreign to the laity of the Roman Rite. The Byzantine Rite, which prevails in the eastern part of the Mediterranean, is even more exotic. It's sometimes called the "Greek Rite" to underline its parallel position to the "Latin Rite" of western Europe. There are about a million members of the Byzantine Rite in the United States and Canada;

---

*Back in 1958, when Pius XII Pacelli died, one of the front-runners was Gregory Peter XV Cardinal Agagianian, Patriarch of the Armenians, who was a perfectly qualified candidate for the See of Peter.

they're in full union with the Pope—that is, their Christian teachings and their organization are the same as everybody else's in the Church. But they use the Byzantine liturgy that differs in some respects from the Mass celebrated in the Latin Rite.

For example, following an ancient tradition that didn't develop in the West, married men can be ordained priests in the Byzantine Rite. Their vestments and liturgies are different from their Latin counterparts, and the Mass is in Greek, not Latin. Byzantine Catholics give communion under both species, bread and wine, and they use leavened bread in the Eucharist. Also, they baptize by immersion, not by sprinkling as in the West.

But the similarities among Greek-speaking Christian sects can get confusing. The Byzantine Rite of the catholic Church is a completely different organization from the Greek Orthodox Church—except that they look almost exactly alike. Both the Byzantine and the Greek Orthodox take their cues from the same leaders, chiefly St. John Chrysostom and St. Basil, who wrote the liturgies they both use. If you go into either kind of church, what you'll see will look basically the same; but the Greek Orthodox Churches separated from the papacy gradually, beginning in the eleventh century. They don't share the Church's teachings in their entirety. It's important to make the distinction because the sacraments administered through any of the Byzantine Rite churches are valid for Christians of the other Rites of the church, but sacraments administered by Orthodox priests are not necessarily. You have to ask a competent authority (usually a bishop in full communion with Rome) about each case specifically.

And, to add to this richness of tradition, the East is home to other Rites, too. The Alexandrian Rite, another part of the universal Church, follows the liturgy of St. Mark, and it's subdivided into the Coptic Rite of Egypt and the Ethiopian Rite, both very ancient and distinctive.

Antioch, where St. Peter first settled, is the seat of more derived Rites than any other place in the world. The Antiochene Rite of the catholic Church follows the liturgy of St. James, and its subdivisions include the Malankarese of India, whose liturgical languages are Syriac and Malayalam—about as far from Latin as a language can be. The Maronites of Lebanon have their own Rite, as do the Syrians, but all of these are derived from the Antiochene Rite. The Armenian Rite uses the liturgy of St. Basil, too, but in Armenian, not Greek. The Chaldean Rite uses Arabic as its liturgical language, and it's descended from the Nestorian Christians who spread the faith as far as Tibet.

The Rite that you belong to is determined by church law. At baptism, you become a member of your parents' Rite, or, if they're of different Rites, of your father's Rite. If you're baptized as an adult (fourteen and up), you get to choose your own Rite, but once there you can't transfer to another Rite unless the Pope gives permission.

Transfer seldom comes up, though. In fact, most people in the Church are probably unaware of the existence of so many Rites. But think of all of these different places, so many customs, so many languages—not just Latin and Greek, but Arabic, Armenian, Bulgarian, Coptic, Ge'ez, Rumanian, Slavonic, Syrian (East Syrian and West), and all of the vernacular languages in the world, from English to Cantonese and back again by way of Vietnamese, Hindi, and Luba.

All in all, the richness and variety of the Church's forms of worship are inconceivable. And each of these Rites cultivates its own style of architecture, painting, music, and all the other arts—each art worth the study of a lifetime. It all adds up to one Church; but a Church always striving to embrace the best customs of the whole world.

CHAPTER 14

THE POPE

What He Does and Why It Matters

WHEN YOU'RE DEALING WITH A revealed religion like Christianity, you have to be sure that you've got it right. You have to know that your religion really does preserve and teach what was revealed, nothing more, nothing less. Everybody who wants to know Christ recognizes that you've got to find the definitive word—and its correct interpretation— somewhere. Some Christian sects separated from the Church ascribe this reliability to one or another version of the Bible, or even to each and every person who reads the Bible in any version. Others rely on a favorite preacher, or the teachings of a certain school or institute. The problem is that all of these sources differ so much on what they say Christ taught.

Well, the Church is understood to be *indefectible*; that's what Christ meant when he said that the Holy Spirit would teach the Apostles all truth and dwell with the Church forever (Jn 14:16, 16:13). It means that the Church will keep the deposit of Christ's revelation intact, with nothing added and nothing taken away, until the end of Time. It means that the Church as a whole has *authority*, which does not imply absolute power to make people believe anything that the hierarchy wants; it means that you can get authoritative information from them when they're telling you what Christ said and what it means—when they're teaching you about faith and morals.* Since the beginning, this authority has centered in the Pope, which is what Christ intended when he built his Church on the rock of St. Peter (*Petros*, in Greek, means "Rock") and added that the gates of Hell shall not prevail against it (Mt 16:17–19).

When you talk about the Pope, you have to take a very long view of the subject. The papacy is an office with two thousand years of history, and it's been at the center of western life and civilization for all that time. It stands at the summit of an international organization that has included untold millions of people in its fold; it operates through its own distinct culture that might look strange to us, standing as we do in a country that isn't half as old as the new basilica of St. Peter's. The incumbents of that office have come from Israel, Greece, Syria, Africa,** and every European nation from England to Poland. They've ranged from ascetic scholars like Pius XII Pacelli to brilliant generals like Julius II della Rovere, from highborn princes like Victor II, Count of Dollnstein-Hirschberg, to ordinary folk like John XXIII (or St. Peter himself, for that matter). The German scholar Von Pastor needed twenty big volumes just to outline its history, without touching its theological or juristic sides. No matter how you look at it, the papacy is an immensely complicated subject.

Not surprisingly, it's also the most misunderstood office on Earth. The news media, the movies, and television seldom get very much right about what the Pope does and what it means, or

*One of the difficulties that Protestants seem to have with this idea doesn't have anything to do with the institutional Church or the Pope, but with the character of faith itself. For the Church, faith means that you accept revealed truths—the doctrines of Christ that the Church preserves and disseminates—on God's word alone. This is called *theological* faith, or sometimes *confessional* faith. For a lot of separated brethren, faith means that you trust in Christ's promises, without reference to any set of doctrines; this is called *fiducial* faith.

**St. Miltiades, who died January 11, 314, and St. Gelasius I, who died November 21, 496. But their race is nowhere recorded, because race has never mattered to the Church—Christ's charge was to preach to all nations, and everybody has the same kind of soul, everybody gets in through Baptism, and everybody gets exactly the same sacraments afterward. No chronicler would bother mentioning a pope's race any more than anybody would care about the color of his eyes.

even about what he's there for. It's important to understand the terms clearly.

Infallibility doesn't mean that every Pope will be absolutely correct on everything that he talks about; it doesn't mean that the Pope knows everything that there is to know in the world, either. Still less does it mean that every Pope enjoys personal freedom from sin, which would be *impeccability*; Christ did, of course, and Mary, but the popes, no. Nobody claims that they ever did. (In fact, every Pope in history has had a personal confessor, a priest permanently assigned to that duty.)

Infallibility is a protection against error, which is a kind of negative guarantee. It means that, whenever the Pope speaks officially as head of the Church on matters of faith and morals, he won't say anything that contradicts Christ's teachings. It means *inerrancy*— that the Pope won't give any wrong answers, not that he'll give all of the right ones, necessarily. The popes occasionally choose to say nothing at all.

So infallibility doesn't cover everything that every pope says. The official definition of the principle, given in the First Vatican Council, July 18, 1870, runs as follows: "the Roman Pontiff, when he speaks *ex cathedra*, that is to say, when discharging the functions of Pastor and Doctor [Teacher] of all Christians, by virtue of his supreme Apostolic authority, he defines a doctrine regarding faith or morals to be held by the Universal Church, he fully enjoys by the divine assistance promised to him in blessed Peter, the same infallibility with which our Divine Redeemer intended His Church should be endowed for defining doctrine concerning faith or morals; and consequently such definitions of the Roman Pontiff are of themselves irreformable".

Speaking *ex cathedra*, from the throne, has its parallels in civil government. When the monarch of England speaks from the throne, for instance, the words have a definite juridical weight that isn't shared by, say, a personal opinion expressed in a newspaper interview. And you don't expect the Queen to call everybody into the throne room and make a solemn pronouncement of something that just popped into her head. You'd expect, instead, that this kind of speech is carefully prepared, with plenty of advice from experts and officials, and that it's not presented until everybody has thought it through and made sure that it's consistent with existing law. You'd expect the same care from the President speaking officially, or even from a Congressman presenting legislation for a vote.

If you'd expect this from civil magistrates whose rulings can be changed at any time, how much more would you expect it from the Pope, who has no mechanism for repeal or modification of any ruling on faith or morals? Once he's defined something officially as an article of faith, that's it, for thousands and thousands of years to come. You can rest assured that the Pope isn't going to say anything—officially as head of the Church on matters of faith and morals—until he and the college of bishops have done everything humanly possible to ensure that it's an accurate definition of what the Church has always believed and taught, a genuine part of Sacred Tradition, and until they've all appealed long and hard to the Holy Spirit for guidance.*

When he speaks as a private person, though, the Pope is on his own, and nobody expects the Holy Spirit to keep him from making the ordinary human mistakes. A pope's personal thoughts are never treated as sacrosanct. Benedict XIV Lambertini wrote commentaries on canon law, for example, that were discussed and disputed just as if they'd been written by a seminarian. Sixtus IV della

---

*It's important to remember that pronouncements *ex cathedra* only confirm articles of faith embodied in Tradition when such clarification is needed; they don't introduce them. The doctrine of the Immaculate Conception (that Mary was preserved from original sin) was formally pronounced by Pius IX Ferretti in 1854, for instance, but it's implicit in early Christian hymns and explicit in the writings of St. Ambrose, St. Augustine, St. Andrew of Crete, St. Germain of Constantinople, and other Fathers right up to St. John Damascene. It was also explicit in liturgy; a feast day commemorating the Immaculate Conception was celebrated annually in the East by the seventh century, formally approved and given a standardized liturgy by Sixtus IV della Rovere in 1476, and extended to the whole Church by St. Pius V Ghislieri in 1568. By then, the doctrine had already been detailed in theological tracts like Gaguin's *De intemeratæ Virginis conceptione* of 1489, which was maintained by the University of Paris and generally accepted as consistent with Tradition. (Of course, it's also consistent with the Bible: Gn 3:15 and Lk 1:26–31, for instance, have always been interpreted as implying Mary's exemption.) It's the same with the Assumption, defined by Pius XII Pacelli in 1950; it's also part of Tradition, reflected in early Christian and patristic writings. By the fifth century it was already celebrated on its own feast day, the very first canonical feast of Mary in history.

Rovere wrote a tract maintaining the authenticity of the Shroud of Turin, but to this day plenty of people disagree with him. John Paul II has said that he personally doesn't like the practice of putting the host into the communicant's hand, but that alone doesn't rule it out.

Still, the popes tend to speak with immense responsibility, *cathedra* or no *cathedra*, and the chances of one's saying anything that's downright wrong are microscopic. One private gaffe that had serious consequences occurred in the pontificate of John XXII d'Euse, who reigned from 1316 to 1334. He happened to say in a sermon something about how the souls of the blessed don't enjoy the full sight of God until after the general judgement. Well, that's not what the Church teaches, officially. His political enemies jumped on this and called him a heretic. They organized a movement to depose him, trying to use his mistake to prove somehow that he couldn't really be Pope. They even got the universities, the King of France, the Emperor of Germany, and lots of other people in on the fray, and in those days it was a short step from disagreement to war.

John defended his position for a while, but then he got a conference of cardinals and theologians together to settle the thing. They showed him that the Mind of the Church had always said otherwise. So, although he had spoken as a private person (even a public sermon by an incumbent pope, you see, is not the voice of the Church), he announced publicly that he'd been misinformed. It happens.

In any case, it's one thing to discuss infallibility in the abstract, to talk about the rationale for it all. But its workings in the day-to-day life of the Church show up clearly in the record. You have to sort through an immense body of papal and conciliar pronouncements—most of them are matters of discipline, dealing with the administrative order of the Church, and since they don't directly touch the deposit of revelation, they're free to move around. Once you get down to matters of faith and morals, you find popes presiding, preaching, promulgating, century after century, often against the full fury of theological rebellion. Human experience tells you that they must, certainly, have contradicted themselves and each other time and time again in the course of twenty centuries. But the fact is that they have not. That's a matter of historical record, and it stands, without parallel.

This record isn't surprising if you take into account an unbroken continuity from St. Peter to the present—in fact, the papacy functions, juristically, on the principle that no pope succeeds his predecessor, but that each directly succeeds Peter. So any pope, first of all, does what Peter did, serve as Bishop of Rome. That puts him in a truly unique position: it makes him the head bishop of the Church. "The college or body of bishops has no authority unless it is simultaneously conceived of in terms of its head, the Roman Pontiff, Peter's successor . . . for in virtue of his office, that is, as Vicar of Christ and pastor of the whole Church, the Roman Pontiff has full, supreme, and universal power over the Church. And he can always exercise this power freely", was how Vatican II put it. That's why ecumenical councils (the ones that include all of the Church's bishops around the world) have always been convened by the Pope, ever since the first one in 325, even though they were rarely held in Rome until the First Vatican Council in 1870. The decisions and decrees of the great councils are authoritative, in fact, because the Pope promulgates them.

And it's why everybody has always turned to the Pope to settle disputes of all kinds. For example, we still have the text of a magisterial letter that Pope Clement I, the fourth bishop of Rome, wrote to straighten out the Corinthians (the Corinthians always seemed to need straightening out). Evidently he wrote it while the Apostles James and John were still alive, and they would have been geographically a lot closer to Corinth; or at least, there were plenty of bishops in that region who had been ordained by Apostles. But still, it was Clement, Peter's successor at Rome, to whom everybody deferred for the definitive word.*

It's also interesting that this primacy has always resided in the See of Rome. In 100, St. Ignatius Theophorus was bishop of Antioch, so he was a lineal successor of St. Peter, too, because St. Peter had set up the church of Antioch before he went to Rome. But Ignatius—like all of the other apostolic bishops in the

---

*The letter was carried to Corinth, incidentally, by Claudius Ephebus and Valerius Vito, two freedmen who had been slaves of the Emperor Claudius.

region—never took that as any reason to claim primacy in the Church. Even in the letters that he wrote when he needed all the importance he could muster (he was being marched in chains from Antioch to Rome to be eaten alive by lions in the Colosseum), Ignatius acknowledges explicitly that it's the Bishop of Rome, alone, who presides over all other Christian communities in the world.

About a century later, St. Irenæus wrote his great tract *Against Heresies*, which is largely concerned with explaining why the Bishop of Rome is head of the Church—heresy being defined basically as any willful rejection of any of the tenets of faith preserved and promulgated by the See of Rome.* Even so, heretics have a habit of appealing to Rome for support, because they usually think that they're teaching what Christ taught and that their opponents aren't (in ninety-nine cases out of a hundred, they listen and learn, and that's the end of it, but sometimes it gets out of hand). Their testimony about the primacy of the Pope is particularly weighty, because they can't be accused of trying to curry favor. By 220 Tertullian had already slipped into his heretical phase, but he still recognized that Pope Callistus had succeeded to the fullness of Peter's office, including the Apostle's special power to forgive sin. Thirty years later, a bishop of Cæsarea, Firmilian by name, took serious exception to the fact that Pope St. Stephen had the right to decide Church policy on the re-baptism of heretics simply "because he held the succession from Peter"—but he still took it for a fact.

The Pope's function as an arbiter carries over into secular affairs, too, either because people are willing to accept the Pope's moral

*Heresy is basically keeping the parts of Christianity that you like and taking away the hard parts—the word itself is from the Greek *haireo*, meaning "I take away." But Christianity, as a revealed religion, isn't like a cafeteria. It's more like a watch, made of many interrelated parts all designed beforehand in the mind of its Creator and intended to function as a unit. If you take out the parts that you don't happen to like (or understand), what's left may look like a watch, but its gears just won't mesh. Unfortunately, interest in heresy is at an all-time low nowadays, because people tend to think that it involves old disputes that nobody takes seriously any more. But one of the major ways that heresy does its damage is by making people think that all of these conflicting views can somehow have the same value, which is known as *indifference*. Completely rejecting Christianity—the next step after indifference—is called *apostasy*.

authority or simply because he's always going to be a well-informed third party who's not allowed to take sides. Even countries with no official religion (or with officially no religion) routinely ask the Pope to decide things for them, and the Holy See has an unsurpassed record in keeping things peaceable. Spain and Portugal asked Alexander VI Borgia to divvy up the New World so that they wouldn't fight over it, which is why Brazil speaks Portuguese today. Louis XIV asked Alexander VII Chigi to settle the rights of his queen to parts of the Netherlands (well, that one did result in a war, but only because Louis had to fight for the rights that the Pope said he had). You probably didn't hear about it on the news, but in 1985 John Paul II mediated a dispute about navigation rights between Chile and Argentina, who were ready to declare war over the matter. Of course, some leaders still see everything in terms of military might—like Stalin, who dismissed the Pope's peace proposals at a Big Three conference by snorting, "How many divisions does the Pope have?" But that's the wrong question. If you're aiming at peace, it's better to ask how many divisions the Pope has put out of work.

He employs legions, though. Like any other chief executive, the Pope directs a formidable array of bureaucrats, and he needs them; not many administrations have nearly a billion people to look after. Only the civil governments of China and India have to handle a comparable load. You can get an idea of the extent of the Church's administration in the Vatican's official yearly directory, the *Annuario Pontificio*, which runs to something over two thousand pages. It lists everybody involved in the papal executive departments, the judiciary, and all of the other offices, which you call collectively the papal court, like the court of any other sovereign. The court's divided into two main parts, the papal household and the administrative offices of the Church.

The household has been thoroughly reorganized recently, as it has been every two hundred years or so anyway, and it runs very smoothly indeed. It still has to employ the chamberlains, stewards, and doorkeepers you need to keep any palace running, and you'll still see a few official costumes that bespeak three, four, or five centuries of service, if not more. (Even the Pope's everyday clothes are determined to some extent by customs, few of which are less than a thousand years old.) And the Vatican used to have, naturally, all of the other officials you'd expect to find at any other Italian Renaissance court. There's still a *Magister Palafrenariæ*, who used to be in charge of the Pope's processional chair and its bearers but now takes care of the "Popemobile". But there's no more Privy Steward, which was a big job back when princely meals had an almost architectural character to them. The present pontiff likes a big breakfast, they say, but only a salad for lunch, with some fruit and maybe a little cheese for dinner. Meals like that don't call for a lot of pageantry.

In fact, during the past few decades, much of the Vatican's temporal pomp has given way to modern circumstances. The papal tiara, the triple crown, is hardly seen any more (although the last one, used at the coronation of Paul VI Montini, is on permanent display in Washington, D.C., at the Shrine of the Immaculate Conception). Other papal accoutrements—the miter, the papal cross, and the rest—still clearly embody their own long histories, but they've been simplified lately. The thick tassels and mossy velvet that had grown all over papal ceremonies for three hundred years have been swept away since John XXIII opened the windows, too. The papal apartments still have an ancient aspect to them, with their lofty ceilings and their beige or ivory walls, set off sparingly with choice artworks from the pontifical collections. But they have a simple freshness and a serenity to them now, a sense of cleanliness and order, that speaks well to an age like ours, so much afflicted by vulgarity and discord.

The business side of the papal court has also been reorganized, but it too draws on ancient roots. It's still referred to as the *Curia Romana*, which is what they used to call the old Roman Senate in the days of the Cæsars. It's made up of all of the *Congregations*—sort of like our cabinet departments—and the tribunals, councils, committees, and other offices that handle the vast administrative duties of the head of the Church. (And, ancient or not, these offices handle things with astonishing efficiency. With nearly a billion people to look after, they can still answer a layman's query within about six weeks.)

Even the titles and formulas that the Vatican chancery uses for official documents have a history longer than the histories of most nations. The civil titles have gone by the way, as the territories that once gravitated toward the Holy See for stable administration have been absorbed into the modern state of Italy. The ecclesiastical titles and distinctions remain. Our word *pope*, for instance, comes from the Greek *pappas*, which simply means "father", and it's been generally used since about the year 1000 (although it was frequent by about 500). *Pontiff* recalls a papal title that's even older than the Church. Originally—so long ago that scholars can't find out when it started—a *pontifex* was a priest of the Roman state religion. *Pons* is the Latin for "bridge", but no one is clear on how the word for "bridgemaker" became the title of a priest. The head of the pontifical college was the Pontifex Maximus, and when the emperors became Christian the Bishop of Rome naturally succeeded to the title as head of the Empire's official religion.

Today, the Pope's official titles are Bishop of Rome, Vicar of Christ, Successor of the Prince of Apostles, Supreme Pontiff of the Universal Church, Patriarch of the West, Primate of Italy, Archbishop and Metropolitan of the Roman Province, Sovereign of the City of the Vatican. Each title names an important part of the Pope's position; each has a long story behind it, and each has immense implications, as you might expect. Still, with all of that to choose from, the popes usually use only one title, first adopted by Gregory the Great in 591: *Servus Servorum Dei*, Servant of the Servants of God. That sums it up neatly.

CHAPTER 15

PRIESTS, BISHOPS, AND DEACONS

The Church's General Staff

O NE REASSURING THING about the Church's clergy is that they've never been self-appointed. The Church's priests, bishops, and deacons don't just set up a pulpit and go into business for themselves. They're called—they have a "vocation", from the Latin *vocare*, "to call".

And the Church doesn't just take their word for it, either. There's a rigorous selection process, a long and demanding formal education, and constant discipline to separate the real vocations from the matters of personal opinion. The clerical state itself is conferred through a sacrament, an act that changes the recipient permanently, irrevocably. It's administered by the laying on of the hands of a bishop who received it the same way himself, hand from hand, in unbroken physical contact from the hands of Christ. So no matter how cranky the clergy get from overwork, no matter how much they may confuse a homily with a financial statement, even when they can't seem to grasp the simple fact that the bridesmaids' contact lenses have to color-coordinate with the carpet in the nave, you can rest assured that you're dealing with the genuine article.

This laying on of hands is called *ordination*, or receiving Holy Orders, which come in three grades: deacon, priest, and bishop.* There are lots of other titles in the Church, but they're mostly administrative titles that describe a job or hierarchic titles that designate a place in the Church's organizational chart. The Pope, for instance, as the successor of St. Peter, is the chief of the Church's clergy, so he has a number of hierarchic titles, like Supreme Pontiff of the Universal Church, Patriarch of the West, etc., etc., as well as administrative ones like Sovereign of the City of the Vatican. But as far as the sacrament of Holy Orders goes, he's a bishop, the Bishop of Rome.

As it happens, that title alone gives him primacy because it puts him at the head of the college of bishops, the corporate successors to the college of the Apostles. But no one is ordained Pope. You're *elected* Pope, which means that (until recently) you only had to be a layman in good standing, with no impediment in the way of your being consecrated Bishop of Rome afterward. Even today, when you have to be at least a priest to be in the running, you can still decline the Throne of Peter or resign after you take it.

Since 1179, the Pope has been elected exclusively by the College of Cardinals, and usually from among them, which helps avert the pressures of external parties like mobs and kings (although as late as 1903 the Emperor of Austria sent his veto to the election of Cardinal Rampolla, and Pius X Sarto was elected instead). But being a cardinal isn't a matter of ordination, either; Cardinal is another hierarchic title. Back when John XXIII was named a cardinal—long before he was elected pope, of course—he said of his red hat, "It is neither a sacrament nor a sacramental; and yet it is a kind of sign that Providence has responsibilities in store for me

---

*There were also four *minor orders*, which weren't part of the sacrament of Holy Orders, so people who took them were free to quit at any time. Minor orders were porter (from *porta*, "gate"; sort of a janitor—which is from *janua*, another word for "gate", come to think of it); lector, who did the readings at Mass; exorcist, who did pretty much what you think; and acolyte, from the Greek for "attendant"—acolytes basically did what altar boys do now. In fact, for the past few hundred years, the functions of all of the minor orders have been performed by other people who don't take minor orders at all, but Vatican II revived the office of lector and that of acolyte under the title of "ministries".

that will require me to give a serious account of myself." Until very recently cardinals didn't have to be ordained deacon, priest, or bishop before being appointed, and they have always been free to resign the cardinalate and go back to their previous state of life.*

The cardinals started out as an informal group of advisers around the Pope, not necessarily ordained but charged with administrative matters, sort of like our cabinet secretaries. They also helped give continuity and stability to the papal administration, as our Senate is supposed to do for our government, but the College of Cardinals never had any legislative function, because that's reserved to the Pope and the other bishops.

Today, cardinals still head the Congregations that constitute the Church's executive departments, and, when the pope dies, they gather from all over the world to elect a successor. They're locked in a *conclave* (*cum clave*, "with a key") in the Sistine Chapel, with no communication to the outside world, and they vote by secret ballot until one of their number has the necessary plurality. Sometimes this seems to take forever—some elections have gone on for years—because the cardinals have to search their own souls and be as certain as anybody can be of the guidance of the Holy Spirit. Even with the best intentions, that has to take time.**

The elections also have to allow for travel time, because most

---

*The last layman to be appointed Cardinal was Giacomo Cardinal Antonelli, who died only in 1876, but there were plenty of others before him. You sometimes find English-speaking historians recoiling in shock at the story of some Renaissance prince who was raised to the purple at an early age and then— horrors!—*ditched his sacred vows* in favor of a politically advantageous marriage. English-speaking historians would recoil a lot less if they checked their facts first. "Raised to the purple", incidentally, refers to receiving the red hat that's the cardinal's symbol of office. The distinctive scarlet garments are purple, too, but that's another story; see chapter 32 about Our Lady's Cloak. The bird is named after the prelate, too, not *vice versa*.

**The cardinals can stall, too, for reasons of their own. Back in the fourteenth century, when the papacy was at Avignon, they dawdled so much that Philippe le Bel, Louis X's twenty-two-year-old brother, was sent down to hurry them up. When Louis died a few weeks later, Philippe invited the College to a memorial service during which the doors and windows of the chapel were silently walled up by his masons. As he left through the one remaining exit, Philippe told the cardinals that if the election weren't made soon he'd take off the roof. John XXII was elected almost immediately.

cardinals nowadays are also archbishops, which means that they have duties far outside of Rome. Archbishop is another hierarchic title, and it's one of the more confusing ones. You might think that an archbishop is some kind of head bishop, but he's really just a *distinguished* bishop. And it's not a personal distinction, either, but an official one.

Here's how it works. The bishop stands in the fullness of priesthood, you might say. There's no higher ordination than that of bishop; the bishop is part of the group that succeeded the Apostles. When the Church started out, all of the priests were bishops (the Apostles, again). They were the ones who celebrated the Eucharist. This worked out fine, as long as Christianity was more or less confined to large cities like Jerusalem, Antioch, Alexandria, and Rome, but as the Church grew, it was clear that bishops weren't enough. You needed assistants who could take care of people in smaller towns and rural areas. So the bishops ordained priests (from *presbyter*, meaning "elder") who were deputized to celebrate the Eucharist and administer the other sacraments, except Confirmation and Holy Orders.

It's important to remember that, while the Church was expanding this way, the Roman Empire was falling. The emperors tried all kinds of reorganizations to simplify administration and keep things running, but the only thing that helped was dividing all of the formerly independent countries into manageable districts called dioceses, which Diocletian did at the turn of the fourth century. As the civil government decayed, the records of the local churches became more and more important—when certificates of birth and death weren't generally available any more, certificates of baptisms and records of funerals took their place, and there were no civil records of marriages at all, after everybody became Christian. After a while, nobody paid much attention to the bureaucracy, and out of necessity the bishops took on all of the administrative duties you'd expect from government.

That's why the territory administered by a bishop is still called a diocese, and it's why the bishop is called the "ordinary" of that territory—from *ordinare*, "to put in order". Each bishop is responsible for all kinds of regulation in his diocese, rules about liturgy, marriages, education, and everything else. They all have to stick to the same creed, of course, but no bishop runs his diocese as vicar of the Pope; each is generally in charge himself, and all bishops are equal in sacramental terms.

But some dioceses are more equal than others, you might say. For instance, they might contain a particularly important city, or just might have a larger population than any of the surrounding dioceses do. A diocese that stands out in its *province*, or group of dioceses, can be distinguished as an archdiocese, and a bishop in charge of an archdiocese is an archbishop. That just means that he has precedence over the other bishops in the province, the so-called *suffragan* bishops. An archbishop can't tell the suffragan bishops how to run their own dioceses, but he can call a provincial council and preside over it (the provincial councils of Baltimore hammered out the catechisms that most of us learned from), and his archdiocesan courts hear appeals from the courts of suffragans. His *see*—from the old English word for "seat", referring to the bishop's throne—is called the metropolitan see, and his cathedral is the metropolitan church. So a person who is an archbishop hierarchically is still a bishop sacramentally, just as the Pope is.

As successors of the old Roman governors, bishops inherited a lot of pomp and ceremony that you don't see in any civil government any more, not even in the territories of the old empire. Ring kissing, for example, might look strange in the modern world, but we've got it easy, these days. You used to have to kiss the bishop's foot. That was the way you showed respect to superior officers like emperors or kings, and, back in the fourth or fifth century, the emperors themselves started kissing the Pope's foot as a sign of deference to spiritual authority. (It wasn't just some papal puppets or little palace-bred wimps who did it, either, but tigers like Charlemagne and Barbarossa, Justin and Justinian the Great.) What happened, of course, is that the Church outlived all of the empires in which this foot-kissing was a normal expression of courtesy. By about 1600 the custom no longer had any parallel in civil ceremonies, and it started to stand out too much. Very gradually, it faded to virtually nothing. Cardinals might still salute the newly elected Pope this way, though, unless he asks them not to (and he probably will).

The ring came into the ceremony because it's the symbol of an unchangeable state of life. That's why Roman citizens had the right to wear one, and why you're supposed to wear one after you get married. Since at least the year 610, when Boniface IV made it definite, the ring has been the primary symbol of the bishop's office—kings get crowns, and bishops get rings. Actually, kissing the ring is a way of showing deference to the office, rather than to the man. But not very many bishops allow it, nowadays, let alone the Pope, and ring-kissing seems to be a dying art.

(Here's how you do it, by the way. You drop to your right knee in front of the bishop. Carefully raise your hand, palm downward, up under his right hand. Bring his hand near your face, take careful aim, and touch your closed lips to the ring. It's perfectly sanitary. The only two difficulties in the maneuver are that you can get nervous and bang the consecrated hand right into your nose, or that the object of your attentions might be wrenched away from you because its owner doesn't quite share your enthusiasm for ancient protocol.)

Between the two sacramental orders of bishop and priest, you sometimes find the title *Monsignor* (from the Italian, parallel to the English *Milord* or the French *Monseigneur*). This is a courtesy title granted to certain priests in recognition of exceptional service to the Church. It's sort of like a knighthood from a secular monarchy; it doesn't involve any specific duties, and it doesn't have anything to do with Holy Orders *per se*. A Monsignor is still a priest.

The priest is on the front lines, really. He's certainly the most visible of all ordained clerics, and misunderstandings at this level seem to have the greatest repercussions. For instance, you sometimes hear of an "ex-priest" who's been given permission to marry. Again, Holy Orders is a sacrament, and no sacrament, properly received, is revocable, so the man is still a priest. But Holy Orders and marriage don't necessarily exclude each other. Celibacy is now an integral part of the discipline of priesthood in the Latin Rite, but it hasn't always been—Pope St. Gregory the Great was legitimately descended from Felix, a priest of the church at Fasciola, and so were Pope Felix III and several noteworthy nuns. Some other Rites of the Church don't require this discipline of celibacy in the same way for their priests, who receive exactly the same sacrament of Holy Orders but are allowed to be married when they do.

Priesthood, then, you get from the Sacrament, but celibacy you take on from a voluntary solemn vow, the exact form of which varies according to your Rite. Therefore, a widower can be ordained in the Latin Rite. The Pope can give permission for a married man to become a priest in the Latin Rite, as he's done for some married Protestant ministers who have converted—the marriage came before the ordination. Or he can excuse a priest from his solemn vow of celibacy: but, in that case, because the Latin Rite doesn't generally have married priests, you can't function as a priest any more. You still *are* one; you just can't *work* as one. A priest in this situation is a *laicized* priest, not an ex-priest.*

How did the discipline of priestly celibacy come about? Actually, it's been around since the beginning, to some degree. St. Paul listed some obvious advantages (1 Cor 7:27–35, for instance). St. Jerome pointed out that "the Virgin Christ and the Virgin Mary have dedicated in themselves the principles of virginity for both sexes. The Apostles were either virgins or, presumably, remained continent (1 Cor 7:29) after their marriages. Those persons chosen to be bishops, presbyters, or deacons are either virgins or widowers; or certainly, once receiving the priesthood, they remain forever chaste." For about the first four hundred years, there wasn't any law about it, but then the example of the celibate monks started to take effect, and it quickly became a real rule. In the East, it was all right to ordain a married man, but in the West it was priesthood or marriage, but never both.

The Eastern practice ran into trouble from the first, because the feeling was that bishops shouldn't be married or shouldn't live with their wives if they were, which caused obstacles to promotion. The western practice may be harder, but forgoing the re-

---

*There are "services" nowadays that dispatch laicized priests to perform weddings and so forth, but they are not legitimate. A priest has to "belong" to a bishop; there are no free-lance priests in the Church. A laicized priest knows perfectly well that his bishop has categorically forbidden him to perform priestly duties except in dire emergency, and the renegade priests who participate in these dispatching services therefore do so under indisputably false pretenses.

sponsibility of a family—which absolutely must take precedence over all other responsibilities—does make possible the almost overwhelming training that priests need, and it frees their time and attention for pastoral matters. Interestingly enough, you don't hear a lot of complaints about priestly celibacy, historically. When objections arise, they seem to come from lay people who aren't directly involved; priests themselves have almost never made an issue of it. And, if you look at the historical record, you get the impression that only those cultures that really need examples of selflessness and dedication clamor to tear down the custom of priestly celibacy.

There's also a lot in the news, these days, about ordaining women, and the Church's perspective on the matter is likewise broader than you might think. Obviously, Christ held women in high esteem, and he broke a good many Jewish taboos when he did so—things like pardoning the adulteress, receiving the penitent at Simon's house, and curing the ritually unclean woman who had the issue of blood (even talking to her was shocking to his onlookers). He treated women with the same respect and sympathy that he showed for men, which was radical in that time and place. But he didn't ordain any, and no Christian church ever has.* Not even Mary, who was with the Apostles at Pentecost, was given a sacramental ministry. Christ never departed from the Old Covenant's precedent of only male priests, and the Apostles followed his unambiguous example, although ladies like Lydia, Phoebe, and Priscilla filled other indispensable roles. There's evidently no previous example of a real movement for the ordination of women, just as there's never been much call to allow priests of the Latin Rite to marry.

Still, things do change in the Church's discipline, but change has always come about through a steady, quiet, universal growth in the recognition of the need for change. It never happens overnight. Persons or groups who advocate change have always had to prove their ideas with actions, not words, working reliably and in strict obedience over the long haul. That's how all of the great orders of

---

*Protestants who appoint ministers don't claim to administer a sacrament, whether the minister is male or female.

monks, friars, and nuns came into being—some of them took generations. Today's vocal advocates of innovation, even if they have a valid point to make, come from only a few western industrialized countries; their movement might turn out to be the beginning of a change in discipline, but right now it's only a beginning.* Of course, if the Church is clearly wrong about some disciplinary matter, she'll listen locally and reform globally; but the record of thousands of years, over dozens of countries, through hundreds of cultures that have come and gone, is really monolithic in the cases of celibacy and ordination. At this point it's hard to imagine compelling evidence for changing the policies.

The problem of declining vocations to the priesthood here and in other industrialized countries is being met by another strategy, the revival of the permanent diaconate. Deacons go back even farther than priests, really—Phil 1:1 mentions bishops and deacons but not priests. The diaconate is a genuine, permanent order; the deacon associates with Christ in his own right and has sacramental powers, as Pius XII put it in 1947. You can't get married after you receive the diaconate, but you can be married already when you do.

The title of deacon comes from the Greek for "servant" or "helper", and we know that the Apostles had them (Acts 6:1–7; 1 Tm 3:12–13). Then as now, they assisted at liturgies, supervising and signaling the conduct of the faithful and giving the dismissal, and they can baptize, preach, and distribute the Eucharist if they have express permission from the bishop. Historically, most of the deacon's duties have centered on matters like helping the poor,

*Generally, successful innovators have always taken great care to show their suggestion's relation to the Church's organization as a whole, as well as its compatibility with scripture and Tradition. The women who seek ordination today presumably do so in good faith, responding to a deep and urgent call to greater service in the Church rather than to any ambition for status, but even sympathetic persons might be puzzled by the fact that women don't often apply for the many important offices in the Church already open to them—everything from Eucharistic minister to Chancellor of the diocese. Also, directors of postulants and novices often point out that the people who insist most vehemently on ordination or reception into an order of nuns are the most likely to wash out during the training; again, the real vocations seem to come quietly, often against the person's initial inclination. See also chapter 16, on the laity.

visiting the sick, and other necessary but time-consuming pastoral functions that would be too much for a single priest to handle.

In fact, the diaconate is the point of entry into the clerical life; everybody on the way to the priesthood starts there. And everybody who enters that life does so through the sacrament of Holy Orders, which is not, as the Council of Trent reaffirmed, just "human invention thought up by men, a kind of rite of choosing ministers", but "truly and properly a sacrament instituted by Christ Our Lord."

CHAPTER 16

A PEOPLE
SET APART

The Laity in the Modern World

I T USED TO BE EASY to be a good American and a good Catholic. You didn't question the hierarchy, in the old days, any more than you questioned Congress. And the clergy, like the politicians, didn't get into the habit of explaining much. Everybody just went along taking things for granted, and you knew where you stood. It was God and Country, one and indivisible, forever and ever, amen.

But then came the 1960s. The cultural revolution tore our civil institutions from top to bottom, and our ideas about life and living didn't seem to be all that clear cut any more. We might have turned to the Church for stability and perspective as we'd done so often in the past, but at exactly that same moment the reforms of Vatican II challenged many people's whole understanding of the Church. Without explanation—without warning, almost—altars were turned around, guitars invaded the sanctuary, and the stately Latin was stripped away in favor of the language of the streets. For many people, even for some priests and bishops, it seemed that there were no rules any more, no guidelines that covered our new situation. All of a sudden, religion was as confusing as politics.

Today, a generation later, there are still lots of big, serious questions about life in this country. You can't pattern your life after any generally accepted social norms, because our society doesn't have generally accepted social norms any more. Ideas about what's politically correct change every day. It's a struggle just to keep up with the vocabulary.

But the Church came through that period of adjustment with flying colors. Alone of all denominations in this country, she kept growing steadily (and at rates far higher than the birth rate, so that includes a good percentage of adult converts). By 1991, she numbered nearly sixty million members in the United States, just about four times as many as the largest Protestant denomination— some 24 percent of the whole population. And it's really easier than ever to figure out what it means to be a member of the Church's laity. None of the Church's teachings changed, of course, but today their expression is deliberately designed to answer the questions of the times.

For example, two decrees of Vatican II addressed the problems of the laity directly, the *Decree on the Apostolate of the Laity* and the *Pastoral Constitution on the Church in the Modern World*. Other conciliar documents, like the *Decree on Ecumenism*, discussed at least some aspects of the life of the laity, and a lot of post-conciliar work followed up on these leads. The new *Code of Canon Law* gives a sort of "bill of rights" for the laity. But then—life being what it is—it also sets out what you might call a "bill of obligations". This section of the Code, running from Canon 208 through Canon 223, is a great place to start if you want to figure out the meaning and purpose of the lay life.

The rights given in these canons include the right to assemble and to found associations for charitable and religious purposes, to get fair treatment under canon law, to enjoy privacy, and other basic things like that. Canon 219 guarantees you the right to choose your state of life—concordant with the rest of Christian morals, of course. The Church's teachings about this last point, particularly, seem to be generally misunderstood.*

---

*The author wants it made clear at the outset that he believes absolutely in the right of all people to pursue happiness any way they want to (as long as the rights of others are preserved, of course). This section simply attempts to be an accurate (but unofficial) report of the Church's viewpoint on these matters, in the context of a society like ours, where personal choices are often made without reference to

For example, alternative lifestyles based on unrestricted or unusual sexual activity get a great deal of attention in the news media, and the Church has taken a lot of flak for what she's been understood to say about them. But consider that the whole point of morality (Christian or otherwise) is that we're supposed to control our impulses and live like human beings, not, as Thomas Merton put it, like stray dogs.

The Church's teachings on lifestyle stand consistent with her teachings on morality in general. It all comes under the basic distinction between what you feel and what you do about your feelings. You might want something, but that doesn't give you the right to steal it; you might feel more comfortable if someone else were dead, but you can't expect permission to kill him. The same distinction applies to sexual activities, no matter whom (or what) you're attracted to; there's no possible license for unchastity in the deposit of revelation. Since the Church exists to preserve and teach that revelation, she can never condone any lifestyle that defines itself by sexual activity that the deposit classifies as illicit. But, just as with shoplifting and murder, it's the activity that the Church calls illicit, not the inclination to do it.*

(Homosexuality, for instance, is defined by the Church as not *normal*—and, just statistically, it isn't—but not *wrong*; that is, it can't be called wrong if you understand the term to mean a set of involuntary feelings that can result from any number of causes, none of which is fully understood. But the gay lifestyle, like any other, is a matter of choice, and nobody has to live that way. It can be hard to see that, especially since people these days often use the words *homosexual* and *gay* as if they meant exactly the same thing,

---

the Church's teachings or, indeed, to consequences. Anyway, it makes sense to listen to the Church when you're picking a lifestyle—no organization has observed more case histories or learned as much about what works and what doesn't—but as far as the author's personally concerned, you're on your own.

*While we're on the subject, you often run into cases where people might not be sinning, but it sure looks like it, as when people of opposite gender live together without intimate relations but also without marriage, or even when an otherwise decent person attends an X-rated event, thinking it harmless. But publicly giving the appearance of sin, or appearing to condone sin, is called *scandal*, and it's a sin, too—leading little ones astray, and all.

but in the Church's view there's a big difference: the same distinction between the inclination to act and the action itself. Here, too, the Church's prohibition isn't about the sexuality—which a person doesn't choose—but about the culture that a person does choose.)

Whatever the situation, the rules about chastity—that is, about self-respect and respect for others—are the same across the board, and God in his wisdom apparently gave some people a tougher time of it than others. But the Church teaches that anybody who has an extra, unchosen difficulty also gets the grace needed to live with it in a manner pleasing to God—but you have to ask for it and try, every day, to live up to that high standard. "If we wish," Paul VI said, "we can keep our body and spirit chaste. The Master, who speaks with great severity in this matter (Mt 5:28) does not propose an impossible thing. We Christians, regenerated in Baptism, while we are not free from this kind of weakness, are given the grace to overcome it with relative facility," a principle that, from the Church's standpoint, practically eliminates any excuse for this stray-dog business entirely.

Paul VI undoubtedly meant that it's easy to overcome all of these lusts and things through the Church relative to how hard it is outside. After all, the Church doesn't just condemn behavior and leave you on your own to stop it. She's got two thousand years of pastoral and psychological skill, to say nothing of spiritual techniques, to help, and it's safe to say that if you seek the necessary graces through the Church you're going to get a great deal of understanding, too, if you go about it with understanding yourself. But it's inaccurate—and unfair—to say that the Church prescribes one state of life for everybody, regardless, because she doesn't. "Only, as the Lord has allotted to each, as when God has called each, so let him walk" (1 Cor 7:17). Celibacy, for instance, is obviously a great advantage to the clergy, but it's just as obviously not for everybody. The Fathers of the Church, like Christ, commended virginity (or failing that, chastity), but they also endorsed marriage, which may not be for everyone either.

In any case, as a member of the laity, you have the right to select your state of life—single, married, clerical, religious, whatever—but no matter how you decide, you're also obliged to strive to lead a holy life and to promote the growth and holiness of the

Church. And you're also required to follow what the bishops declare as teachers of the Faith or determine as leaders of the Church; to promote social justice; to assist the poor from your own resources; and to see that the message of salvation reaches all humankind. That's a tall order, but you don't have to go it alone, and the Code itself points the way to success in these endeavors by obliging you to maintain full communion with the Church. That means regular attendance at Mass, for one thing. In fact, the very word *liturgy* is from the Greek λαος, meaning "people" (which is where we get the word *laity*), and έργον, which means "work". So the liturgy is "the work of the laity"; it's your job, something that you do, not something that you just sit and watch. "Why do you seek to sit there," demanded Thomas à Kempis, "since you are born to this work?"

In fact, there's a lot more to the laity's job than going to Mass. Canon 212, for instance, says that you have the right *and the obligation* to make your needs and desires known to your bishop, and the right to make known to the bishops and to other Church members your opinions regarding the good of the Church.

So you've got to speak up, and they've got to listen. Maybe you don't like something that goes on in your parish—the music, maybe, or the homilies. Maybe the priest refused to let you have your way about a wedding or a funeral, and maybe he didn't explain or seem very helpful. You don't just sit there and take it, and you don't get up and go to another parish, still less to another denomination. It's your job to fix it, or, looking inward, to fix whatever misunderstanding you brought with you. Handle it, basically, the way you'd handle a disagreement with any civil official, a mistake on your water bill, say, or an unfair assessment of your property. Whether the case is civil or religious, you'd try to see both sides of it, and you'd use your common sense—remember that, just as everywhere else, if you get an answer that could be called "rude", you may have asked a question that could be called "stupid". But if you've researched the matter, and given it lots of thought before speaking, and you still think that you've got a valid point, go back to the pastor, and to the parish council, and talk about it.

You'll get an answer right then, in all probability, and maybe even an apology (in the sense of an *apologia*, an explanation). If you don't, or if you don't understand the answer or still think that it's wrong, address your question to the bishop. Tell him, in writing, what the issue is and how often you tried to get a response and from whom. The bishop will almost certainly answer in a reasonable time. If he doesn't, follow up your complaint; get the correct address from the *Annuario Pontificio* (university libraries have copies) and write to the Pope about it, or really to the Congregation in charge of those matters.*

Again, document briefly but completely your attempts to get an answer from your pastor and your bishop. Enclose copies of any correspondence on the matter. You'll get an answer, usually within six weeks. If the problem was that you didn't understand the rules and their rationale, you will be instructed in no uncertain terms; if the fault was with the clerics who failed to respond, they will get called on a very important carpet indeed. Either way, you've fixed the problem, and everybody's learned how things work, so it probably won't happen again. You've done your duty.

But you probably won't need to exercise your apostolate in such a contentious way. Remember that Canon 208 guarantees that you have the right to expect true equality in dignity with everybody else in the laity. Think about what that means. For one thing,

---

*The hierarchy's response to some problems has seemed tragically inadequate, but they're not necessarily being obtuse. Because priests are there to listen and sympathize, some disaffected persons of all conditions—bereaved, traumatized, lonely, elderly, children and men as well as women—do develop disproportionate feelings toward them. Predictably, a small percentage of these people, disappointed perhaps in their expectations, will accuse priests of some kind of wrongdoing, perhaps even illicit sex. One person making one complaint to a bishop, or—worse—harassing a bishop by repeating unsubstantiated charges, therefore, may reasonably be assumed to fall into this category (canon law treats such accusations specifically, in Canons 982 and 1390). Normally the priest is entirely innocent, which is presumed, and the complainants can be helped adequately and humanely by purely pastoral means; if the local hierarchy hears nothing more about it, they can only assume that the matter has been handled appropriately. But canon law mandates severe penalties for any priestly impropriety, particularly for violating the Sixth Commandment or even *proposing* to violate it (Canons 1387, 1394, 1395). So if there is a real problem, people need to register it *in writing* to help distinguish it from the distraught or vindictive false alarms. Of course, with hindsight, it's easy to make that distinction, but the laity must not fail in its duty to follow up at the time, referring it upward to Rome if necessary; the obligation to denounce such an occurrence is considered grave.

most offices in the Church can be filled by lay people. If you're qualified, you can run for parish council, or be chancellor of your diocese, or top financial officer, or lots of other things, regardless of race, color, or national origin—the Church understandably prefers some conformity on the matter of creed.

Regardless of gender, too—"since both [men and women] are in a similar servitude to God, both are reckoned as of equal status", as St. Jerome said back in the fourth century. (Granted, some of the things St. Paul wrote sound a little antifeminist, but remember that he came out of a tradition that said things like, "Let the words of Torah be destroyed by fire rather than imparted to women," so he was something of a liberal, really, for that place and time. And he was articulating matters of Church discipline against specific abuses, not talking about faith or morals, there.) Probably the major reason that there aren't more female chancellors or minority diocesan CFOs in this country is simply that the laity figures that somebody else will do it while they sit there in the pews. If you have some skills that you're not using, the Church really needs them. Most parishes and dioceses, and all of their agencies, have a rough time finding qualified people to fill positions. Just sitting there isn't fair to yourself, either; Church agencies involve large budgets and lots of people, so experience gained in managing them is marketable in the secular world. Keep an eye on the parish bulletin and the diocesan newspaper, and see what you can do.

Even if this sort of thing isn't for you, you still have a life to live, and you've got your apostolate to work on, no matter what your state of life. If you're in charge of children, for example, raising them and teaching them, you're fulfilling an indispensable role, not just in the Church's life but in the life of society as a whole. If you work in an office, or in construction, or anywhere else, you can perfectly well concentrate your apostolic efforts where you are. You don't have to preach or anything; you just have to set a good example. Check the Code, the Vatican II decrees, and the rest for guidelines. Then all you have to do is be such a good Christian, so reliably fair in all your dealings, so radiant with the quiet light of virtue, that everybody will want to know how in the heck you manage it. It's probably easier than trying to be politically correct, anyway.

CHAPTER 17

A DIFFERENT
ORDER OF LIFE

Monks, Nuns, and the Rules
That Guide Them

WHEN YOU READ THE HISTORY of the Dark Ages, from about, say, 400 until the Renaissance, you run into some remarkable characters with very strange-sounding names. You meet Abbo and Benzo, Boso and Lioba, Tutilo, Offa, Molua, Hardmut, Notker, and Poppo—two Poppos and a whole string of Notkers, in fact (Notker the Stammerer, Notker Labeo, and Notker Physicus and his nephew, just plain Notker). You encounter people with outlandish names like Sebbi and Wazo, Illtyd, Bugga, and Byrhtnoth (who always looks like a misprint), and the man with the most unfortunate name in history, Wipo. It was pronounced "Veepo", but somehow that doesn't help.

The thing that these people all have in common is that they were monks or nuns, or they worked very closely with them. Their names sound like they're from another planet because they came out of a culture as foreign to our own as it was to that of ancient Rome. In fact, they were busy building that culture on the ruins of old Rome, and the way we live today is based directly on the work of these people and others like them. Even the countries of Europe owe their foundation and much of their character to them.

But, originally, monks were about the least likely people to change the world. The basic idea, back in the fourth century, was to just get away from it all, to abandon this world entirely and concentrate on the next one. Apparently it was some Egyptian Christians who had the idea first, and, as there was plenty of desert available, they took to it. They sought the angelic life: neither married nor given in marriage, the sole object of their existence to sing the praises of God.

All in all, they lived pretty much the way holy men have lived in the East since time immemorial, but there were some important differences: they had a very clear view of Christian theology, and they had a profound respect for the authority of the Church. Their rejection of the material world was a discipline, not an escape, and they had rules about it. In fact, it's the rule that makes the monk; monks (and nuns) are called *regular* clergy because they live according to a rule—in Latin, *regula*. They are therefore distinct from the *secular* clergy, those who live in the world—the ordinary hierarchy of parish priests, bishops, archbishops, deacons, and so on.*

The rules came originally from two remarkable men. One was St. Anthony, who died in 356 at the astonishing age of a hundred and five, after eighty-five years in the desert. He was a Copt, a native Egyptian, and he defined what you call the *eremitical* mode of monastic life. That's where you live alone (the word is related to our word *hermit*) in contemplation, trying to return to Christ by way of perfect prayer, with some general conferences and individual advice from time to time.

The problem was that St. Anthony's approach depended entirely upon the personal character of the leader, and the gifts that define characters like St. Anthony are really rather rare. So monks don't live eremitically, as a rule. They live as *cenobites*, from the Latin word for "cell".

This was the idea of the other fourth-century monastic rule-

---

*Strictly speaking, "clergy" means people who have received the sacrament of Holy Orders; we're using the term here in its everyday sense, meaning people who, in conformity with the Church's regulations on the matter, have adopted a state of life dedicated to the service of God. And the term *monks* here includes nuns, too. What is true of one group is true of the other.

giver, St. Pachomius. Like St. Anthony, he was a Copt, and he had no philosophical training whatsoever. But his order popped up virtually overnight in its full organization: several thousand people, in separate communities for men and women, with a superior general, visitations, general chapters—the whole works.

Pachomius's monks and nuns had to meet some very high standards—they had to know the Psalms and the entire New Testament by heart, for instance—and they took vows of poverty, chastity, and obedience. Poverty may not sound terribly attractive, but you can put it to good use. It follows Christ's oft-repeated indictment of riches (Mt 13:22, for instance, or Mk 10:21–28). Also, when you get plenty of practice giving up material things—which are external to your nature—it's easier to live in chastity, which involves giving up the strongest earthly ties of all, as well as conquering the animal side of your nature.

That's also why fasting is so important in monastic culture; learning to control the permissible appetites teaches you how to control the ones that aren't so permissible. (You don't have to be a monk to manage this, incidentally; anybody can do it, and it works.) Obedience is spiritually necessary, too, not only because it follows Christ's mode of operation (Mt 16:24) but because it brings you the supernatural strength that you need to conquer self-will.

Oddly enough, Pachomius's rule didn't have much influence in the East, but St. Jerome translated it into Latin, and it hit the West like a ton of bricks. St. Augustine put together a sort of rule based on Pachomius's, and a lot of regular clergy still live by it. He was the one who thought of making some monks priests (not all of them are; you can take simple vows and be a monk for a while, just as you can be a nun for a while. So you shouldn't necessarily be shocked when the newspapers refer to a woman as an "ex-nun". It's a mark of distinction, really.)

But the man who really built on Pachomius's ideas was St. Benedict of Nursia, who lived around the middle of the sixth century. His *Rule* hit a perfect balance between the ideal and the practical, the life of prayer and the hardheaded management of a large organization, and it has worked superbly for more than fifteen hundred years, now. It calls for something like a family, with an abbot (from *abba*, "father") heading up a community of equal brethren. This makes the *Rule* a wonderful source for the Christian formation of anybody's family, by the way, and it wouldn't hurt businesspeople to read it, either.

In fact, St. Benedict's *Rule* defined the basics of the monastic way of life forever after, and—although nobody suspected it at the time—it outlined the social mechanism by which western civilization itself was preserved and nurtured for the next millennium. You have to remember that in Benedict's day, and for centuries afterward, Europe was exactly like the American West used to be. The monasteries, all begun by southerners or easterners, were like frontier forts: there was plenty of regulation on the inside, but no law at all on the outside.

So, when Benedict's troops moved in, the nomadic tribes of northern Europe found themselves peeking around the trees to see silent, hooded figures clearing ground and planting crops and cutting stone to make into buildings, ideas that never occurred to the natives. And, in a short time, they were surprised to find that these aliens led a way of life almost exactly the opposite of their own— we'd find it unbearably austere, but it was infinitely more comfortable, reasonable, and stable than anybody's wild tribal ways.

Remember, we're dealing with people that the Roman legions could never conquer, people whose idea of politics as usual was to kill their king because "he was wont to spare his enemies and forgive them the wrongs that they had done as soon as they asked him," as the Venerable Bede noted in the eighth century. Try teaching the Lord's Prayer to folks who operate that way.

But a couple of centuries later, "after their acceptance of Christianity," wrote Adam of Bremen—a northerner himself—"they have become imbued with better principles and have now learned to love peace and truth. . . . Of all people they are the most temperate both in food and in their habits, loving above all things thrift and modesty. . . . There is much that is remarkable in their manners, above all Charity . . ."

Of course, monks like Abbo and Hardmut, and nuns like Bugga and Lioba, could turn people like that around only because the northerners were good by nature and understandably eager for a more agreeable way of life, just like everybody else. Also, the clerics didn't act superior to the people, although they necessarily held themselves apart from the world at large. With their vows of poverty and obedience, they couldn't be seen as particularly high and mighty; since they weren't allowed to bear arms, they couldn't be seen as a threat to the local order of things.

They just taught by example, taking what was there and using it to greater advantage. And this goes for the arts of civilization as well as the natural resources and the people themselves. The monasteries attracted hordes of recruits from all segments of the tribal societies, from royalty like Illtyd, Sebbi, and Offa down to perfectly ordinary people. Once they got settled and disciplined, they quickly raised local modes of expression, like the epic, to new artistic heights, and, through the international scope of their orders, they introduced these forms to the rest of the world.

We're still living on the incidental side effects of that process. Apart from introducing agriculture and permanent architecture into those lands, monks kept all of the other arts alive—sometimes almost single-handed. Tutilo of St. Gall, for one, was renowned as a "poet, orator, architect, painter, sculptor, and metalworker, but most of all a superb musician", and there were plenty of others like him. They were the ones who invented the "Gothic" style, including stained glass.

They were also the ones who developed the first hospitals (from *hospes*, "guest"). St. Benedict wrote in the *Rule* that "every humanity must be shown to guests . . . all who arrive are to be welcomed like Christ . . . (and they are always coming to a monastery)". Since the monks couldn't turn you away, and since they were required to care for you like that, it made sense to go to a monastery if you were sick. Besides, a lot of the monks could read and write, so they had access to more medical information than anybody else.

Even now, monks sometimes take on educational duties, but for more than a thousand years in Europe (and for a long time in some parts of America), the monasteries were the only places where you could learn to read and write. The monasteries, in fact, were literacy factories, turning out the treaties and deeds for everybody else, practical works like little discourses on agriculture—to say nothing of the illuminated Bibles, Gospels, breviaries,

and books of hours—and the only histories around, which is how
Notker the Stammerer and Wipo made such names for themselves.

In short, when it comes to books, we owe the monks everything. Without them, we wouldn't have one meaningful scrap of
literature from ancient Greece and Rome. It was the monks who
recognized that the brilliant culture of antiquity was crashing
down around them (and that's not easily seen, believe it or not—
you usually just find yourself remembering the Good Old Days,
when the plumbing worked). And it was they who decided to preserve the best of it, particularly those monks who followed a man
who deserves to be better known: Cassiodorus, a Roman of senatorial rank who turned his villa into a monastery. With one foot
in classical antiquity and the other in the Middle Ages, he's personally responsible for anything that we know today about Greece
and Rome.

The transformation of Europe was more or less completed by
the year 1000. Five hundred years later, the frontier outposts of the
monasteries had grown into great cities—from Rouen to Brzevnov—that had built their civilization as they had built their streets
and houses, on foundations laid by the Church. And just when
this great work of civilization had reformed the known world, a
new world opened up.

The story of the European missions to the New World still stirs
people's hearts today, one way or another. But whatever motives
may have drawn the secular states of Europe to stake out territories
in the New World, the Church's mission there was the same as it
had been in the Old World, and she undertook it in the same way.
In those relatively small areas controlled by the colonists, she did
what she could to restrain the secular powers.* And, striking out
on their own far beyond the territories secured by European armies, again with precious little personnel and exactly no material,
regular clergy walked once more into a wilderness peopled with
tribal societies where warfare was a way of life.

---

*The evidence strongly suggests that the Church really did stand guard over
her converts here. In countries colonized by Spain, Portugal, and France, the
population today is almost entirely made up of Native Americans, while in those
former colonies of countries that were outside the Church's jurisdiction the natives were virtually exterminated.

This time, though, the missionaries weren't exactly monks. They were Franciscans, friars who, with canons regular, clerks regular, and congregations, round out the ranks of regular clergy. Their names had a more familiar ring to them: Junípero Serra, Marcos de Niza, Gaspar de Portola. But the accomplishment was the same. Carrying no weapons, not even speaking the language, they walked barefoot two by two into Indian country. Some were killed instantly—some horribly—but apparently the sheer novelty of these visitors held people's interest most of the time, and their religious teachings were usually embraced quickly by people eager for a new way of life.

As Christianity spread across the New World, missionaries and natives together built an entirely new way of life for themselves. The achievements of this new culture stand today, embodied in the rosary of mission cities that stretches from Vera Cruz to San Francisco, through El Paso to San Antonio, Santa Fe, San Diego, Los Angeles, and Sacramento. The culture itself is still very much alive, a major influence on American music and art, on our holiday customs, and even on the food we eat. It can't be called a European culture, and it is not entirely native; but it is clearly the child of both, fostered by the Church through her regular clergy.

What's their next move? Well, there is always the need to preserve the best, the need to communicate it to the rest of the world. There are always places where good education can make a material improvement in the way people live. For the monks, nuns, and friars of this world, there's always a new frontier.

CHAPTER 18

SAINTS

How You Get to Be One

I F YOU DEFINE A SAINT as anyone who's died and gone to Heaven, then the idea of sainthood is older than the Church. There are Moses and Elias, who appeared in company with Christ at the Transfiguration, as well as Onias and Jeremias, who interceded with God for their Earthbound brethren (2 Mc 15:11–16). Christ himself told us about how the rich man communicated with Lazarus, who had died and gone to be with Abraham (Lk 16:19–31). And Revelations tells of saints (5:8) who present other people's prayers to God (angels do the same thing—Tb 12:12, Rv 8:3—but they're different in that they've never had bodies).

So, with a suitable attitude of respect, just as you ask your friends here on Earth to pray for you and with you, you can ask friends who have died—those that you know died "in friendship with the Church", anyway. You can probably assume, or at least hope, that they're with God, face to face, and therefore in a much better position to pray than we are down here where this mortal clay looks through a glass so darkly.

But how do you know for a fact that somebody's with God, particularly somebody that you don't know, who lived long ago and far away? The Greek Orthodox Church goes by general public opinion, and other Christian sects are fairly casual about it. But the Church experienced long ago the abuses that can arise when people are elevated to the honors of sainthood just by popular acclaim, and her regulations on this matter have grown by the same kind of crystallization that characterizes all of her work on Earth. In fact, the Church is the only religious organization in the world that has a regular, legalistic process for determining who's with God.*

As it stands now, the declaration of sainthood is reserved to the Pope. The procedure leading up to this declaration is long, complicated, and very, very strict, although it's been streamlined in recent years. But almost none of it runs the way that you might think it does.

You might think that conspicuously holy people get a red-carpet treatment (after they die, of course), but in fact the more spectacular the sanctity the longer it takes for the official decision. You have to wait for the dust to settle, and often for everybody who knew the candidate personally to die, so that the evidence will stand on its own, uncolored by personal affection or hostility. Padre Pio, for instance, had it all—reputed cures, bilocation, even the stigmata—but his canonization isn't automatic. There's never much hurry about these things, and the Church has all the time in the world.

And, as it happens, latter-day saints, far from being the darlings of the hierarchy, are almost always regarded with the chilling eye of suspicion. You can't have some spellbinder leading crowds of people astray. St. Francis of Assisi was always in hot water, but it turned out that he really was right when everybody else was wrong, and his ideas eventually touched the whole Church. St. Ignatius of Loyola was hauled up before the Spanish Inquisition more than once. St. John Bosco was denounced by local clergy as a lunatic—who else would take in all of those stray children with absolutely nothing to sustain them but faith in God's providence?

---

*Some separated sects in this country say that they accord the title on the basis of mention in the Bible, but that comes down to popular acclaim, too. Plenty of people in the Bible (Onan and Judas come to mind) probably wouldn't make the grade, no matter how charitably you look at it.

And when the deputation of priests charged with committing him came along to invite him "for a little drive in the country", he politely got his hat and coat, opened the carriage door, and let them get in before him. Then he slammed the door, yelled to the driver, "To the asylum!", and went back to work.

Saints do tend to be a lot more cheerful than you might expect, too. In fact, one of the things that the commissions reputedly look for is "evidence of joy", even if this spiritual elation usually comes mixed with the severest kinds of penitence. St. Thomas More was Chancellor of England, and he had to dress the part, but his hair shirt crept out from under his velvet doublet once because he was laughing so hard. His embarrassment only made him laugh harder. Until then, nobody had suspected its existence except his daughter, dear Margaret, who used to wash all of the blood out of it for him every day. St. Teresa of Avila, Teresa of the Strict Observance, Teresa of the Unmitigated Rule, taught her nuns to dance in the cloister on feast days—with castanets, no less. (But she knew passages like Psalms 150 and 29:12, 2 Kings 6:14, and Lk 1:44 perfectly well, so it's all right.) Mother Cabrini, she of the legendary spankings, was enough of a character to keep a reporter from sneaking into her hospital by batting him in the face with a wet mop (she was chief administrator there, but she was taking her turn as janitor in the wee hours that night, just as all of the other nuns did). People still smile when you mention St. Philip Neri.

They're funny, the saints are, but there's no nonsense about any of them when it comes to the Faith. They have their foibles, just like the rest of us humans, and they have distinct personalities that range all the way from girlishly sweet, like Thérèse of Lisieux, to really rather crabby, like Jerome—but they all show the very strictest obedience to the Church and all her laws. True, many saints have persuaded certain hard-nosed prelates to change their minds, but they obeyed those prelates even as they changed them, which is a much more delicate accomplishment. During the formal inquiries that precede canonization, investigators look long and hard for the slightest sign of disobedience, as well as any departure from purity of doctrine in whatever writings the candidate has left behind. (There used to be a "devil's advocate", a lawyer charged with deflating the cause, but that's really superfluous because the whole point of the inquiry is to find possible ways to disallow the declaration, to be on the safe side, and to entertain any—any—counter-evidence.)

The main thing that you look for in a candidate for sainthood, though, is "heroic virtue", the practice of all Christian virtues in a truly perfect and exemplary manner—to the point of heroism. Martyrdom is one good sign of heroic virtue, but even that has to be proved. It's not enough to be a Christian (in full communion with the Church) and be skinned alive by someone who isn't. There's got to be proof that the killing was done *in odium fidei*, in hatred of the Faith. That isn't always easy: whom can you call as witness?

But heroic virtue comes in quieter ways, too. If St. Thomas More hadn't been publicly beheaded for refusing to go along with the things that Henry VIII pulled, nobody but God would have known the full scope of his sanctity, even after the hair-shirt episode. The stunning spiritual life of people like St. Catherine Labouré (the classic example) is all the more astonishing because of the element of surprise. Nobody who knew them ever suspected.

Saints like these only point up the immense importance of quiet heroism, of fighting the good fight inside yourself every day, without making a fuss about it. After all, how very few of those in Heaven are officially canonized—most people who make it must come straight from the pews, after leading a life hidden with Christ in God, as it says in Colossians. Well, bear that in mind, and take another look at the lady who always cleans up after church suppers.

But supposing your sanctity becomes public knowledge anyway, that you get through all of the inquests, all of the reviews, and all of the other interminable procedures. There's still one more thing that the Church requires before declaring confidently that you're with God: miracles. People sort of expect miracles from those who get a reputation for holiness ("Miracles they want now!" snapped Pius X. "As if I didn't have enough to do already!"). If any happen during the person's life, they can be adduced as evidence, but the ones that really count toward canonization have to happen after the candidate's death.

The idea is that if God wants this person known as a saint, he'll permit an extraordinary event in answer to prayers to the candidate, and he'll do so in such a way as to leave no reasonable doubt that the event was accomplished through the candidate's intercession. (Of course, if you don't get the miracle, that doesn't mean that the candidate isn't in Heaven. It might mean that God doesn't want to make the fact known publicly, for whatever reason.) The difficulty of proving reported miracles brings into play the full battery of scientific and medical techniques, everything that can possibly be used to probe the event from top to bottom, as well as theological, juristic, and historical techniques, to exclude any possible natural explanation—to exclude any *possibility* of a natural explanation, really. That takes a long time, too, and it's certainly the most rigorous inquest on Earth.

Then, if you've got your evidence of sanctity, you're deceased, and you've passed all inquiries (including certifiable miracles), you get declared "Blessed". If further evidence comes to light, you get put through the process again, and then, if you pass, you go to full canonization, which means that your "memory should be kept with pious devotion by the universal Church," as the official proclamation says. You're enrolled in the canon of the Church calendar—"canonized"—you have a Mass and an Office in your honor, and you can be named patron of parish churches, oratories, and cathedrals.

In short, you get what's called a public cult, but we don't have an exact word in English for the veneration that a saint gets— English tends to be kind of stodgy when it comes to matters of the heart. Centuries ago, you might have said that a saint gets "worship", because the word comes from the Old English *weorthscipe*, which just means "worthy of honor" or "worthy of respect". That's why British speakers of English used to say "Your Worship" as a title of courtesy to anyone with whom they spoke politely.

Nowadays, of course, *worship* means only our attitude toward God Almighty. In Latin, which is richer when it comes to these things, the worship owed to God alone is called *latria*, a word that has its roots in the ancient Greek word meaning the adoration that humans owe to the divine. It's a matter of acknowledging your total dependence upon God. But the respect that we owe to the saints is an entirely different kind of attitude; it's called *dulia*, which means "appropriate" or "fitting and proper," as when you say that someone acts *dutifully*, or that a trial was handled with *due* process. In an everyday sense of the word, *dulia* is your demeanor in court or meeting the President; it's much more like what you'd call courtesy than what you'd call worship.

(There's a variation of *dulia* that's often misunderstood: *hyperdulia*, a higher kind of reverence that's accorded only to Mary, first among saints. Note that this is basically *dulia*, only higher. It's an entirely different thing from *latria*, and it can't diminish the unique honor owed to God. It's never correct to say that the Church *worships* Mary—it hasn't been correct since people stopped speaking Old English, anyway. You can only say that, in recognition of her unique relationship with God, the Church renders to Mary a unique reverence notably higher than the respect accorded to other saints.)

Dulia, even in its exaltation as *hyperdulia*, is a familiar, comfortable kind of devotion that lets you develop a close acquaintance with those who are in a very good position to help you. Once you start looking, you'll find at least one saint who had exactly the same problems you have, only worse, and then you can find out how to overcome them. You'll find another who had the same kind of job that you have, or the same kind of singular failing— they all have heroic virtue, but remember their heroic eccentricities, too. Just reading about their lives helps put things in perspective and indicates how high you can set your sights and how you can rearrange your own life to welcome the will of God. That's what saints are there for. The whole point is that anybody can do it.

CHAPTER 19

FÁTIMA, LOURDES, AND ELSEWHERE

The Story of Apparitions

BACK IN THE SIXTEENTH CENTURY, there was a woman in a little Spanish village who claimed that the Holy Spirit appeared to her every day and gave her all kinds of revelations—the futures of people in town, new prayers and practices, all kinds of things. She naturally attracted a lot of attention, and the local bishop sent St. John of the Cross, even then known as a wise and trustworthy man, to investigate.

John found the woman in front of her house. "Are you the woman to whom the Holy Spirit appears?" he asked. "Yes!" she smiled. "I am!"

"God bless you, Señora!" he said. He returned to his monastery and reported to the bishop that the woman was either a fake or deluded.

The Church's investigations of alleged apparitions aren't usually so informal, and they're not usually so quick. But John knew one important thing about people who really do have supernatural experiences: they don't brag about it. They don't readily admit their visions; they don't run around giving interviews and blessing people. If they run at all, it's to get away from the crowds.

Of course, you can't take the word of a visionary as evidence, anyway, on purely logical grounds. A vision can be diabolical in origin, or pathological; even a devout person can be fooled by the subconscious. And just going by ordinary human rules of evidence, the Church understands that you can't say unequivocally that a supernatural being appeared on Earth. That's why the Church is very, very cautious in investigating reports of apparitions, and that's why the most you ever get is a *negative approval*—a statement that there's nothing in the account contrary to faith and morals, and that therefore it's "worthy of belief." But visions aren't part of the Church's teaching, and acceptance of the ones that pass investigation is not imposed but only permitted.*

Now, the Church recognizes three main types of apparition (*apparition* may sound strange, but it's just a noun form of the verb "to appear"). St. Augustine classified them first, and St. Thomas Aquinas articulated more details of each type in his *Summa Theologica*. St. John of the Cross and his contemporary St. Teresa of Avila wrote simply and stunningly about visions, too, and from their own experience. (These are four of the most intelligent people who ever lived, incidentally, which is pretty strong evidence against dismissing visions as mere superstition.)

One kind is the *corporeal* vision, when you see something that's normally invisible, as when the angel Gabriel appeared to Mary (Lk 1:26–38) or when Paul got knocked off his horse on the road to Damascus (Acts 9:1–9). These are caused by God directly or through an angelic power or—here's the catch—by the devil, as when he showed Christ "all the kingdoms of the world and the glory of them" (Mt 4:8). On the other hand, corporeal visions can also happen just in terms of nature, as when certain atmospheric conditions let you see something that's normally hidden behind landscape features. Visions of this kind, or any other kind, can be tricky, and they're all serious business. St. John of the Cross outlines the damage that they can wreak, in his *Ascent of Mount Carmel*, and you'd better read it.

Another kind, the *imaginative* vision, happens without the aid of sight. You can be asleep or awake, but you can't produce the vision when you want to or get rid of it—St. Teresa resisted her visions

---

*By the way, apparitions are reported every day; the overwhelming majority are obviously not valid, so they're disapproved and you never hear of them again.

with all of her considerable willpower and devotion for two whole years, but they came anyway. This kind of vision may be symbolic, like Jacob's ladder (Gn 28:10–22); it can be personal, like St. Margaret Mary's vision of the Sacred Heart; it might also be dramatic, like the Mystic Marriage of St. Catherine. And it can also be diabolical in origin or simply natural.

It's called an imaginative vision because it imprints an image on your consciousness. St. Teresa didn't like this term, because it's related to the word *imagination*. "That this vision from God could be the work of the imagination," she wrote in her autobiography, "is the most impossible of impossible things; it is utter nonsense to think so . . . because they go far beyond what we can comprehend here on Earth." She describes this kind of vision in a profoundly stirring passage that begins with the twenty-fifth chapter of her autobiography, and if you're interested in visions you ought to read that, too.

The third kind, as St. Teresa wrote, "is called an *intellectual* vision; I don't know why." St. John of the Cross explained that it gets this name because "all that is intelligible to the intellect, the spiritual eye of the soul, causes spiritual vision, just as all that is corporally visible to the material eye causes corporal vision." The intellectual vision is a simple intuitive knowledge that you just *know*, without any natural means like study, with no help from your senses. "It's as though the food were already placed in the stomach without our eating it or knowing how it got there," St. Teresa said. As with an imaginative vision, you can be asleep or awake, but an intellectual vision can last hours or days. The best thing about the intellectual kind is that only God can produce it, since only God has access to the human intellect. But then again it's the hardest to identify, the most difficult to describe.

No matter what kind of vision it is, the experts can usually distinguish the divine from the diabolical (or the false) by certain characteristics. In fact, the apparitions that get the Church's cautious certification run to a certain pattern, just like the behavior of the seers—but then adherence to the pattern isn't necessarily proof of anything, either. And, really, when you get down to cases, the pattern holds *except*; there's always at least one feature that departs from what you'd expect from looking at the others.

The best-documented examples of visions are the more famous apparitions of Mary. Almost all of them happened in isolated areas, tough, infertile places where people scrape a living from ungenerous soil. The visions tend to occur in ordinary, but quiet, places; a barren hillock on a dry Mexican mountainside, a rocky grotto by a river, a little oak tree in a pasture. In this, they are consistent with the stable at Bethlehem. Of course, the exception is St. Catherine Labouré's convent oratory in Paris (1830), but even that was an island of calm in—well, in Paris.

Speaking of Paris, these apparitions also occur in areas that urgently need correction—areas where skepticism, worldliness, mockery, and blasphemy set the tone. Even Guadalupe (1531) happened in an area still largely in the hold of indigenous cults, steeped in the blood of human sacrifice and tied closely to idols. The others happened when revolutions were about to break out, when Communism was about to erupt, or when Hitler was preparing to ravage Europe and the world. Lourdes (1858) stands as an exception here; things were fairly stable then, relatively speaking.

Also, the visionaries usually live in places that don't have many paintings and statues, no images that would soak into their imaginations to come forth later (except, of course, the visionaries of Pontmain in 1871, who saw the Lady as she was shown in the unique arrangement of their parish church, but that makes sense as it was the only way they'd recognize her). Their families tend to be irreligious, or at least casual about religion, except St. Bernadette's family, the Soubirous, who were deeply devout. The seers also tend to be children, except Juan Diego of Guadalupe, who was fifty-one, and a widower—but then, he had the natural innocence of a child, and he never lost it.

None of the visionaries ever expected it; it would never even cross their minds that such a thing could happen. Except St. Catherine Labouré, who said that another nun's discourse on the Blessed Virgin "gave me so great a desire to see her that I went to bed that night with the thought that I would see my good Mother that very night—it was a desire that I had long cherished." Still, it's clear from her words and—more important—her life that she wanted it not as a special favor but for the sheer spiritual joy of it;

not to make herself more important but to bring herself closer to God. But, generally, people who expect this kind of favor never seem to get it, which tells you something about Pride.

And those who do see credible visions are not usually the kids that people pick out as being particularly holy or remarkable in any other way. Medical, psychological, and ecclesiastical examinations show them completely normal, just as analysis of the waters of the miraculous springs shows ordinary water. The seers are, as a rule, completely uneducated, certainly too ignorant of theology to come up with the messages on their own—all of the approved apparitions, without exception, deliver messages, as Moses and Elias did at the Transfiguration (Lk 9:28–31). Sometimes the seers don't even speak the language that the Lady uses. At Banneux (1933), the Lady spoke the official language, French, but the seer, Mariette Béco, spoke only the local Walloon; at La Salette (1846), the Lady also spoke official French, but the children spoke only their local mountain lingo. The children of Fátima (1917) understood the Lady's Portuguese well enough, but they'd never heard some of the theological terms that she used.

Most of the visionaries, in fact, are—how should one say it—not excessively bright. The prioress at Châtillon routinely refused to take into the postulancy a person with so little promise as St. Catherine Labouré. St. Bernadette was a constant exasperation to her teacher; she was a very poor student, to say the least.

(This teacher, by the way, is a good example of a fairly usual reaction to credited visionaries. She was a nun who invented all kinds of penances for herself. For most of her adult life, she slept on a bare board and for only a few hours a night; she mortified every desire. She thought that she'd earned some mark of divine favor, and then when the Blessed Virgin appeared in the neighborhood, it was to this illiterate little good-for-nothing who didn't even know her catechism! The nun was furious; apparently there was no one to point out that God had chosen her, above all other nuns, to instruct a great saint who urgently needed a good teacher. Her charge was divine, the potential reward immense; her singular favor analogous to that of St. Joseph himself—and she just didn't see it.)

So the visionaries tend to be innocent of all learning. And who

would believe a college-educated visionary? There's not much reason to credit a supernatural source for the sayings of a learned person who had plenty of natural means to develop a message of this
kind, no matter how meaningful and theologically sound, and no
matter how unconsciously it was done.

The Lady warned them all that they wouldn't be happy in this
life, and they certainly had a hard time of it afterward.* Bernadette
and Catherine Labouré put up with emotional and even physical
abuse for decades, without a word. But they don't all have the
stamina for this. When news of Mariette Béco's visions leaked out,
the other kids started genuflecting before her, calling her "Bernadette", or just beating her up. She didn't take it well; before and
after her visions, she was rated by her teachers as downright
farouche—"savage", we'd say in English. The seers of La Salette,
Maximin Giraud and Melanie Mathieu, their teachers noticed,
nourished an active dislike for one another, and neither came to a
happy end.

Maximin never found a career and died a failure at forty.
Melanie at first acted as you'd expect; she indignantly refused to
take the money that people pressed on her (although she could
have used it), she was horrified by the idea of blessing people who
asked for it, and she wanted only to stay away from the crowds.
But eventually she gave in to the adulation, and she started to like
it. She tried more than once to enter religious life, but she
couldn't make the grade—humility and obedience seemed to be
her weak points. She became something of an itinerant crank, rail-
ing against the clergy for failing to appreciate her tremendous importance. Apparently these two visionaries had no vocation to
heroic virtue like the others; but their very failures in every other
facet of life only point up another definite characteristic of credit-
worthy seers: their remarkable lifelong precision in relating what
happened to them that day.

The visionaries never forget what Christ or Our Lady tell them
during the visions. They repeat it verbatim for the rest of their

*You'd expect people so favored to become saints, but that's by no means au-
tomatic; to get canonized, they have to go through exactly the same rigorous
procedures as any other candidate. See chapter 18 on saints.

lives, when required to, and they don't trip up by misquoting themselves. And remember, it wasn't always in a language that they spoke themselves. They even kept straight all the tiny details of voice and appearance. Policemen, bishops, parents, and—most brutal of all—other children can't make them change a word of it. And they never add anything, either.

The messages all center on themes of repentance, reparation, and prayer. They never add anything to the Gospels; that alone would be grounds enough for classifying the purported vision as a hoax, because it would assert that Christ did not do his work completely while he walked among us. Naturally, the approved ones contain nothing, and imply nothing, that's contrary to the faith as taught by the Church.

All of the countries involved were predominantly, and tradition-ally, in full communion with the Church—well, except Mexico in the early sixteenth century, and that was rapidly on its way. These things do not occur among separated denominations, and there don't seem to be any exceptions to this. Pius XII, in fact, noted that the miracles that followed the apparitions at Lourdes "con-firmed the catholic religion as the only one given approval by God."

And the approved apparitions are indeed followed up with genuine miracles. Not the "Oh-look-my-rosary-has-turned-pink" sort of thing, which doesn't count. There's nobody to certify be-forehand that the rosary wasn't pink to start with, and even if there were, there are countless ways that skill or a mistake made in good faith could accomplish this. Rather, the miracles that follow appa-ritions have to do with cases like people terminally ill, consigned to hopelessness by their doctors, who get well immediately—sometimes before your very eyes—while visiting one of the Lady's springs.

There are thousands of these cases, documented and even pho-tographed, in the records of Lourdes, compiled by unimpeachable doctors, some of them faithful to the Church but also many others who are members of separated sects, non-Christians, or even ag-nostics. The proof is there. You may find it all hard to rationalize, but you won't find it easy to dismiss.

CHAPTER 20

WONDERING ABOUT SIGNS

Does the Madonna Really
Weep Through Images?

I N 1953, IN SYRACUSE in Sicily, in the worst possible neighborhood in the city, a cheap plaster bust of the Virgin cried copi-
ous tears for four days. The rest of the little statue stayed dry,
but the eyes wept even when the figure was detached from its
mounting and held in the hand, buckets. Thousands of pilgrims
came to see, and to pray, taking the phenomenon as a call to repentance. The occurrence was declared "worthy of belief" by the
local Ordinary, the statuette was moved to a special church built to
house it, and a huge marble plaque was set into the wall of the
house where the event occurred.

In 1992, in Lake Ridge, Virginia, the figure of the Blessed Virgin in a fiberglass statue of the Holy Family was reportedly shedding tears. Reporters, curiosity seekers, and crowds of people
whose emotions had been brought to the boil pushed into the little church. Later, stained-glass windows appeared to drip tears,
too. The local Ordinary put a stop to the fuss, and, after a few
weeks of intense media coverage, the story dropped from sight and
life went back to normal in the parish.

Why the difference? Well, the cases were different. Just in a
general sense, these two occurrences followed the distinction between religion and superstition, between devotion and hysteria. In

Syracuse, delegated witnesses saw the statue weep as they held it in their hands; under constant observation, more liquid came out than the statue could have held, physically. Medical analysis of the fluid showed that it contained all of the salts and complex proteins and other substances found in normal human tears, in the right proportions. Otherwise inexplicable cures were effected, crime waned, and the city turned to a generally more punctilious observance of its religion. In Lake Ridge, nobody saw the statue weep; they just saw puddles on the floor "afterward". The phenomenon happened only in the presence of one certain person, and it followed him when he went to another parish. Nobody was cured of anything.

But in both cases, the Church's reaction was really the same: reservation. Her first presumption is always that these things are completely natural but unexplained, events best handled by scientists whose study confines itself to the hidden workings of nature. Religion, after all, has nothing to fear from a genuine scientific explanation of anything.

(You often hear professional magicians and other self-appointed "debunkers" carping about how "The Church" doesn't let them touch the images in question, "because they don't really want to know the truth" or "they get a lot of money from it." Wrong. For one thing, there's no global procedure or policy here, and the Vatican doesn't have much to do with it, so you can't fairly talk about how "The Church" handles it. Investigation of this kind of thing is reserved to the local bishop, and he's required to undertake it. There's probably no phone call any bishop looks forward to less than the one about a weeping statue, but they get more of them in a year than you'd believe. A bishop's tribunal for these matters is extremely precise and exacting in its investigations; the members have to be very conservative about the qualifications of the experts consulted. You have to be an accredited scientist, degreed and respected, not merely an entertainer who can figure out a mechanical way to reproduce the effect of the event, which, logically, wouldn't prove anything, anyway. And, naturally, the crowds have to be kept a reasonable distance away from the phenomenon, to avoid purposeful or accidental tampering.)

In any case, you can't rush off and say, yes, this is a miracle, and then find out that it was a subtle fraud. You can't jump up and say, no, this is not a miracle, and then find out that it really must have been. Nor can you easily exclude every possible natural explanation, because science only goes so far. So, even if the event stands up under investigation, as the one in Syracuse did, the Church doesn't say all that much about it: only that it's worthy of belief. The Church never comes right out and says, "This is a miracle from God." The most the Church will ever say is that it hasn't been possible to find an ordinary natural explanation for the phenomenon, so you can consider it a sign from God if you want to. But belief in miracles, outside of the ones in the Bible, is not required for membership.

In fact, the only real value of things like this (if they're genuinely worthy of belief) is that they can attract attention to the substance of the Faith. That's how Christ used his signs and wonders. "Now, when he was at Jerusalem for the feast of the Passover, many believed in his Name, seeing the signs that he was working. But Jesus did not trust himself to them" (Jn 2:23–24). Attraction to a miracle and attention to faith are two very different things.

But look at Nicodemus (Jn 3:1–4). The miracles got his attention, and he followed up on them. "Rabbi," he said, "we know that you have come a teacher from God, for no one can work these signs that you work unless God be with him." But Jesus changed the subject, abruptly. "Amen, amen, I say to you," he said, "unless a man be born again, he cannot see the kingdom of God," and the very incongruity of the answer stopped Nicodemus short. "How can a man be born when he is old?" he asked, and they were off. They never did get around to discussing the miracles.

Unexpected things like images that weep or bleed can do the same thing today—get attention. But the problem is that a lot of people, unlike Nicodemus, get so excited about the image itself that they never get around to the religion. It doesn't take much to attract attention, either. Even things that obviously occur purely by chance, like a human face in a burned tortilla or a figure in the grain of wood, are enough to make some people cry "Miracle!" Simple public veneration of a beloved icon that doesn't even do anything can be a distraction from the substance of religion, too, because there are plenty of people whose way of life doesn't give them the means to distinguish between using an image and worshiping an idol.

But the Church, embracing as she does every possible culture on the planet, knows the difference. The urge to make images of sacred subjects is older than the Church (older than history, for that matter), and it's a natural expression of faith and joy and hope for most people. Since the Apostolic Age, Christians have used images to help them communicate their faith or as a focus of devotions—the catacombs are full of them. In fact, people used to think that God put his seal of approval on sacred images by making them himself: there were plenty of them that had the reputation of having just come into existence by the agency of Heaven, without anybody's painting them or anything. (You call one of these an *acheiropoeton*—"ah-kee-roe-PAY-ton." It means something not made by hands.)

There was the *Mandylion* ("man-DIL-ee-un"), an inexplicable image of Christ's face (which was probably the cloth that we know today as the Shroud of Turin); there was the *Keramion*, a tile that had taken on the same image, reputedly by being in contact with the Mandylion during its stay in Edessa in Syria. And there was the *Kamoulianai Christos*, another cloth with the face of Christ on it, supposedly created when Christ appeared, washed and dried his face, and disappeared again at the church of Kamoulia in Cappadocia in about 570. All of these images were kept in the Holy Palace of Constantinople, and they were trooped out at the head of the armies whenever the Emperor went forth to fight heathens. So everybody knew about them, and they were objects of national pride, like our Liberty Bell and the original Declaration of Independence. Nobody seriously disputed their miraculous origin.

This might sound like the rankest superstition, but we're in the same boat—our science doesn't explain everything, either. And when the Fathers of the Church had to formulate an official opinion about images, they did it with remarkable good sense, considering that controversy about the role of images in worship was tearing Christendom apart at the time.

It all started in the year 726, when the Byzantine Emperor Leo

III decreed that all sacred images should be destroyed. Nobody knows where he got the idea, but he came from a rather backward part of the country, as did most of his army, and maybe the bright lights of Constantinople were just too much for him. On his own authority, he ordered the troops to remove and destroy all of the icons in public places—in the churches, in the palaces, the market-places, everywhere. They smashed or burned every picture, statue, and reliquary that they could find—even relics. They even went so far as to destroy any plain crosses that they found.

There were riots; the elite of the city, like the people in the streets, opposed the sacrilege, but nobody could get very far against the army. The popes who reigned during this sad time objected strenuously, because the move had no theological basis whatever.

Leo paid no attention. The scene got uglier and uglier, with hundreds killed in the riots, clergy humiliated, patriarchs beheaded or beaten to death. It got worse day by day for the next fifteen years, at which point Leo died. There was a moment of hope, since Leo had begun the movement capriciously all by himself, but his successor, Constantine V, was a brute, too, and he really cracked down on images.

But in the end a few *iconoclasts* (from the Greek meaning "people who smash images") couldn't buck eight centuries of Christian custom. Constantine died, too, finally, and his widow, the Empress Irene, assumed power as regent in the name of her son. She was determined that the ancient traditions of Christianity would never again be oppressed.

Irene called for an ecumenical council specifically to come out with an official statement of the Church's policy on images. She contacted Pope Hadrian I, who convened the Second Council of Nicæa and sent two delegates, Peter the archpriest and Peter the Hegemon from the Greek monastery of S. Saba. The Byzantines sent three hundred and fifty delegates, which was fair, because the controversy had been most intense in the East. (The papal legates signed all of the documents first, and they were always listed first. Everybody knew who was in charge.)

The Council got down to business on September 24, 787, and it sat for about three weeks. Things went as you'd expect, with the council reaffirming the propriety of religious imagery. But there was a terrible confusion in the West when the Council's documents got there, because of the hideous translation that was sent. It sounded like the Council was prohibiting images, everywhere, even in the West. This was outrageous. The Pope and even Charlemagne got terribly upset, and all kinds of decrees thundered across Europe and back to Greece. Armies were mobilized from Paris to Constantinople. It finally got straightened out (history does not record what happened to the translators, although we are dying to know), and the Council's decrees on images have remained ever since as the foundation of the Church's opinions on the matter. Basically, the Second Council of Nicæa drew the distinction between *proskynesis* and *latria*.

Latria is the Latin word meaning the worship that's owed only to God, and not given to anybody else, not even saints. *Proskynesis* ("pro-skin-EE-sis"—everybody spoke Greek at the Council) is a polite gesture. It can be anything from a bow to a genuflection or a kiss on the foot to a simple greeting. The Sign of the Cross is a form of proskynesis. It's a cultural matter, not a point of religion; some gesture or mark of respect that you do to acknowledge a ruler, as they used to do for the Emperor. (The emperors at that time, by the way, didn't allow proskynesis toward themselves on Sundays, thinking it unsuitable for a creature to receive such a salutation on the Lord's Day, and just to show that it differs substantially from worship.) The term also covers any posture of intense prayer, like kneeling, or a gesture of penance or of greeting a holy person. In short, it's some ritual way that you courteously humble yourself.

Well, the Council reaffirmed that latria, worship, is for God alone, period, but that proskynesis (of some kind) is as appropriate a mark of respect for holy pictures and statues as it is for anything else that represents something superior like a saint. In other words, it's all right to respect an image of the holy, and to use it in your devotions, as long as you know that you're not worshiping it.

The interesting thing is that the Council set these guidelines for *any* religious image. It doesn't matter who made it or where it came from. As long as it's a regular, proper, edifying image— tortilla veneration is out—you may use it for your devotions if you want to, provided that you do it in a proper manner. If you don't want to, you don't have to. The Fathers of Nicæa II knew the power of images to focus people's thoughts and to move them to deep and meaningful emotions like repentance (try watching the Crucifixion sequence in *Ben Hur* with a dry eye). But they also knew that you don't need any *things* to prove the truth of Christianity.

So if the Shroud of Turin is the actual burial cloth of Jesus, that's fine, but it doesn't change anything that he taught. If it isn't, that doesn't mean that what he taught was wrong. Either way, it's totally unconnected to the Deposit of Faith. Same with the image of Our Lady of Good Counsel at Genazzano in Italy, or the *tilma* of Juan Diego with the image of Our Lady of Guadalupe. An image can weep spontaneously or not. It's nice if these phenomena are genuinely miraculous, but, barring outright fraud, it doesn't matter if they aren't. They're just images, and they have to be used in the context of proper devotions, no matter who made them or what they're purported to do. That's why the Church has always maintained a steady reserve on the genuineness of allegedly miraculous images, leaving those questions to qualified scientists. She doesn't really have anything riding on the outcome.

But she'll do everything in her power to keep people from going overboard with alleged miracles, from getting all enthusiastic about some spectacular sign instead of developing and growing in the steady path of Christianity. After all, Christ himself handled this issue in advance, too. "Blessed are they," he said, "that do not see, but believe."

PART FOUR

CUSTOMS

CHAPTER 21

HOW BEAUTIFUL THY DWELLING PLACE

The Basic Forms of Churches

S INCE THE SECOND VATICAN COUNCIL, church buildings in the United States have started taking on all kinds of shapes. They turn out round or rectangular, triangular, "free-form", or just about any other shape an architect can dream up. But a church isn't just another building. It's a sacramental, a material article that the Church uses to dispose people to the reception of grace. It's a holy object, a thing that's set apart for the service of God, just as a chalice or an altar is.

So an architect can't go about designing a church as if it were a gymnasium or a meeting house. There are plenty of regulations, embodied in ritual and in law, governing layout, materials, procedures, and everything else. In fact, every detail is *substantially* determined by regulation, although every detail can be *stylistically* determined with great freedom—there's an infinite number of floor plans and architectural fashions that will accommodate liturgies suitably and conform fully with regulations. The problem you run into, if you're designing or remodeling a church, is that the regulations lie in more than one place, and there aren't as many convenient manuals about as you might think.

For new churches, you can consult the recent guides put together since Vatican II,* but you might also want to have a look at St. Charles (Carlo) Borromeo's *Instructions for the Building of Churches (Instructiones Fabricæ Ecclesiasticæ)*, first published in 1599. The *Instructions* never had the force of law, and we've been through a great deal of re-regulation since then, but your parish church was probably designed to its specifications, if it was built before about 1950. And the book still gives a good practical frame of reference that includes all kinds of things you wouldn't have thought of. It's certainly the most comprehensive and concrete directive on church building ever assembled in the western Church.

Even with the help of publications like these, you still have to know the Missal, the Pontifical, the *Code of Canon Law*, all kinds of rulings by the Sacred Congregation for Sacraments and Divine Worship, and, permeating all of this, two thousand years of custom.

In fact, for most of that time, custom was enough to draw the main lines of church buildings. You can see this for yourself in Europe, in Latin America, or even here at home, if you're in an area where the Church has been settled in for a long time. You'll find that churches will either be in the form of a long rectangular hall leading from the door to an arch over the altar, or they'll be in a "centralized" form—a circle, a square, a six-sided or eight-sided shape, or perhaps in the form of a "Greek cross" with its four arms equal in size and shape. Almost all of these centralized churches have domes.

The difference between the rectangular church and the centralized church has to do with the liturgies that were celebrated in these buildings. After all, no matter what the size or shape of a church, no matter what kinds of other ceremonies it may have to accommodate, it's built primarily to house the Mass. And when it's a question of the Mass, the first place to look is in the Roman Missal.

*Among them *The Dedication of a Church and an Altar* (altars are considered entirely separate structures from the churches that house them) in the *General Instruction of the Roman Missal* and the statement put out in 1978 by the United States Bishops' Committee on the Liturgy, *Environment and Art in Catholic Worship*. Your diocesan library, or any Catholic bookstore, will probably have these publications.

The Roman Missal, whether in the older editions or the one revised after Vatican II, gives the liturgies of two kinds of Mass: regular *parochial* Masses of the Church calendar; and *votive* Masses for special intentions—for thanksgiving, for funerals, or to ask the aid of Our Lord or the intercession of a certain saint in a case of need. The fact that there are two classes of Mass, parochial and votive, brings about the distinction in traditional church types.

Parochial Masses are the general framework of the Church's public worship. The whole hierarchy of the Church is arranged, basically, to see that everybody has these Masses available, and from the rising to the setting of the Sun, therefore, the world is mapped out in dioceses, definite territories presided over by bishops and mitered abbots. Each diocese is subdivided into parishes. Each parish—from the Latin *parœcia*—has its own church, which is where you'll turn for marriages, funerals, baptisms, and the other ceremonies of life, and it's where you go to attend Mass on Sundays (or every day, if you're lucky enough to have that kind of schedule). You're supposed to be registered there, and canon law prohibits your just picking a parish church that you like and driving over there every Sunday. If you don't like something about your parish, it's your job to help improve it; you can't just complain about it or attend Mass someplace else.

Your parish church is where the Masses of the regular church calendar are celebrated throughout the year. Each parish church has to be designed to accommodate the congregation made up of the people who live in the territory of the parish.* And the most efficient form for this purpose is the familiar rectangular hall with the altar at one of the short ends and the entry at the other.

When you think about this form, though, it's really a radical departure from the religious architecture that pre-Christian religions

---

*There is such a thing as a "personal" parish, which is erected within the boundaries of a diocese but defined by the persons it includes, not by particular territorial boundaries; it accommodates persons of existing rites other than the Latin, or those having a common language or national origin, military or university personnel, etc. A cathedral, by the way, is a special kind of parish church; it's the principal church of the diocese, and the bishop is its pastor. So it holds a *cathedra*, a bishop's throne, and it is usually designed somewhat differently from a parish church, to accommodate special ceremonies like ordination.

had. Pagan Greek and Roman temples weren't places where people congregated. They were too small inside for that, and too dark. They were like fancy little boxes that held a cult image, and nobody but caretaker priests went in. Public sacrifices were held in the courtyards in front of these box-buildings—the open-air space that was actually called the *templum*—but you didn't have to attend. It was enough, in those religions, for the sacrifice to be made.

This wouldn't work for Christian liturgy. The sacrifice of the Mass is a joint effort, with an indispensable teaching function (the Bible readings and the homilies) and with priest and people acting in unison as well as responding to one another. And a central point of it is the distribution of the Eucharist. No classical temple would accommodate this kind of thing. Synagogues wouldn't, either; they were set up for public readings of Scripture, but they didn't have to accommodate everybody in town. Besides, early Christianity took pains to separate itself in the public mind from Judaism. And it outgrew the Holy Land so fast that by the time the Church started building for herself she was already working in territories where most congregations had never even seen a synagogue. So Christians had to look elsewhere for ideas on planning parochial churches.

The logical model was the Roman law court, because the Mass works, mechanically, much like a civil proceeding, where crowds of people assemble to stand or sit in the rectangular hall while the trial was conducted on a raised platform at one end, where the judge sat. Everybody could see what was going on. The hall itself often had a wooden roof and ceiling, to resonate with the speakers' voices so that everybody could hear everything. It was a familiar sort of building, too, because every large city and most small towns had one, just as every American county has its own courthouse today.

As a model for Christian churches, the Roman law court made sense symbolically as well as practically. These courthouses were called *basilicas*, from the Greek word meaning "majesty", because they were the places where the majesty of the Roman state made itself visible, embodied in the person of the judge and in the book of the law. The basilica was where the law became active among the members of the human community. This is perfect symbolism for the place where Christians come to hear the Law of Scripture and to see the Incarnate Law make himself physically present in the Eucharist to flow forth in communion with the population at large. It isn't by coincidence that our rising up and our sitting down are so similar at Mass and at trials, or that you only find pews in churches and in courthouses.

So the basilica lived on, long after the Empire fell, in the shape and the symbolism of the traditional parish church. That's why so many churches, in any style, follow the so-called basilican plan,* consisting of a long hall-shaped *nave*—from the Latin word for "ship", because that's what carries all of us passengers safely to our destination—ending in a raised platform with a big arch over the altar.

This basic scheme underlies the countless variations played through late Roman, Romanesque, Gothic, and Neo-Classical churches around the world, even some in traditional Chinese or Indian style. This pattern probably set the foundations for your parish church, too, if it's more than twenty or thirty years old. But what about all of those other churches, the round ones that started springing up all over Europe after the Renaissance? Do they mean that you can make a church any shape you want, from rectangular to round?

Well, no. Even today, we're supposed to follow the regulations as well as "the principles and norms of liturgy and sacred art" (Canon 1216) that centuries of Christian usage have established. And the Renaissance architects weren't just fooling around with meaningless or arbitrary forms. Their taste for little round churches had to do with who paid for the buildings, what kind of philosophy was in vogue at the moment, and, above all, with what the buildings were for: here, too, the plan reflects the kind of Mass that the building was supposed to hold.

Just as churches built on a basilican plan are for regular parochial

*The titles of churches sometime gets confusing because an important church building like St. Peter's or the Old Cathedral in St. Louis, Missouri, is called a "basilica", but that's just an honorific title that important church buildings get, as a person can get a knighthood. It doesn't necessarily mean that the building is shaped like a Roman basilica.

Masses, those built on a centralized plan are built for votive Masses, the "extra" Masses in the Missal that are celebrated for special intentions in addition to the regular parochial Masses. And, strictly speaking, these buildings aren't "churches" at all.

It all started about a generation before Columbus set sail. Europe had just shaken off the Middle Ages; trade was gearing up, and there was suddenly a lot of money in circulation. Of course, there were plenty of local charities who could use help, but if you really struck it rich, it was considered a worthy and pious act—and socially *de rigueur*—to pay for your own private church by endowing a foundation to say votive Masses for your intentions. You'd deed over some land that would earn rent, or you'd set aside a sum of money at one of the newfangled banks to earn interest, and the proceeds would support a priest or two (in those happy days of abundant clerics) to celebrate your votive Masses for you in perpetuity.

Votive Masses can perfectly well be celebrated at the altar of the parochial *church*; that's the usual way in this country now. Sometimes, though, you'd build or decorate a *chapel*, a smaller subdivision of a larger church building, that had its own altar or altars for your votive Masses. And starting in the Renaissance in Italy, if you were really rich and really powerful, the fashion was to construct a freestanding *oratory*, a building specially constructed to house votive Masses.

Actually, oratories are as old as Christianity. The worship spaces in the catacombs are too small to be congregational churches, and in fact they were only the sites for Masses for the dead, which are one kind of votive Mass. You find this devotion continuing down through the ages, as it does today, but the high and mighty of the Renaissance tried to outdo each other building fantastic architectural jewels to house endless Requiem Masses for the repose of their departed relatives. Sometimes a prince might promise to build an oratory in thanksgiving for favors received—winning a battle, concluding a favorable peace treaty, or seeing his people's prayers answered for relief of a plague or famine—so the oratory would have a public monumental character, too.

Sometimes a prince or an association, or maybe a religious order or confraternity, would want to mark the spot where something significant took place (a martyrdom, perhaps, or the burial of a beloved saint) and they'd found an oratory, too, putting the building over the holy site. Maybe a confraternity included people from many parishes, and they wanted a special place dedicated to the celebration of Masses for the intentions of the group, in addition to Sunday Mass at their individual parishes.

But the problem was that this kind of foundation hadn't been customary in Europe for about six hundred years. Experienced architects were consequently scarce. Besides, architecture had undergone a neo-Roman Renaissance. So, if you had the money and the ambition to build an oratory, you'd have to turn to one of the new best-sellers: theoretical books on architecture that told you precisely how to structure a building according to the latest fashion.

One of the first of these books, entitled *On Building (De re ædificatoria)*, was written in 1452 by a Florentine canon lawyer by the name of Leon Battista Alberti. It's still worth reading, but you have to keep an eye on Alberti. He was kind of a snot, to be perfectly frank, and he mixes old pagan and Christian beliefs freely, just so you'll see how well educated he is in the classics. Unless you know the *Corpus Juris Canonici* and the *Missale Romanum* backward and forward—as he assumed you would, if you were involved in building churches—you can hardly sort out the really useful information from the parts where he's just showing off. In fact, he went out of his way to include bizarre new instructions on how the Mass should be run and lots of other editorial asides that fall far beyond the scope of his expertise. These parts of his book were put on the *Index of Prohibited Books*, and they never had any effect whatever on the way the Church builds.*

---

*Still, for the past hundred years, Alberti has led astray countless architectural historians who take the *De re ædificatoria* as Gospel. The confusion is compounded because *votive*, like its Latin root, *voveo*, means two entirely different things. Votive masses, like votive candles, are *applied to a purpose*. But votive also means "resulting from a vow", and a number of oratories for votive Masses were built in fulfillment of vows. Of course, you can build any kind of church (or offer a candle or anything else) in fulfillment of a vow, but Masses of this particular kind, and the oratories built to house them, are always "votive" in the sense of application, whether there's a vow involved or not.

Alberti was the first to get the new fashion in church buildings down in black and white. Some churches, he writes, "are *principal*, as is that wherein the chief Priest upon stated Seasons celebrates some solemn Rites and Sacrifices". If you cut through his Neo-Platonic verbiage, he's talking about the parochial churches and the Masses of the regular calendar. These buildings, he says, should be handled in the traditional way: he reminds us that the priest "might be more distinctly heard in a Basilique ceiled with a Timber Roof". That's about all that he needed to say. After all, they'd been building them that way in Italy for more than a thousand years.

But he really gets busy with plans for the other church buildings, those "under the Guardianship of inferior Priests, as all Chapels in Town, and Oratories in the Country." He had a great deal of freedom in confecting plans for these designs, because votive Masses are "extra" Masses—an oratory doesn't have to accommodate much of a congregation. It just has to hold an altar (or any number of endowed altars), a priest for each, one or maybe two ministers to make the responses, and perhaps the odd patron now and again. And it's this fact that determines a great deal about the plans of oratories.

For one thing, size just doesn't matter with an oratory. Some oratories are immense. St. Peter's at the Vatican, redesigned in about 1500, is one of the biggest churches in the world, but it was never a parochial church or cathedral; it's an oratory built to mark the grave of St. Peter. The domed oratory of the Invalides in Paris towers over the cathedral of Notre Dame, and the Shrine of the Immaculate Conception in Washington, D.C., holds its own against any other gigantic church on Earth. Other oratories are tiny. S. Pietro in Montorio, on the spot where St. Peter was martyred, is only about fourteen feet in diameter. Some aren't much bigger than a phone booth.

But what's more important than size is the arrangement of an oratory's plan. Since the architect didn't have to worry about where everybody would sit, symbolic considerations could override everything else. And the fashionable philosophy of the Renaissance mandated the symbolism of a plan based on the geometric symmetry of the circle.

"It is manifest," Alberti wrote, "that Nature delights principally in round Figures . . . why need I instance the Stars, Trees, Animals, Nests of Birds, or the like Parts of Creation, which she has chosen to make generally round?" Why, indeed. Every architect knew about the perfection of the circle—"having its parts similar to one another . . . the extreme being found in all its parts equally distant from the middle," wrote Andrea Palladio in his *Four Books of Architecture* in 1570; "it is exceeding proper to demonstrate the infinite essence, the uniformity, and the justice of God." Other theorists wrote about how "the round form is the perfectest of all others", meaning the circle and other centralized forms derived from it, like the square and the octagon. Philosophers at the time figured that these shapes reflected the "unique and absolute" nature of the unchanging God, the self-enclosed perfection of the foursquare Gospels, and so forth.

Excited by the chance for pure symbolism, and well funded for once, Alberti and his colleagues went to work, turning out a kaleidoscope of geometries as elegant as snowflakes and about as practical. To crown their oratories, they favored the dome. This is the logical consequence of a centralized plan—an arch rotated on its axis to take on a third dimension—and it carries the symbolism of the circle to new heights. A dome, they pointed out, is a model of the heavens, a representation of the firmament, a vision of the Throne of God.

And because these oratories were privately endowed, they usually have greater artistic quality than the average parish church. The ones that got finished do, anyway. Princely families (or just pretentious rich people) spared no expense in the competition to out-Roman the ancient Romans, bidding for the most famous artists the way football teams and movie studios bid for stars nowadays. Plenty of them bankrupted themselves in the process, and Europe was littered with the broken hulks of unfinished domes, standing like the shattered shells of some fantastic race of snails. (Another theorist, Sebastiano Serlio, noting that "there are no more great Churches begun to be made, and that men finish not them which in former times have been begun," filled his own book with projects "so small, as they may pass in reasonable manner, for that with small cost, they might in short time be made," which helped make his book the most popular of all.)

The more reasonable oratories, though, were usually built quickly and controlled by a single patron, or by a small, knowledgeable committee of well-heeled *dilettanti*—which made it easier to keep the project on track, without the squabbles and compromises that can happen so easily with a public building of any kind. As a result, the old votive oratories are often marvels of decoration, from the floor right up to the dome, covered with the finest work of our best artists, done consistently in a way that makes clear sense.

And this, too, is in line with the theory. "To conclude," said Alberti, "a Structure of this Kind ought to be so built as to entice those who are absent to come and see it, and to charm and detain those who are present by the Beauty and Curiosity of its Workmanship."

The steady stream of theoretical and practical books on how to plan your princely oratory swept the fashion all over Europe and, eventually, to the Americas, where countless examples sprouted. After about 1870, though—the time of the First Vatican Council—people started to think twice about these little blossom-churches. By then, spare money or credit from one locality could be applied to a pressing need in another country or even on another continent; it no longer seemed entirely responsible to channel resources into largely ornamental buildings when you could set up a foundation for votive Masses to be celebrated at an existing altar in your parish church.*

So, if you're involved in planning a new parish church, check out the regulations, and don't overlook the ancient efficiency of the basilican plan; nobody's likely to invent a better layout, not

---

*Even so, instituting a votive oratory is still one way to raise money when plans for a new parish church exceed the parish's resources, because you can cast your nets wider. You just emphasize the devotions centered on the oratory, which cut across parish lines, and build a composite building that houses the oratory's devotions and the parish's Masses. That's how the people of Florence raised the huge sums needed for their new cathedral in the thirteenth century. The faithful of Monterrey, Mexico, used the same strategy only a few years ago to build a striking modern church dedicated to Our Lady of Guadalupe in the city's booming suburbs. You can usually identify the older examples of these composite churches because they have a dome atop a basilican plan.

without two thousand years of experience. And, if you're interested in the more exuberant side of the Church's art, seek out the domes and take a look inside.

CHAPTER 22

PRIESTLY
VESTMENTS
Their Origins and Meanings

"**D**O NOT BE ANXIOUS, saying, . . . 'What are we to put on?' "

Christ's instruction (Mt 6:31) means basically that we shouldn't concentrate on our clothes, getting all wrapped up in the newest fashions. Of course, the clergy has taken this to heart, wearing plain, simple clothes of black, brown, or gray, and often sticking to the same cut and pattern for centuries. This leaves them free to devote fuller attention to their ministry—they never have to coordinate their outfits.

Some clerics, like the Franciscans, achieved this austere convenience by reverting to an extremely simple robe that was never in fashion, but others adopted the ordinary dress of their day and retained it no matter how fashions changed. The old-fashioned habits of many orders of nuns and religious sisters, even those with the extraordinary headdresses, started out as the basic clothing of women at the time and place the order was founded. Now, even with easy-care fabrics, the elaborate folds and flounces of some habits take hours of ironing and fussing, hours that could be spent working. True to the spirit of their founders, some orders have retired these old-fashioned garments and adopted a simple, more modern form of everyday female dress.

But in one activity, a change of habit is highly unlikely. The vestments that priests and deacons wear to the altar are, basically, the ordinary clothes of Our Lord's time and more than a thousand years thereafter (fashions changed very slowly in those days). If they were worn on the street today, priestly garments would certainly stand out in a crowd, but people really used to dress like that. As late as 255 Pope Stephen I had to issue an order that "priests should not use their consecrated garments for daily wear, except in the church." Apparently nobody would have noticed if they did.

Once these vestments were set apart for sacred use, though, they were retained as a venerable tradition and updated at a glacial pace. The Second Vatican Council allowed the territorial bodies of bishops to make adaptations in vestments and propose them to the Holy See, but the Council also condemned "novel and improvised" vestments as "foreign to catholic worship". So any radical change is unlikely, although the past twenty years have seen a trend toward lighter, more elegant, more sophisticated design in vestments that everyone, whether right or left of center, can welcome.

Naturally, some of the same vestments are worn while hearing confessions or administering other sacraments, but we most often see the full panoply at Mass. The first vestment that the priest puts on is the alb, the "vestment common to ministers of every rank", as Vatican II put it. This is a long, simple robe of linenlike cloth, with long sleeves. It's always white. In fact, its name is from the Latin *albus*, which means "white". It's the descendant of the inner tunic that the Romans wore.

(The alb is sometimes worn by altar boys or other nonclerical ministers, but you may also see them in a garment called a *surplice*, which has wide sleeves and reaches to just below the hips. It's sometimes ornamented with lace. Sometimes priests wear a surplice over their cassock—the long black garment—in processions, at blessings, or administering any sacrament when the alb isn't prescribed.)

Then there's the amice, also of white linen. It's shaped like an apron but worn across the back and tied around the neck. It began as a sort of muffler, or a headcover, or as a garment that could be used as either—its Latin name, *amictus*, simply means "garment".

In most Rites, it's worn under the alb, but over it in the Ambrosian Rite. Nowadays, it's optional because some albs have collars, and that makes the amice unnecessary.

The stole is a long, narrow band a few inches wide and about eighty inches long; the stole that a priest wears will be the same color as his other colored garments, red, green, violet, black, or white, as prescribed by the service books. It goes over the priest's neck, like a necktie that hasn't been tied. Deacons, too, wear a stole, but over the shoulder like a sash. Smaller stoles are kept in sick-call cases, to be ready when the priest is called to anoint the sick.

The stole also takes its name from a Latin word, *stola*. But it doesn't seem to be an ancient Roman garment like so many of the others. The earliest recorded stoles, as liturgical vestments, showed up in the sixth century, looking exactly the same as they do today. But they didn't come into general use, apparently, until around the time of the great emperor Charlemagne, who was crowned in the ninth century—which gives you some idea of how long it takes for innovations in vestments. Over the centuries, though, the stole became such an indispensable mark of the higher orders of the clergy that almost all Protestant sects rejected it, even when they retained other clerical garments for liturgical use.

The cincture is simply a sort of cord or belt that goes around the alb and stole to keep them in place. The maniple was a sort of napkin for the altar service. It started out as the handkerchief carried by Roman dignitaries, and it was worn across the left forearm. It was first ordered for deacons by Pope Sylvester I some time between 314 and 335, but it isn't much used since Vatican II.

Over all of these garments the priest puts a chasuble, an ample robe of a color suitable to the liturgy of the day. Ample, indeed— the name comes from the Latin *casula*, "a little house". Normally, it's used only at Mass; it's very rarely used otherwise, and then only at some other ceremony closely associated with the altar. It's derived from the common Roman cloak everybody wore in antiquity. Priests who swelter under the chasuble today might reflect that, with the alb, it was the everyday dress of clerics for the first eleven centuries of the Church's life, and be thankful, perhaps, for small favors.

Over the years, the chasuble has changed a little, too. To make it easier to perform the manual tasks of the Eucharist like handling the chalice and paten, the parts of the cloak covering the arms were gradually cut away. The fabric became richer, stiff with embroidery sometimes, which also made it easier to handle, if less ample in its folds. Now, with a return to more traditional forms, the chasuble is again somewhat wider, somewhat plainer, and made of lighter cloth, but it's still the characteristic garment of a priest at Mass.

Deacons at Mass wear a dalmatic, which follows the chasuble in fabric, color, and ornament, but differs in cut; it's a long, sleeved robe. It's a relative novelty among vestments. It came into fashion in the second century, and only two hundred years later Pope Sylvester I ordered it adopted as the typical liturgical garment of deacons (this must count as the quickest the Church has ever taken up a new fashion). As its name implies, it came originally from Dalmatia. In the Middle Ages—in fact, right up to the nineteenth century—the dalmatic was sometimes covered with decorative embroidery. Now, of course, it usually shows up in its original simplicity.

These are the garments you are likely to encounter at Mass. There are other liturgical garments, too, like the bishop's miter, sandals, and buskins, and the *pallium*, a little white stole, something like a loosely knotted necktie, worn by the Pope, by archbishops, and by some privileged bishops. And sometimes you might see a different kind of chasuble, one that's open down the front and held at the chest with a big decorative button. That kind of chasuble is called a cope, and it's worn by the celebrant at nearly all solemn functions except the Mass.

The color of the chasuble (and of the burse—the square case sometimes used to hold the corporal, a white napkin spread under the chalice and paten—and of the veil that covers the chalice) tells you a lot about the particular Mass that's being celebrated. The colors of clerical vestments bear a rich and venerable symbolism, and they're governed by canon law, so it isn't just a matter of taste. You have to use specific colors on specific days and for specific purposes.

The vestments used for the liturgies of Ordinary Time, for instance, are green. "Ordinary" here means those days that aren't special feasts, so green is the color you'll see most frequently at church. Green, in the traditional imagery of the western world, is a color of vitality, the color of fresh leaves and grass, the color of life. This meaning of the color green was already an old idea when Christ used it to make a point (Lk 23:31), and it's a symbolism that would be understood always and everywhere. And green is the color of hope. In fact, in European religious paintings from the Middle Ages until the First World War, you can identify Hope just because she's the lady in the green garments.

White is used for the liturgies of the seasons of Easter and Christmas and on other feasts and memorials of Our Lord, such as Ascension Day, that don't commemorate the Passion. White is also used on feasts of Our Lady, the angels, or saints who weren't martyrs, and on certain specified holy days. Why? Well, white is obviously the color of purity, which explains why it's appropriate for Mary's feasts and those of angels (have a look at Mt 28:3), and certain saints.

But white is also the color of joy, of triumph. Check the account of the Transfiguration (Mt 17:2, Lk 9:29). In Revelation, the elders who sit in perpetual adoration around the throne of God are dressed in white (4:4), and so is the returning Christ at the head of his white-robed armies (19:11–14). These passages suggest the appropriateness of white for the vestments of Easter and the other triumphs of Jesus, and for those of saints' commemorations. It also explains why, in the United States, white vestments may be substituted for the traditional black for funeral Masses—they emphasize the Christian's triumph over death rather than focusing on the death itself.

Black also used to be preferred for Good Friday, just as it was for private funerals, but it's not the only traditional color for Masses for the dead. Sometimes, you'll see deep violet vestments on such occasions, because violet is the Church's color of mourning, the color of penance. That's why it's used during seasons of preparation like Advent, even extending, during Lent, to the veils that covered the statues and pictures in churches in the old days. And, speaking of violet, a word of definition is in order.

In the everyday language of United States, we tend to refer to the color violet as "purple", but in speaking liturgically we have to be more precise. Violet is the deep, rich blackish-blue you get when you mix equal amounts of red and blue; in Latin, it's called *violaceus*. But liturgical purple—in Latin, *purpureus*—is a deep, rich red, sort of what we might call a clear maroon. This purple is the color of the old imperial robes of Rome, the official color of the Byzantine emperors, and, today, the color of the princes of the Church, the cardinals.

That's why you'll still hear, occasionally, the phrase "raised to the purple" when a man becomes a cardinal. And when a priest receives the honorary title of Monsignor, he's allowed to wear a purple sash and purple piping (which can be any of several shades of rich red) on his cassock, a sign of his distinctive proximity to the princely rank.

So purple, strictly defined, isn't used in priestly vestments at Mass, although you may see a deacon's stole in the dark imperial red. You do see a bright, clear red during the feasts of the Passion, including Good Friday, and on the feasts of martyrs, the Apostles, and the Evangelists. As the color of blood, red is the obvious choice for these uses; but it's also the color of fire, so it's used on Pentecost, when the fire of the Holy Spirit descended at the birthday of the Church.

Green, white, violet, and red are the basic colors of the liturgy, with black optional for some uses. Violet or white, as we've seen, can be used in place of black, and in fact white can generally be used as a substitute for these other colors. Some other substitutions are possible, though, adding still more color to many liturgical functions.

The third Sunday of Advent, for example, is called *Gaudete* Sunday, because that Sunday we hear the Epistle to the Philippians, beginning with the fourth verse of chapter four: *Gaudete in Domino semper*—Rejoice in the Lord always. Because the message of the Mass that day has to do with rejoicing, the violet vestments of Advent seem inappropriate, so rose-colored garments may be substituted. They're a related color, since violet is a combination of rosy red and blue, but they're certainly more cheerful than the traditional color of penance. And, again, just as with cardinals' robes, the rose of Gaudete Sunday recalls, in a diluted sort of way, the dark red of imperial purple.

The message of this Mass, by the way, is the reason for the single rose-pink candle among the violet tapers on Advent wreaths. Similarly, because the Introit of the fourth Sunday in Lent, in the old Roman Missal, quoted Isaiah 66:10—Rejoice, O Jerusalem!—you'll sometimes see rose vestments on that day.

Most spectacular of all are the vestments made of precious metal. Gold and silver can be drawn out into very, very thin wires, thinner than a thread, and still be strong enough to work with. And because these metals are so soft, these precious threads have the consistency of heavy silk. You can embroider with them just as you would with silk floss, which you see today on the uniforms of admirals and other military grandees.

In fact, you can make truly spectacular lace, or you can set up a loom and weave cloth that can be tailored into vestments. It's called "cloth-of-gold" or "cloth-of-silver". Like white, gold and silver vestments may be substituted for just about any other color, if the ceremony is particularly solemn. Nowadays, you might see a cloth-of-gold miter at some pontifical functions, or a chasuble enriched with gold crosses or embroidery. But imagine the great royal functions of the Middle Ages, when whole sets of vestments were woven of bright gold, prelates walked on gold carpets, and, believe it or not, entire churches were covered inside with draperies entirely made of gold. It must have been beyond description.

There's not much left of these rich fabrics from past ages. Usually, despite the unimaginable amount of work involved in drawing out all those threadlike wires, weaving them into ponderously heavy cloth, and even embroidering them over with more gold thread, the vestments were melted down after a while so that the metal could be reused. Heavy taffetas and velvets were often embroidered with precious thread, but these were usually burned after one use so that the metals would melt and could be washed out of the ashes.

Well, that kind of extravagance, like that kind of craftsmanship, is out of the question these days. Yet the simpler colors remain.

They're the clear, definite colors we learn as children, always the same yet always new, reappearing like the colors of nature in a reassuring cycle through the liturgical year.

CHAPTER 23

LIKE UNTO
PURE GOLD

*The Meaning of the Precious Metal
in the Service of the Church*

T HE GOLD ARTIFACTS FROM ANCIENT tombs like King Tut's
tend to dazzle us nowadays, when everything seems so
utilitarian. But it's easy to be blinded by the glare of these
treasures, and it may be hard to notice that the gold of the pharaoh
was not used extravagantly, but very precisely—to convey a specific meaning.

The things that Tut used in his daily life were not made of gold.
Those things were all made of wood, stone, clay, or basketwork,
like everybody else's. Apart from some jewelry, you wouldn't see
much gold around a pharaoh's court. The stupendous gold items
in King Tut's tomb were royal ceremonial items like the scepter
and throne, used when Tut showed himself as an incarnate god, or
figures of the other gods of Egypt, or things needed for religious
rituals, such as sacred vessels and priestly ornaments. Not one of
the golden things was for a mortal man to use; all had to do with
the gods, and specifically with making invisible, immortal beings
visible to mortal men.

Gold is the perfect way to show that a god—any god—an angel,
or any other immortal being is showing himself forth to us on
Earth. Because of its molecular structure, gold never tarnishes,
never corrodes. It stays clean, bright, and shining forever, or at

least until the end of Time. So gold is ideal for making things that have to do with everlasting life. Halos on the heads of immortal angels and souls have been made of gold always and everywhere. So are crowns and coins, the halos of kingly offices that outlast the death of the mortal men who hold them. So too are idols, figures that give immortal "bodies" to pagan gods. The Children of Israel, backsliding in the desert, made a golden calf that probably looked a lot like the gilded figures of the cow-goddess Hathor found in King Tut's tomb, which were evidently made shortly before the Exodus.

Even when the Israelites turned away from their golden idol, they didn't forget the symbolism of the metal. Look through the Old Testament. Wherever the visible majesty of God was to reside, the Israelites arranged that the background should be gold—a proper setting for the glimpse out of Time into Eternity that these divine epiphanies allowed. For instance, the inside and the outside of the Ark of the Covenant, which held the tablets that embodied the Law of God, was "plated with gold, and a molding of gold was put around it" (Ex 37:2). Solomon's Temple, where the "majesty of the Lord settled in", was bright with gold—the Holy of Holies was entirely plated with gold (3 Kgs 6:20–22). And you don't find much else made of gold in the Old Testament; like the Egyptians, the Israelites reserved their gold for the divine, the immortal.

Of course, the Church follows this pattern, too. Christians have always known that the chalice of benediction, as St. Paul put it, is the Blood of Christ, and that the bread that we break is the partaking of the Body of the Lord (1 Cor 10:16). That's why the Church has generally reserved gold for those things most closely associated with the epiphany of Christ in the Eucharist. But it hasn't always been easy.

When the Church was just starting out, the chalice for the wine and the paten (the dish for the bread) were of any durable material, the finest that the congregation could afford, and they seem to have been shaped like the ordinary utensils of the day.

They were often much more ornamental, though, in keeping with their exalted function, and glass seems to have been favored—it let the congregation see the Blood during the liturgies. In fact, Pope Zephyrinus, in about the year 200, "made a regulation for the Church, that there should be vessels of glass before the priests in the church, and servitors to hold them while the bishop was celebrating Mass", according to the *Liber Pontificalis*.

But, whatever its liturgical advantages, glass didn't make the grade on practical grounds. For one thing, it was horribly expensive in those days, and it's just too fragile, too easily chipped and broken. Only about twenty years after Zephyrinus came down in favor of glass, Urban I ordered that all of the vessels of communion—the chalice, the paten, and all—should be of silver, a noble metal more durable than glass, yet within the economic reach of any congregation, even in those unsettled times.

Even then, gold was still reserved to the service of the undying divinity, as it had always been, and apparently some congregations stretched themselves to provide it. Official records of the persecutions under Diocletian show that on the nineteenth of May, 292, one Munatius Felix, high priest (pagan, of course) and mayor of Cirta in Armenia, ordered the local bishop to hand over his Christian scriptures to be burned. The bishop refused, and the subsequent police search of the premises turned up nothing of value—just a lot of clothes and shoes for the poor—except the few gold vessels used for the Eucharist.

But by the ninth century, the Church had stabilized as an international institution, and the liturgical vessels had definitely begun their slow evolution to the forms we know today. By then gold was the general rule; for at least three hundred years the Church had been embraced by the emperors east and west, and she had been receiving immense donations of gold and silver vessels from whatever government was in power. That imperial tradition made it fashionable for the rich and powerful to supply suitable furnishings to their local churches around the Mediterranean basin and northward through France and Germany.

So the Church, now benefiting from the generosity of wealthy patrons, was free to incorporate the ancient symbolism of gold into the normal celebration of the Mass. Silver, tin, or pewter were still allowed, for good economic or pastoral reasons, but even then the inside of the cup and the face of the paten, the parts that touch Christ's Body and Blood, were supposed to be of gold.

But it took a surprisingly long time to work out exactly what utensils you needed and exactly what design they had to have. By the ninth century, the bowl of the chalice had become hemispherical, and a base had been added, broad enough to keep the chalice from tipping over accidentally. Chalices about this time also tended to have two handles, relating them to the ancient tradition of the loving cup—appropriately enough—that would be passed from hand to hand at victory celebrations.

This passing the chalice had always caused problems, from a pastoral point of view. There were big fights about it. Some theologians held that everybody had to communicate under both species (that is, you had to receive both the Body and the Blood of Christ at communion). Therefore, they said, you have to distribute the bread from the altar and pass around the chalice. They saw this "unity of chalice" as an important sign of the unity of the faithful. St. John Chrysostom was of this opinion; "not only do we drink the same drink," he pointed out, "but we drink it from the same chalice."

Other theologians agreed about both species, but they said that it was all right to distribute from more than one chalice. After all, with large congregations, a single chalice took a very long time to circulate, and it had to be so huge that it was not easily handled. Some early chalices hold nearly half a gallon. Handles or no, spills were frequent, and to many churchmen the impracticality outweighed any possible symbolism.

As a result, there were all kinds of strategies developed to manage the distribution of the Blood. The most usual was to have ministers distribute from more than one chalice, sometimes with a golden straw (which you still see at some papal masses), as a way of avoiding spills. *Intinction*, where you dip the host into the chalice, was another way of working it out, and by the ninth century it had become standard practice in the eastern Rites. Sometimes this is done by hand, with the priest or the communicant dipping the host, but the East also has a long tradition of golden Eucharistic spoons to manage this. The hosts are simply put into the chalice and spooned out by the priest one by one. The Russian and Ruthenian Rites still use spoons this way, but generally, as with the Melkite Rite, the tendency is to do away with the liturgical spoon altogether, for considerations of health.

Immersion is another way to do it, putting a piece of the host into the chalice, as happens at the breaking of the bread *(fractio panis)* in the Mass of the Latin Rite. Some Rites anoint the host with a few drops from the chalice before distribution; this is called *consignation.*

None of these strategies really worked out too well, for symbolic or liturgical reasons (they could take forever, too, and working with liquids and spoons was generally impractical). Intinction, for example, was already prohibited by Spanish churches two hundred years before it became standard practice in the East—apparently, the Spanish bishops had some problem with it.

But everyone understood that it wasn't really necessary to distribute the chalice at every Mass. It's preferred, of course, because Christ spoke of the two together; unless you eat the flesh of the Son of Man, *and drink his blood*, you shall not have life in you, he said (Jn 6:54). But he also called himself, repeatedly, the bread of Heaven, with no mention of the wine; he who eats this bread shall live forever. And the Church has always understood that Christ is fully and truly present in either the host or the chalice.

So, by about the twelfth century, distribution of the chalice was normally omitted in the West. This led to some misunderstanding; people started to think that the chalice *must not* be distributed. Well, the Council of Trent clarified that in the sixteenth century, and the Second Vatican Council upheld those regulations, although now the ancient practice is generally reserved to certain particularly solemn occasions. But, if the congregation is small enough and there are enough Eucharistic ministers to distribute chalices, you may see it happen at ordinary Sunday Mass.

All of this had a profound effect on the design of chalices. When the symbolism of a single cup began to fade, chalices got smaller very quickly. The bowl got egg-shaped or conical, because it needed to hold less. A stem was put between the base and the bowl, to help the priest elevate the chalice at the consecration, and then a knob was added in the middle of the stem to make it easier to hold securely. A few more centuries passed, and the bowl of the usual chalice became lily shaped, with a rounded bottom and a flaring upper section; you still see this Baroque form today—it's the very symbol of religion, in western art.

The paten had a similar evolution. Patens used to be huge trays that could carry a lot of bread. The *Liber Pontificalis* lists, among the immense donations of the emperor Constantine to Pope Sylvester I, several patens of gold weighing ten pounds and one of silver, "overlaid with gold and set with jewels", weighing fifty. Even though the Roman pound was only twelve ounces, those are some very hefty patens. (All of Constantine's church furnishings were massive. Life must have been hard for fourth-century altar boys.)

In any case, as liturgy evolved in the West, the custom arose of reserving the paten for a single, larger host that's elevated at the consecration, with the smaller hosts for distribution kept in a *ciborium*—a sort of chalice with a larger bowl and a lid. This, too, helps simplify the liturgy and make things go more smoothly.

Every church also has a *monstrance*, a tall vessel that holds a single consecrated host so that it can be seen by the congregation for ceremonies like Benediction and at the Exposition of the Blessed Sacrament. It has a base and stem like those of a chalice, but at the top it has a circular glass case for the host, usually surrounded by rays of glory.

But no matter what shape these liturgical vessels take, they're generally made of gold or at least plated with gold, because of the metal's same ancient symbolism of immortality. And because gold is, for all practical purposes, immortal, it's also appropriate for reliquaries, which the devout princely families of Europe began giving to churches in the Middle Ages. By the eighteenth century, some churches were criticized for storing up massive amounts of gold in altar furnishings and reliquaries and in vestments made of cloth-of-gold.

But you have to remember that before the French Revolution this gold had been treasured for its symbolic meaning, not its economic significance, and that it had a limited economic significance anyway. When famine hit before the dawn of capitalism—before the First Vatican Council, really—all the gold in the world was useless without the communication networks that we use to publicize need, and without the transportation networks that we use to alleviate those needs. Horses and wagons from, say, France or America could hardly help the hungry in Poland or China, no matter how much gold was lying around. In fairness, too, we should remember that those same churches and abbeys, not the secular governments, maintained full granaries that were opened in time of public need.

In most cases, the reliquaries didn't belong to the churches, anyway. Nobles and merchant princes would have elaborate gold reliquaries made up from coin metal; they'd deposit these in the churches—not donate them, just deposit them—so that the public could view the relics, but also so that their gold would be safe during wartime and recoverable in time of need. After all, a reliquary isn't necessary for any liturgy, and it doesn't even need to be blessed. You could melt one down any time, as long as you safeguarded the relics. Well, by the time of the French Revolution, people started concentrating on the metal's purchasing power, and we lost a lot of reliquaries.

But this destruction, perhaps, helped focus things a little better for us. Today, it still seems entirely natural that incorruptible gold should be used for the chalice that holds the Blood of the everliving Christ, and for the patens and monstrances that hold his Body. But, even in a rich parish, you won't see much gold apart from the altar and its furnishings—unless you look at the pictures.

Most of the pictures that you see in churches have to do with things that happen in Heaven. People have always associated Heaven with the sky, but a blue background won't do if you want to show, say, Christ in majesty. Christ is always in majesty—"of his kingdom there will be no end"—but our natural blue sky won't last forever. It will be "rolled up" at the end of the world. It says so in the Apocalypse (6:14). This presents a problem to artists: how can you represent the everlasting heavens, the heavens of Endless Time?

Gold, of course. A gold "sky" in a picture tells you that the scene takes place outside of Time. Illuminated manuscripts frequently use gold-leaf backgrounds, as do mosaics, which are the most glorious way to use gold in sacred art. When St. John saw the heavenly Jerusalem, he described it as being "pure gold, like fine glass" (Rv 21:18). This combination of features may seem physically impossible on this Earth, but gold mosaic comes close. A gold mosaic is made of small squares of thick, rough glass, usually no bigger than about an inch on a side, that are backed with gold leaf as an ordinary mirror is backed with silver. These tiny squares are set into mortar, one by one in the best mosaics, on a wall or ceiling. Each is set at a slightly different angle, scattering the light and turning the wall into a flat, glowing cloud of shimmering gold that, it seems, you could put your hand through.

You can imagine that gold mosaic is even more impressive on a wall than solid plates of gold like those the Israelites used in the Temple, and there are places where you can still see what it looks like. The new cathedral in St. Louis, Missouri, is covered inside with one of the largest collections of mosaics in the world. The National Shrine of the Immaculate Conception in Washington, D.C., is one of the largest churches in the world, and the extent and glory of its mosaics beggar description.

Still, there are words to describe the overall effect. In the sixth century, when the Emperor Justinian built the Church of the Holy Wisdom in Constantinople—another of the largest churches on Earth—he covered the whole inside with plain gold mosaic. On his first inspection tour, Justinian strode into the immense church; he looked up into the radiant dome, a vast artificial sky scintillating with a billion crystal stars. Raising his hands to Heaven, he spoke. "O Solomon!" he cried, "I have outdone thee!"

CHAPTER 24

THE VATICAN
A Holy City

WHEN ROME WAS just a little country town, people used to cross the Tiber River to the west to dig for clay at the base of the Vatican Hill, one of the seven hills on which Rome was built. The river cut across the bottom of the hill and exposed the clay, so they could get at it easily and ship it to the potters who used it for wine jugs, bricks, and roof tiles. But the bottom of the Vatican was swampy, and the ancient Romans considered it too unhealthy for habitation. So it was given over to the clay quarries and, like many a "potter's field" in other cities, to burial.

The Roman matron Agrippina cleaned up the area, draining the swamps and building terraces up the hill for public gardens. After she died—in the same year as the Crucifixion, 33—her son, the mad emperor Caligula, built a stadium (in Latin, a *circus*) on the Vatican Hill for public chariot races. About twenty-five years later, another mad emperor, Nero, expanded the stadium for even bigger chariot races, but he also held more imaginative spectacles there, like impaling Christians on stakes and smearing them with tar so that they could be set ablaze. Nero found the Christians a convenient scapegoat for the great fire that destroyed Rome in 64, so, in his mind anyway, this was poetic justice.

What was left of these martyrs was buried in the cemetery that stretched alongside the stadium. Because it was so close to the city, it became Rome's major cemetery, and the tombs of some of Nero's favorite slaves, famous charioteers, and even famous chariot horses were built there.

Then something happened to change the history of the Vatican forever. Among the Christians that Nero had executed after the fire was one Simon bar-Jonah, called Peter. He wasn't burned but crucified, although he had requested some other form of execution because he didn't consider himself worthy to be killed as Christ was killed. His executioners therefore crucified him upside down—if anything, a more excruciating death. Peter's followers took his body out to the burial ground at the Vatican and began holding memorial services out there.

Soon, more and more Christians were buried around St. Peter's tomb, in group mausolea, in individual graves, or stacked one atop the other in sequential graves. From this time forward, it was the Christians, not the pagans, who dominated the Vatican Hill. The bishops of Rome after St. Peter were customarily buried there as St. Peter had been—although they lived in the city, because nobody lives in a cemetery. By the time Christianity became tolerated by the Roman emperor Constantine, there had already been four centuries' worth of Christian tombs and memorials crowding the top of the hill.

When Constantine and his mother, Helena, started building Christian churches all over the empire, the emperor ordered a princely new church built over the tomb of St. Peter on the Vatican Hill, which was begun in about the year 330. Of course, everybody had always known where the tomb was, but, for some unaccountable reason, the twentieth-century excavations that opened St. Peter's grave and revealed his bones surprised a lot of people, as if they had figured that the unbroken two-thousand-year history of the site were some kind of legend.*

---

*Apart from the Church's unbroken occupancy of the site, everything about the building itself points to the existence of the tomb at that exact spot. Constantine's engineers, who liked to do things just as cheaply as they possibly could, had to shore up the slope of the hill with about a million cubic feet of fill to build St. Peter's, but they left the site of the circus right next to it vacant—a

Constantine built the first basilica of St. Peter's right over the saint's grave, and he built a new cathedral, St. John Lateran, in the city itself. The Lateran is still the official seat of the Bishop of Rome. (St. Peter's skull is buried there, although the rest of his remains are still at the Vatican. The skull is considered the principal part of human remains, and its location determines the place of burial, usually; so while the original grave deserves commemoration, the skull was transferred to the cathedral of Peter's successors.)

But while these new churches were rising, Constantine moved the civil government of the empire from Rome to a new capital at Constantinople. Little by little, people turned to the only organized administration left in the city—the administration headed by the Bishop of Rome. By the beginning of the Middle Ages, the Pope was temporal lord of a broad band of territory stretching from the sea west of Rome all the way to the Adriatic coast south of Venice.

These territories, the "Papal States" or the "Patrimony of Peter", were ruled by the popes from their residences within the city of Rome—the official seat at St. John Lateran and the palace on the Quirinal, another of the seven hills. Rome became once more a major political center as the capital of the Papal States and, what is more, it became an international city as the focus of worldwide Christianity. Its bishop was, after all, the successor of Peter, the Vicar of Christ and head of his Church.

As the capital of Christianity, Rome became the seat of the apostolic patriarchs, those prelates whose episcopal sees were founded by Apostles. Each of these patriarchs has a major basilica in or near Rome assigned to him. The Pope is of course assigned St. John Lateran, while the other major basilicas, St. Mary Major and St. Paul's Outside the Walls, have the Patriarchs of Antioch and Alexandria as their titular pastors. The basilica of St. Peter on the Vatican Hill was assigned to the Patriarch of Constantinople as his official church and residence when he came to Rome.

---

good, flat, clear space at the top of the hill, with plenty of massive foundations already in it. Obviously, that precise location in the cemetery was of paramount importance from the beginning.

This arrangement continued until about 1438, when an ecumenical council met at Ferrara in Italy to try to reunite the western Church with the eastern Church governed by the Patriarch of Constantinople. The attempt failed, and the Greeks went home, to remain separated from the Latin Church to this day, despite continuing efforts on both sides.

But a little while after this attempt at union failed, Pope Nicholas V Parentucelli moved his residence from St. John Lateran, the cathedral of Rome, to St. Peter's on the Vatican Hill, as if to demonstrate that, as sovereign Pontiff and head of the universal Church, he was assuming the duties of the separated Patriarch of Constantinople.

By the time Nicholas moved to the Vatican in about 1450, Constantine's basilica was over a thousand years old. Its walls, standing on the patchwork foundations of old tombs and rubble, were nearly six feet out of plumb—leaning so far out that the mosaics on the walls had been lost under a blanket of dust. Nicholas V propped them up as well as possible, and, because no prelate had resided on the Vatican Hill for decades, he added a little to the palace there. ("Palace" sounds rather posh, but it was just a few big rooms strung along behind a colonnade. It had been built two hundred years before by Nicholas III Orsini, as part of a stronghold against marauders in Rome. You wouldn't have wanted to live there. You wouldn't have wanted anyone you knew to live there.)

Not much later, the Constantinian basilica started slipping again, and it couldn't be repaired any more. In 1506, Julius II della Rovere took the drastic steps of pulling it down completely and beginning the new St. Peter's that we see today. This new church was planned around a dome like a Greek church, appropriately enough, given its Constantinian history, although the Renaissance fashion of funeral oratories in this form was also a major influence on the design.

Donato Bramante laid the first plan, for a church that would have easily held the one you see today. But he didn't get very far; he only finished the four great piers that he'd designed to hold up the biggest dome in the world. It was slow going because they'd decided not to build it the way churches were built in the early sixteenth century but as the everlasting ancient Roman monuments were built. That meant concrete, not stone or brick, and nobody knew much about concrete any more. They hadn't really used it in more than a thousand years.

After Bramante figured it all out again, of course, concrete was used for everything down to overpasses and parking garages, but that's getting ahead of St. Peter's. Bramante's plan was just too big, a complicated mountain of concrete. After he died, Raphael and a number of other artists were called in, one after another, to formulate new plans around the four big piers, but none of their ideas worked out. Finally, in 1546, forty years after Bramante's piers were begun, Paul III Farnese told Michelangelo to finish the building. The great artist figured out how to use Bramante's great piers as the central feature of an architectural masterpiece that embodies all that he knew of the plastic forms of sculpture, the light and shade of painting, and the meter and eloquence of poetry.

Michelangelo's idea for the dome, though, was a little flat. He engineered it to be hemispherical, which would have made it seem to press down on the rest of the building. You can't really blame him for that—nobody on Earth had ever put up a dome that big that high, or anything even close, so nobody could really tell what it would look like. Michelangelo didn't get it finished; he died. His assistant, Giacomo della Porta, carried the project up to the point where the dome begins about thirty years later, and he could see the problem. So he re-designed the dome to have a more parabolic swing to its silhouette, which makes it seem to spring upward from the rest of the building rather than pressing down on it. Every western dome you can name after that, from the U.S. Capitol to your local courthouse (if it has a dome) follows the pattern of St. Peter's.

While the popes still preside at St. John Lateran as bishops of Rome, they've ruled the universal Church from the Vatican since about 1450, and the new St. Peter's has been their principal ceremonial church since about 1590. That's why this single building has been the object of the attentions of every major artist in the western world from the High Renaissance until the First World War (and it's had any number of masterpieces created for it since then, come to think of it). Its general appearance owes a lot to one man, though; what Paul III did for the exterior through Michelangelo, Urban VIII did for the interior through Gianlorenzo Bernini.

One of the first things Urban VIII did when elected in 1623 was heap honors on Bernini; "You are fortunate to live in the pontificate of Urban VIII," he told the artist as he knighted him, "but we are even more fortunate that the Cavaliere Bernini lives in our pontificate." Indeed, for nearly half a century, Bernini filled St. Peter's with a coherent program of superhuman masterworks. He designed and engineered the miraculous bronze altar canopy, ten stories tall, that brings focus to della Porta's dome and envy to the hearts of structural engineers. He produced the great reliquary in the apse that shows the four great Fathers of the Church holding up the ancient Throne of Peter, which is the perfect image for the spot even though everybody knows that the chair it encloses is a couple hundred years too late for Peter.

And in between, Bernini created scores of other statues, cherubs two feet tall and great saints forty feet tall; the mosaics; the frescoes; the bronze fittings; the pavements—everything, even the candlesticks and censers and vestments. He even lived long enough to build the tomb of his great patron, Urban VIII, and another for Alexander VII Chigi, who died a generation later. And Bernini built the great colonnades that stretch outward from St. Peter's, welcoming arms that reconcile the old Apostolic Palace with the church's new nave. (This nave is an extension to the original centralized church. It was finished in 1615 by Carlo Maderno, and since Maderno was patronized by Paul V Borghese, that pope's name appears front and center on the church now, almost as if he built the whole thing himself.)

It's on St. Peter's hill, too, that popes are elected by the College of Cardinals, in the Sistine Chapel built for the purpose by Sixtus IV della Rovere and decorated by Michelangelo under Sixtus's nephew and successor Julius II.* And it was from the Vatican that

---

*To hear Michelangelo tell it, he worked out this cosmic system of interrelated images all by himself. If it were true, it would be the only time in the Renaissance that a major patron let an artist have that much say in setting out the theme, and it doesn't stand to reason. Julius II never did anything else that casually in his life, not where money was involved; Michelangelo was no fool, and only a fool would have excluded the brilliant humanists of Julius's court, men

the Papal States were governed until Italy was unified into a modern secular state in 1870. Naturally, the new Italian kingdom couldn't be divided by another state stretching from sea to sea and covering a third of the peninsula. So the Papal States were seized and incorporated into the state of Italy, while the pope, Pius IX Ferretti, decided to stay within the walls of the Vatican complex, the "prisoner of the Vatican".

This tense situation lasted until 1929, when the secular Italian government—already headed by Benito Mussolini—signed the Lateran Treaty with Pope Pius XI Ratti. The treaty recognized the sovereignty of the "State of the City of the Vatican", a tiny monarchy covering 108.7 acres. It's the smallest country in the world, according to the *Guinness Book of World Records*.

This little country is the administrative headquarters of the universal Church, and everybody who lives there is in that business. ("How many people work in the Vatican?" someone asked John XXIII. "Oh, about half," he answered.) The city-state has its own passports, its own flag and postage stamps, its own law courts, a drugstore, a railroad station of pink and green marble, and a radio station that was built by Marconi himself. It even has a heliport.

The Vatican has its own army, too, the efficient little remnant of the Pope's legions. The Swiss Guard was formed in the early sixteenth century, about the same time that Michelangelo was doing the Sistine Ceiling, and he's supposed to have designed their uniforms. Today there are about a hundred Guards, and they really are Swiss, because one of the requirements is that you've gone through the mandatory military training of that country. Candidates for the Guard also have to be members in good standing of the Church and come with a recommendation from their pastors, and of course there's a rigorous selection process. They learn to use all kinds of weapons and to be proficient in hand-to-hand combat; many have black belts, but they don't wear them with the

---

like Bembo and Castiglione. Well, whoever figured it all out, the Sistine frescoes—with Genesis and prophecy stretched out above the altar and with the Last Judgement standing behind it—set the Mass properly, as the crucial event between the beginning of Time and the end.

uniform. They do two-year tours of duty, usually, although some become permanent residents of the city-state.

For going on five centuries now, the Swiss Guard have been defending the Pope and the Vatican. They were the only military unit available, for instance, to defend St. Peter's from the pillage of Emperor Charles V's armies, and they lost 147 out of 189 Guards that day—May 6, 1527. The anniversary of that battle is commemorated in the annual induction of new Guards.

Now the Guard defends against individual people, madmen, mostly, who try to attack the Pope. There aren't so many blatant military attacks any more. The Vatican City is more like a garden than a country. Within its old fortified walls, it has elegant little summer houses from the Renaissance and playful Baroque fountains along miles of paths that wind through groves of lemon and laurel. And, stretched along one side of this lush park, right next to the great church of St. Peter, there's the Apostolic Palace, greatly expanded since Nicholas V put up a few rooms for himself. Now the palace joins St. Peter's at a staircase built by Bernini, includes the Sistine Chapel painted by Michelangelo and the other great painters of his century, and connects, through a loggia decorated by Raphael, with the Vatican Museums.

These are the museums begun in the Renaissance to house the best of the Church's art alongside masterpieces from all ages and places. There's the Belvedere, with its famous ancient Roman Apollo; this building, begun in 1485 by Innocent VIII Cibo, was remodeled by Julius II into the first real museum, in our sense of the word. Clement XIV Ganganelli and Pius VI Braschi later added new sections, now logically called the Museo Pio-Clementino. There are also the Gregorian Etruscan Museum, added by Gregory XVI Cappellari after a treasure-filled Etruscan tomb was found in 1836 at Cerveteri; the Gregorian Egyptian Museum that he opened in 1839; and the Gregorian Pagan Museum, a newer division that houses primarily Roman antiquities that used to be in the Lateran Museum until John XXIII moved them to the Vatican. And a Picture Gallery, a Missionary-Ethnological Museum, an underground Historical Museum, and a collection of modern religious art, to name only a few.

The Museums, in turn, connect to the vast Vatican Library, arguably the greatest on Earth, with millions of books and unpublished manuscripts on every conceivable subject from the dawn of recorded history. The same complex of buildings also houses the Archives that hold countless documents of state spanning the past eighteen centuries.

(Here we need to clear up another sinister rumor, the one about the "secret" archives that are supposed to contain all kinds of sneaky things. In fact, every parish keeps a secret archive that contains things relating to matters of conscience that have to be recorded but must never be made public—things like tribunal cases that involve the privacy of persons and all kinds of other spiritual and moral matters that are nobody else's business. The Secret Archives of the Vatican contain things like that, too, and not much else. The word *secret* in this usage is derived from the Italian *segreto*, which means in this case something more like "segregated", set apart, than "suppressed" or "hidden"; a *giardino segreto* is a private garden, for instance, and the Vatican has those, too. Well, the same root gives us our word *secretary*, which is nothing more than someone to whom you entrust your private business—your secrets.)

There are many, many other interesting things in the Vatican, too. There's the Pontifical Academy, whose members are outstanding scientists of every nation and creed, many of them Nobel-Prize Laureates; the seminary for Ethiopian students; several pontifical institutes; and countless chapels and oratories filled with artworks impressive in quality and unimaginable in quantity. You could spend a lifetime there and still not have seen a fraction of all that's noteworthy.

Nowhere else on Earth have so many extraordinary things been gathered in so small a space for so long a time. Those few buildings in that princely garden in that tiny state shelter the finest products of the human mind. It is, of course, the seat of Christ's Vicar on Earth; but, just as truly, the Vatican is the memory of mankind.

CHAPTER 25

RELICS

The Church Remembers

A UNIVERSITY CHAPLAIN GOT AN excited call in the middle of the night. "Father!" cried an elderly lady of his acquaintance. "Is it true that anything handled by a saint is a relic?" "Why, yes," the priest replied. "Anything we know to have been touched to a saint's body is what you call a third-class relic. Why?"

"Well!" she said proudly. "I was once spanked by Mother Cabrini!"

That was stretching it a bit. But relics have always been important to Christians, and many are still in the news today.

First, let's have some definitions. Traditionally, a "first-class" relic is the corpse of a saint or any part of it. Second-class relics include any object intimately connected with a saint or Our Lord, and we've already discussed a third-class relic, albeit one unlikely to be set up for public veneration. Each of these classes has a rich and ancient history, filled with anecdotes, arguments, and sometimes controversy.

In earliest times, Christians risked life and limb to gather up the remains of their brothers and sisters who had been killed for their faith. It was dangerous, not to mention grisly, to sneak into a guarded arena or marketplace to pick up the remains, but the belief in the importance of decent burial has always been strong in the Church, and nothing is more natural than the desire to lay our loved ones to rest.

And it was traditional, as far back as anybody can tell, to celebrate the Eucharist at the site where martyrs were buried—see the sixth chapter of Revelation, verse 9. It was a special way of honoring them and including them in the prayers. By the third century, this practice had become universal, as reflected in St. Augustine's remark: "It is not to any of the martyrs, but to the God of the martyrs, although in memory of the martyrs, that we raise our altars." In other words, there's a martyr buried in the altar, but we go to worship *there*, and not to worship *him*. (Or *her*, as the case may be.)

By St. Augustine's time, in fact, Christians had already extended the practice and developed a new custom that was foreign to Roman traditions but common in some other parts of the ancient Mediterranean world. They began to preserve the bodies or remains of martyrs and holy people for separate veneration. And this is where a good deal of controversy came in.

A lot of important churchmen thought that it was proper to venerate the site of burial, but on the other hand they also thought that everybody should *have* a site of burial; others disagreed and said that you could move relics around as needed or even as convenient. As usual, controversy intensified study of the question, and St. Cyril of Jerusalem, Origen, Chrysostom, and most other Fathers of the Church came down in favor of the idea that, while the sites of martyrdoms could be memorialized, the obvious holiness of martyrs and saintly people gave them a distinction that could be marked properly through the respect shown to their earthly remains, wherever they were.

Also, the custom of celebrating the Eucharist on the gravesite of martyrs was growing steadily more powerful. In fact, when churches were built in places that had no martyrs, it had already become usual to ask for some small fragment to be buried in or around the altar table, or at least somewhere in the building.

St. Ambrose, St. Augustine's friend and mentor, said that, as Christ who suffered for us all is on the altar, "they who have been redeemed by his sufferings are beneath the altar." The Second Council of Nicæa in 787 absolutely required that relics be installed in a church before the building could be consecrated, and this directive still holds. The 1917 *Code of Canon Law*, crystallizing the ancient practice, mandated a little "sepulchre" cut into the altar stone to contain relics.

So, beginning very early in the Church's life, the bodies of martyrs and other saints have always been preserved and divided for distribution. This was, of course, an exception to the Church's custom of burial, but it was handled with discretion, decency, and a special ceremonial that helped ensure that accurate records were kept of the distribution of first-class relics. And the Church has been very conservative in judging a relic's certification. Today, if you see an object publicly displayed in a church as a bone of a saint, you can be certain beyond any reasonable doubt that it really is genuine.

But do these relics have any relevance for our time? Well, the Second Vatican Council echoed Augustine and reminded us that, while "the martyr's body does not bring honor to the altar," it is true that "the altar does honor to the martyr's tomb." And relics are still buried in altars, in accordance with the ancient practice endorsed anew by the 1983 *Code of Canon Law*: "the ancient tradition of keeping the relics of martyrs and other saints under a fixed altar", the *Code* says, "is to be preserved according to the norms given in the liturgical books."

Also, in this age when medieval stories of the miraculous preservation of saint's bodies can tempt anybody to scoff, there are some messages that sink in to our skepticism only through relics. In Paris, for example, there's the body of St. Catherine Labouré, and in Nevers, France, that of St. Bernadette, uncorrupted in glass-sided altars, and there's ample documentation to prove that these friends of the Blessed Mother were never embalmed or treated for preservation. This is completely at odds with what most of us expect to happen to a body after death, and it can remind us that there are causes and purposes beyond nature —which is what relics are for.

Second-class relics, too, have histories that continue to intrigue scholars today. The Pillar of the Scourging, for example, was a bone of contention for centuries among the churches in Rome, Constantinople, and Jerusalem that all claimed to have it. The

Holy Shroud now in Turin was stolen, probably more than once, which makes it very difficult to find documents showing that it's the original winding-sheet of Christ.

Usually, the study of second-class relics generates a healthy study of many fascinating traditions along the byways of the Faith, and, in many cases, those who have gone before us turn out to be much less gullible about relics than you might think at first. The triple "pillars", for example, turned out to be three fragments of, apparently, the same stone column—another example of the division of relics. And the Shroud of Turin, according to one recent study, holds its own against microscopic inspection of its fibers, its stains, and even the pollen it bears from plants growing in the area when it was woven—things no medieval faker could have known.

And, with a little thought, we can lay to rest the old one about how there are so many purported fragments of the Holy Cross that you could put them together and build a wooden Empire State Building. Think about it for a minute. An upright timber maybe six to eight inches in diameter and ten, maybe twelve feet long, is sunk into the ground to support a man's weight, with another timber perhaps seven feet long, to hold his outspread arms. Now, mentally divide those timbers, each into one thousand pieces. You'd still have fair-sized pieces of wood, each of which could be divided into a thousand again. Then you'd still have pieces big enough to recognize as wood, and you'd have two million of them. The creditable pieces aren't even that big.*

But pieces of the Holy Cross can't outnumber third-class relics, by far the most numerous kind. They're the conceptual descendants of things in the New Testament that conveyed a special closeness with a holy person, like the tassel of Christ's garment that cured the woman with the hemorrhage (Mt 9:20–21). In Europe and even here, it's still fairly common to keep snippets of the clothing of prominent people, almost the way people like to collect autographs. Scraps of Napoleon's coat, or his hat, are still

---

*People who keep track of such things tallied up all of the certifiable relics of the Cross in the world, including all 537.587 cubic centimeters that are kept in various reliquaries and cardinals' crosses in Rome, and figured that they'd add up to a wooden cube maybe six inches on a side.

sought by collectors, and a suit of Thomas Jefferson's clothes was recently offered in the international antiques market.

It's no different with religious figures. Padre Pio, for instance, was hounded by people who asked for a bit of his clothing, as part of prayers for healing or simply as a souvenir. Even when twentieth-century popes lie in state, the guards can't always keep mourners from snipping off pieces of the burial garments, which sometimes have to be replaced because of these attentions.

This is part of an ancient tradition, too, related to the universal desire for mementos. But objects like the Seamless Robe, the Crown of Thorns preserved in Paris, the five ancient boards at Our Lady of the Manger inside the Basilica of St. Mary Major in Rome, and the iron links at the church of St. Peter in Chains have a value far beyond that of the souvenir. Science may still test their authenticity, but no matter what, they serve as immediate, solid, and highly evocative reminders of the origin of Christian faith.

CHAPTER 26

THE SIGN OF
THE CROSS

*The Surprising Story of Christianity's
Best-Known Symbol*

THE ADMINISTRATION OF ONE OF those standardized pre-college tests brought students from all over the region to a large Catholic high school. As the test proceeded, a student from across town noticed others turning frequently to glance at the back wall of the auditorium. Later, he turned, too, to find out how much time he had left for a particularly difficult section of the test. But instead of a clock he saw a large wooden crucifix.

Christ crucified is one of the Church's most familiar images. The crucifix helps focus attention on Christ and his sufferings whenever you want to pray or, like the students, simply raise your thoughts to God. We see so many of them so often that, possibly, we take them for granted. But it took Christians a long, long time to adopt the crucifix at all.

Think about it. Christ was beaten nearly to death, dragged through the streets, and nailed naked to a cross so that everybody could see him hanging there. With his wrists and feet pierced, his life's blood drained away slowly; with his arms raised, after such a flogging, he was unable to breathe, and his wounded feet could not relieve his arms of their burden. It was enough to kill a person three times over, but it was contrived to kill you slowly, very, very slowly. Truly, crucifixion is the most agonizing, the most humiliating form of criminal execution ever devised. And the Romans were so practiced in it that they knew exactly when to stop scourging, exactly where to drive the nails, executing thousands of people with a grim craftsmanship.

Only the worst criminals, and only those who weren't Roman citizens, were crucified: murderers, habitual bandits, and traitors—those who, like Spartacus or Jesus of Nazareth, posed a threat to the government. When Our Lord said, "he who does not take up his cross and follow me is not worthy of me" (Mt 10:37–38), he must have sent shivers down his disciples' spines. The cross was what the electric chair is now, and in the early years, the crucifixion of your leader wasn't something that you could easily explain about your religion.

(While we're on the subject, the fact that Christ cried out, "My God, my God, why have you abandoned me?" on the Cross is hard to explain, too, usually. It wasn't a cry of despair; God couldn't abandon Christ, since Christ is God. It's the first line of one of the prophetic Psalms—21 or, in some numberings, 22. As it happens, people used to learn all hundred and fifty Psalms by heart; until fairly recently, it was one of the ways that children learned languages. And quoting the first line of a poem is how you remind your listeners of the whole thing—Christ was certainly in no condition to recite the entire psalm. Read it, and you'll see why he made the witnesses remember that particular psalm at the moment of his crucifixion.)

This association with unthinkable punishment was why, in the early years, the cross as a symbol only provoked mockery. One of the earliest representations of Christ on the cross was scratched on the wall of an ancient school in Rome. It shows a young man in prayer before a man with the head of an ass who is nailed to a cross. The caption reads, "Alexamenos adores his God." So shameful was the idea of crucifixion that the early Christians were very careful about representing the Cross. They disguised it by adding to it the features of a trident or an anchor, or they left it out altogether.

But all of this changed in a flash. Back in the early fourth century, the Roman Empire was torn by civil war. Two candidates for emperor, Constantine and Maxentius, were about to meet in a decisive battle at the Milvian Bridge. The night before the battle, Constantine saw a bright vision in the sky: a great cross with the legend "in this sign you shall conquer"—*in hoc vinces*, or *in hoc signo vinces*.* By the next night, Constantine had won the battle and become sole emperor of Rome.

Grateful for the divine aid, he took an interest in Christianity, supporting it with gifts of land and treasure, building immense churches (including the first St. Peter's), presiding at synods of bishops in his palace, and, apparently, receiving baptism on his deathbed—he postponed it for political reasons. But by the end of his reign, Christianity was fairly well established as the official religion of the Roman Empire. And by then crosses appeared on tombs, monuments, coins, noble insignia, and official documents all over the known world.

In light of this renewed interest in the cross as a symbol, Constantine's mother, Helena, decided that the True Cross should be recovered. She toured the Holy Land, visiting Jerusalem and building the Church of the Holy Sepulchre over the tomb in which Christ lay from Good Friday until Easter. And she ordered careful excavations on the hill of Golgotha nearby, where, according to Christian tradition, the Cross of Christ had been buried on the first Good Friday. Helena was undoubtedly ecstatic when the excavations turned up a whole cross, well preserved despite its two hundred and eighty years in the dry soil. But things got confusing when another cross turned up in the same excavation.

And then another! But Helena figured that she'd come up with the Cross of Christ, all right, and the crosses of the two thieves, too. To distinguish the True Cross from the others, Helena halted a funeral procession that just happened to be passing the site. First one cross, then another, was held over the dead boy; when the shadow of the third fell upon him, he stirred, sat up, and came back to life. No doubt remained in Helena's mind. She had found the Cross of Christ.

---

*This Latin inscription still shows up on churches, altar cloths, and vestments, as well as on some crosses. You might also see the three letters IHS in the same places, but they're not directly related to *In Hoc Signo*. They're Greek, not Latin, an abbreviation of the Holy Name.

This discovery confirmed the cross as the primary symbol of Christianity. But the horror of crucifixion faded very slowly, and Christians were still a little shy about depicting the suffering and death of Our Lord. Artists just showed Christ and the two thieves standing there with their arms stretched out, and they left out the crosses altogether.

By the end of the fourth century, though, crucifixion as a public execution was virtually unknown, and people started to see the Cross differently. Crosses of gold or of precious wood were studded with pearls, jewels, and carved gemstones, and a *crux gemmata* was carried in imperial and pontifical liturgies. This kind of image exalts the cross, transforming it from a symbol of shame into the sign of triumph.

But the Church gradually moved away from this image of imperial splendor and came to prefer the crucifix—a cross with a *corpus* or figure of Christ attached. It focuses attention on Christ's sacrifice rather than on the glory of the image itself. By the year 692, the Council of Constantinople ordered the use of crucifixes in place of ornamented crosses. Still, a good many patrons naturally still had the taste that brought about the old *crux gemmata*, and they ordered crucifixes showing Christ alive, standing before the Cross with his arms outstretched, wearing imperial robes, a kind that you can still find today.

But the trend toward realism continued steadily, and by about the year 1000 the familiar crucifix was becoming standard in Christian art—there was a popular impression that the world would end in the year 1000, and it made people think more about penitence and suffering than they did before. The corpus, crowned not with gold but with thorns, was shown hanging in pain, cut by the lash and bleeding. Realistically painted crucifixes showing the Suffering Christ are still made in Spain, Germany, and elsewhere, often reaching extremes of agony and blood—powerful images, certainly, if not to everyone's taste.

By contrast, the tendency in Italy, France, and England in the Middle Ages was to make crucifixes of plain wood, metal, or stone, representing Christ calm and at peace, the sacrifice consummated: Jesus dead on the Cross. These two types of crucifix, the agonized and the tranquil, have predominated in Christian imagery ever since. Indeed, the crucifix had by then established itself as the predominant symbol of Christianity, perhaps even more than the simple cross. Even during the storms of the Reformation, the "high-church" Anglicans and the Lutherans continued to use crucifixes.

But some radical Protestant sects saw the crucifix less as a symbol of Christ's sacrifice and more as a symbol of the Church's hierarchy, against which they rebelled. Others distrusted any religious image as an idol, even a plain cross. Either way, the result was the same: they destroyed every crucifix they could find. If they made any symbol at all for their meeting places, it was a plain wooden cross with no ornament and no corpus. There's an apparently similar tendency, nowadays, to forsake the traditional crucifix in favor of the plain cross. This may sometimes seem to be a needless rejection of a very old tradition, but then again it might just reflect a growing taste for art that's symbolic in a more abstract way.

It speaks well of people's values that the Cross is displayed now where it didn't show up before, but it can be disturbing to see it used on disposable items, where it might soon be treated as trash, or on wholly secular items, where it might be combined with unsuitable secular images. But, as long as the image is treated with respect, the symbolism is the same whether expressed through cross or crucifix, simple or elaborate, large or small.

No changes in taste and fashion could ever reduce the Cross to the symbol of shame it once was. It's hard to imagine a Christian who would disagree with the attitude of the old Roman Missal's antiphon for the first vespers of the Feast of the Holy Cross:

> *O Cross, brighter than all the stars!*
> *Famed throughout the world,*
> *Lovely unto men,*
> *Of all things the most holy,*
> *Who alone was worthy to bear*
> *The Ransom of the World!*

CHAPTER 27

SACRAMENTALS
Souvenirs of Sanctity

THE CONTRAST BETWEEN VISUAL CULTURES and literal cultures is nowhere clearer than at prayer. Christians from visual cultures might kneel, their gaze rapt upon a statue or picture that sums up, for them, some truth of their faith. Christians of a more literal mentality might kneel with their hands clasped hard upon a Bible, their knuckles white as if sheer pressure could pop their thoughts right into the book itself. But in either case the actual prayer, we hope, is of the same nature: not praying to the object but using it, word or picture, to help focus the heart and mind on the real object of your prayer.

As it happened historically, the Church grew up in both kinds of culture, the anti-image, literalist culture of first-century Judaism and the richly figured culture of first-century Rome. Of course, it's not a matter of either-or. The Romans had a brilliant literature at the time, too, and they loved to write down laws and histories and instruction manuals. The Hebrews used plenty of visual images—see Ex 25:18–22, 3 Kgs 6:23–29, 7:36, etc., etc.—and plenty of *things* to aid them in their devotions. Even today, pious Jews and Muslims use objects like phylacteries, mazuzahs, and prayer beads, although they understand very literally the biblical injunctions about graven images.*

After St. Peter established his seat as Vicar of Christ in Rome, the Church inherited all of these modes of expression, and she's used them all to bring the message of God closer to people, and people closer to God. Apart from the Bible (and millions of other books), the Church has given the world an abundance of things—objects, images, ceremonies, or actions that she uses to dispose people to the reception of grace.

And a few religious objects are so important in the Church's daily liturgical life that we may take them for granted: the candles and vestments used at Mass, for instance, the holy water used on entering the Church, the palms of Palm Sunday and even their ashes, which are distributed as a reminder of human mortality on Ash Wednesday. A Bible is itself one of those objects, if you look at it that way. Other things are just as familiar in the home: just about every member of the Church owns a Rosary, and perhaps a little medal or figure of the saint who bears the same name or who is the patron of some particular cause. But all of these objects, and many familiar images, ceremonies, and actions, belong to the same class: they're all sacramentals.

When discussing sacramentals, we have to be very careful with terms, because a sacramental is a very different matter from a sacrament. It can get confusing, especially when the same material object is used in both. Blessed oil, for example, is used by a priest administering the sacrament of the Anointing of the Sick, and some members of the laity visit the sick and anoint them with blessed oil, too. But when the laity anoint, it's just a way of praying: the blessed oil in this case is like blessed water, having no effect in itself.

The distinction is really very clear. The seven sacraments are visible acts of worship established by Christ: Baptism, Confirmation, the Eucharist, Reconciliation, Matrimony, Holy Orders, and

---

*Even some modern fundamentalists, touchy in the extreme about idolatry, gratify the perfectly normal urge to objectify their prayers, sending out prayer handkerchiefs and other objects to their followers. It has to be noted, though, that these things are not said to work the way the Church's sacramentals do.

the Anointing of the Sick. Sacraments produce grace in and of themselves. The Church teaches that, in a sacrament, Christ gives grace directly to the person receiving the sacrament, provided that the recipient is "properly disposed" to receive it—that is, the person has to be in the right relationship to God. The sacraments always have to be properly administered, but their effects depend not on the doer but on the deed itself.

The effect of a sacramental, by contrast, depends not on the deed but on the doer; not on the thing, but on the person who uses the thing properly. A sacramental produces grace, through the intercession of the Church, indirectly: sacramentals arouse us to the acts of virtue that draw God's graces to us. You don't need any sacramental for salvation, but they can inspire you to greater devotion.

Through the prayers of the Church for those who use sacramentals properly, you can obtain forgiveness of venial sins, as well as remission of temporal punishment. Their use also brings actual graces, protection from evil spirits, and health of body and material blessings. And there we need another word of caution, because we need to distinguish between proper use of sacramentals and superstition.

Sacramentals are not good-luck charms. The power to do good is in you, not in the sacramental itself. And using a sacramental to say prayers in the belief that you'll get what you want, just by saying those prayers, is more like casting a spell than it is like praying, and the Church frowns on that. So it's a good idea to make sure that you're dealing with an approved sacramental and performing legitimate devotions through it. Enthusiastic people come up with a lot of things that aren't.*

In any case, reviewing the stories of legitimate sacramentals makes a fascinating study. The history of the Rosary and the Stations of the Cross are outlined here in separate chapters, as are the

---

*So do manufacturers. They're in business like anybody else, and they rise to meet demand. But even "Catholic" stores sometimes sell articles related to unapproved (or disapproved) apparitions or to devotions that are officially discouraged. Naturally, the institutional Church has no control over these manufacturers and merchants, and she wouldn't want it: after all, the approved devotions almost all started as popular movements among the laity.

sacramental uses of water, incense, vestments, and so on. In fact, you can get whole books on these subjects. Sacramental actions are ancient modes of courtesy that the Church has embraced as appropriate manifestations of respect for God, actions like genuflecting (as in Mk 1:40—in the Latin Vulgate, the leper comes to Christ *genu flexo*, "on bended knee"), fasting, or ceremonial footwashing (Jn 13:1–16). Their histories, too, are wide beyond the Bible, and much older. And there are so many sacramentals in the form of prayers and blessings that their stories would fill a library.

Shrines like those at Lourdes and Fátima count as sacramentals, too, as do church buildings in general, whose history lies at the root of the whole glorious history of art and architecture. All of the great paintings and statues of the West that you see in art-appreciation courses were called into being as sacramentals. In fact, even some "everyday" sacramentals have more of a history than you might think. Medals depicting Christ, Our Lady, or the saints, for example, are as popular today as in centuries past, and examples have been found in the catacombs.

Other familiar sacramentals have histories that aren't so long but just as interesting. The scapular, for instance, developed from the habits of certain orders of monks in the Middle Ages, which consisted of a tunic and a "scapular" that hung over the shoulders (*scapulæ*, in Latin) like a sort of narrow poncho. People who wanted to strive for Christian perfection in the spirit of an order, but who had to remain in the world without taking any permanent vows, joined a sort of auxiliary organization and had the right to wear a modified form of its habit—they're the so-called "Third-Order Seculars", and you can still be one.

As time went on, though, it wasn't really possible to wear the habit of your favorite order as you went about your daily life, so it got shaved down, little by little, over the centuries, and replaced by ordinary street clothes. Finally, the only thing left of the original habit was a miniature scapular, the two little stamp-sized pieces of rough cloth and two strings connecting them. You still have to be "invested" in the scapular by the proper religious authority, much as you have to formally receive the habit—in fact, there are just about as many scapulars as there are religious orders.*

Then there are all of the other images—statues large and small, "holy cards", prints and pictures, even refrigerator magnets and light switches. We all know people who collect and cherish such little sacramentals, and we all know people who draw the line at key chains of the Sacred Heart. Where do these little bits of popular piety fall in the great scheme of things?

Well, you have to remember two things. First, any image is simply a reminder, like photographs you might keep of absent friends. You might like to look at the picture and think about your friend, or keep it before you when you talk on the telephone or write a letter. But thinking that the photo actually is the friend, or talking to it instead of to your friend, would be pretty disordered thinking—and it's the same with religious images. They focus our attention during prayer or meditation, but they don't have any power in themselves. In the beautiful phrase of St. John of the Cross, the devotion should be directed "spiritually toward the invisible saint in immediate forgetfulness of the statue".

Second, remember that your preference for any sacramental— Renaissance bronzes, dashboard figures, mosaics, key chains, books, music, whatever—is all a matter of taste. And, as the saying goes, it's no use arguing taste.

---

*It used to be fairly routine to enroll children in a scapular at their First Communion, so you might check your records to see if you were. Certainly the history of any scapular is worth knowing, because of the many lovely stories connected with the devotion, like the accounts of Our Lady's appearance to St. Simon Stock at Cambridge in 1251 and the promises she made in reference to the scapular.

CHAPTER 28

WATER

Holy and Plain

Cleanse me of sin with hyssop, that I may be purified; wash me, and I shall be whiter than snow (Ps 50:9).

W HAT'S HYSSOP? It's an herb, about two feet tall, with treelike woody stems, slender leaves, and blue flowers. What's it got to do with cleansing people and washing them whiter than snow?

In Egypt and the Middle East, people used hyssop plants the way we might use brushes: the tough, leafy plant can be dipped in any liquid you need to spread or sprinkle. So the Lord ordered Moses to prescribe a sprinkler of hyssop for the water and blood used to purify a house infected with leprosy (Lv 14:49–52). Anyone having contact with a corpse, likewise, had to be cleansed with water sprinkled from a bunch of this common herb (Nm 19:18).

So that's what hyssop is about. It's used to sprinkle cleansing water. You may have noticed a priest sprinkling holy water on a congregation or a building using a small metal ball with holes in it, sort of like a tea infuser set on a handle. Nowadays, this *aspergillum* probably encloses a sponge to hold the holy water, but it used to be filled with hyssop leaves—the Church has always remembered the Old Testament practice in these acts of purification by water.

And purification is immensely important in all of the Church's traditions, not just because it's an obvious symbol of the forgiveness of sins, but also because it's a sign of reverence in approaching God and things related to God. The Hebrews used to insist that the priests wash their hands before and after they handled the sacrifices in the Temple, and that anyone approaching the sanctuary had to wash up. That's why Solomon built so many containers for water at the Temple in Jerusalem. The Third Book of Kings lists a "sea" of bronze, fifteen feet in diameter and seven and a half feet high, holding about ten thousand gallons of water, as well as an impressive battery of smaller lavers, cauldrons, basins, pots, and bowls. Ritual washing was—well, a ritual with the Jews of the Old Testament, and Christians followed this example of cleanliness, both symbolically and practically.

In fact, Christians used to think that washing your hands before you prayed was mandatory. This idea was so widespread that Tertullian, in the second century, had to point out that it wasn't necessary. Still, the idea of purity in approaching God stayed so strong that, two hundred years later, St. John Chrysostom wrote, "though our hands may be already pure, unless we have washed them thoroughly, we do not raise them in prayer."

Of course, the early Christians incorporated washing into the liturgy of the Mass, and it's still there, right after the gifts are presented. But early church buildings included in the porch or courtyard a fountain or a little "sea" so that people coming to Mass could wash their hands. Artists and architects lavished great care and attention on these facilities, and some of them must have been marvels of workmanship and design. Often, the verse from Psalm 50 that stands at the beginning of this chapter was inscribed on the fountain, but one remarkably big "sea" had a more inventive inscription.

It was a huge basin in the courtyard of the sixth-century Church of the Holy Wisdom in Constantinople, then the largest church in the world. It was inscribed, in Greek, "Wash not only your hands but also your souls"—and the Greek letters of the inscription were contrived so that the words read the same whether you went around clockwise or counterclockwise.

Today, with the convenience of modern plumbing, we don't need to wash in public. But water is still the Church's most frequently used sacramental. Through the medium of blessed water, the Church transfers a priest's blessing to the faithful, remitting venial sins, just as the water sprinkled by Hebrew priests purified unclean persons and places. For the same reason, we touch a drop of holy water to ourselves when we make the Sign of the Cross on entering a church—but not necessarily when leaving after Mass, because receiving the Eucharist remits those same venial sins. You need to be cleaned on the way in to the sacred mysteries, not on your way out to the sordid world.

(By the way, there are more than one kind of holy water. Besides the "ordinary" blessed water you find in a font in church or at home, there's "water of consecration" or "Gregorian water", which is mixed with wine, salt, and ashes, used only in the consecration of a church. There's also baptismal water, containing oil of catechumens and holy chrism, although plain water is often used for baptism, too.)

In baptism, of course, the symbolism of water's purification is most clearly seen. John the Baptizer walked his followers into the running waters of the Jordan, a symbolic act that they'd clearly understand as washing away their sins (Mk 1:4–6). The early Church continued this procedure for the sacrament, using rivers and the same symbolism.

From about the fourth century, though, the sacrament moved indoors, and Christians started using an artificial container for the water. With this shift in procedure, the emphasis in imagery started to shift from the idea of washing, so natural for baptism in free-flowing water, to the idea of rebirth, emphasizing Christ's words: "unless a man be born again of water and the Holy Spirit, he cannot enter into the kingdom of God" (Jn 3:5).

After that time, this idea of rebirth became primary in the symbolism of baptism. When you'd completed your basic training, you'd come forward to the deacon or priest who was to baptize you. Apparently, the person being baptized, the person doing the baptizing, and anybody who assisted all stood in the water naked, following an old custom consistent with the symbolism of death and birth: by the year 200, St. Hippolytus of Rome had already prescribed, "Let them remove their clothing . . . and put aside any gold or silver ornaments they may be wearing. Let no one take any foreign object into the water with him." It runs counter to our feelings nowadays, but before private plumbing people were used to this sort of thing, from the public baths. And for female catechumens there were special women ministers there, for the sake of propriety.

Once in the water, you'd hear the formula of baptism and be completely immersed, not once but three times, because it's essential that there be plenty of symbolism of the Trinity in the ceremony—"for indeed, legitimate baptism is had only in the Name of the Trinity," as Origen noted in 244, when a lot of heretics were baptizing differently. Many of the Fathers of the Church, such as Gregory of Nyssa, Athanasius, and Leo of Rome, noted that this triple immersion also serves as a symbol of Christ's three days in the tomb. "For," wrote St. Paul to the Romans, "we were buried with him by means of baptism into death, in order that, just as Christ has arisen from the dead through the glory of the Father, so we also may walk in newness of life" (Rom 6:4).

This idea of rebirth through baptism was reflected in art. The tanks, or "fonts", used by the early Christians looked like modern bathtubs, except that they were big enough to be comfortable—about three feet wide, six or seven feet long, and maybe two feet deep. The font was often built into a niche in the wall, so that it had an arch over it from head to foot.

Interestingly enough, this is exactly the same arrangement that you find in any number of tombs built at the time. The arch, in the symbolic language of western architecture, is the same as a halo, showing that the person under the arch has everlasting life, so it's an appropriate symbol for a Christian tomb—when you rise again to everlasting life on the last day, you'll be right under the arch, where you belong. The arch is also appropriate for a baptismal font, where the same idea of resurrection to new, everlasting, life prevailed. So are the paintings and inscriptions that you find on both wall tombs and baptistries—in fact, the two kinds of structure are so similar that archæologists sometimes can't tell which is which.*

In modern times (relatively modern, anyway), the sacrament of baptism has been administered most usually by "infusion", with a priest pouring water on the head three times while saying the words, "I baptize you in the Name of the Father, and of the Son, and of the Holy Spirit." There have been a lot of controversies about this—in the past, some have even left the Church because they thought the only proper way to baptize was by immersion or by sprinkling (a genuine case of throwing out more than the water).

But the old *Rituale Romanum* allowed all three methods, although it did note that pouring and immersion are the most widely used. The 1973 document on Christian initiation from the Sacred Congregation on Divine Worship even states that "either the rite of immersion, which is more suitable as a symbol of participation in the death and resurrection of Christ, or the rite of infusion may lawfully be used in the celebration of Baptism." Not too many churches in the United States or Europe are fitted up for baptism by immersion, but the important things are the words—and the water, which has never lost its force as a symbol of regeneration.

*Even today, the symbolism and images seen at funerals echo those seen at baptism; see chapter 10 on funerals.

CHAPTER 29

THE ODOR OF SANCTITY

Making Sense of Incense

THREE HUNDRED YEARS BEFORE THE birth of Christ, when Alexander the Great was just a boy prince of Macedon, he had to preside at a sacrifice at a pagan shrine. Generous as always, Alexander threw a big handful of frankincense on the altar's fire. His tutor, Leonidas—who's gone down in history as just about the meanest teacher in the world—snapped, "Don't be so free with precious things unless you're master of the lands they come from!"

Well, Alexander never forgave his tutor. The young king of Macedon later went off to conquer the world, sending back millions of pounds of gold and silver. But he didn't send anything to Leonidas until he'd conquered the lands at the very end of the known world—and then all he sent his stingy tutor was a hundred-pound sack of frankincense.

It was intended as a graceful insult, but it really wasn't such a bad present. In those days, frankincense was worth more than its weight in gold. Just as today, everybody loved the incomparable rich, spicy scent. Fifteen centuries before Christ, Egyptian pharaohs sent expeditions to find it in the mysterious lands on the southern end of the Arabian peninsula—today's Yemen and Oman. All over Greece, Rome, and Palestine, the mysterious crystals were coveted as a basis for perfume, as a medicine, and, most of all, as a way to honor the gods.

What is frankincense, exactly? It's a resin produced by a family of desert trees, scrubby little bushes with sparse, tiny leaves and bloated branches. Frankincense trees grow scattered across the rocky, broiling deserts of southern Arabia. Traders find the trees and scrape patches of the bark from the trunk and branches. This irritation stimulates the flow of milky-white sap that hardens into droplets of resinous gum. These are relatively weak in scent, and the traders generally throw them away when they return to the trees. A second scraping gives low-quality frankincense, but the third stimulates the flow of sap that dries to amber-gold crystalline lumps, and that's the finest frankincense.

The land of frankincense is just about the hottest on the planet, excruciatingly dry. For three thousand years this region was an almost complete mystery, simply because so many people who tried to get there died trying. Alexander's army suffered tremendously as they passed this way on their way back from India, and a Roman legion sent to conquer these lands twenty-four years before Christ gave up and straggled back to Egypt—something that never happened to Roman legions anywhere else. Apart from the trackless deserts, there are ranges of sharp, rocky mountains that guard the few oasis cities, islands of life that tower with "skyscrapers" of lacy elegance, some a hundred and fifty feet tall, and all made out of the only thing available, mud brick. You couldn't get there by water, either, very easily: even Pliny the Younger advised traders that it was customary to carry a company of archers on board when you tried, because the trading routes were "greatly infested with pirates".

These frankincense kingdoms flourished for centuries, relatively secure from invasion or even communication from the outside world, just because nobody could get in. But the natives knew how to get things out. Every year for hundreds of years, hundreds of tons of frankincense were carried by camel to the shore to be loaded on ships—so much that the beaches smelled of ancient perfume. "The whole country is scented," wrote Herodotus five hundred years before Christ, "and exhales an odor marvelously sweet." It still does, reportedly.

The names of these fragrant cities of frankincense still evoke
the exotic mystery of the East: Nabatæa, Qataban, Sheba. "And
The Queen of Sheba, having heard of the fame of Solomon in the
Name of the Lord, came . . . entering into Jerusalem with a great
train, and riches, and camels that carried spices . . ." (3 Kings
10:1–2). Frankincense must have figured prominently among the
"spices" that the Queen of Sheba brought, not only because nothing else grows there, but because Solomon was already one of her
best customers. The Hebrews used tons of frankincense in the services at the Temple. God himself had ordered a special Altar of Incense set up before the tent sanctuary that Moses built, which
Solomon copied for his Temple. "For burning incense you shall
make an altar of acacia wood. . . . Its grate on top, its walls on all
four sides, and its horns you shall plate with pure gold. Put a gold
molding around it. . . . On it, Aaron shall burn fragrant incense"
(Ex 30:1–7).

The prescribed incense—the name comes from the Latin meaning "to burn"—was compounded largely of frankincense—"true"
incense—mixed with other, less-expensive, aromatics (Ex 30:34).
"Morning after morning . . . and again in the evening twilight . . .
throughout your generations this shall be the established incense
offering before the Lord" (Ex 30:7–8).

By the time of Solomon, this twice–daily sacrifice of precious
incense had been going on for nearly five hundred years. That
adds up to a lot of frankincense. Incense was understood by the
Hebrews to be a "pure offering" pleasing to God—who, after all,
promised "never again to curse the ground on account of man"
when he "smelled the sweet odor" of Noah's sacrifice after the
Flood (Gn. 8:21). The Book of Leviticus makes repeated references to sacrifices of "sweet-smelling oblations" and "pleasing
odors" of cereal and meat burned with incense. The prophecy of
Malachi (1:11), that "from the rising of the Sun, even to its setting
. . . everywhere they bring . . . a pure offering", has sometimes
been taken to mean that Christians would one day offer incense to
the God of Israel. And, in fact, frankincense has been with Christianity from the beginning.

At the Nativity, of course, "Magi came from the East to Jerusalem . . . and opening their treasures they offered him gifts of

gold, frankincense, and myrrh" (Mt 2:1, 11). Christians never really adopted the Hebrew concept that the fragrance of frankincense pleased God materially, the way it pleases a human who smells it. Instead, Christians' incense, still compounded largely of frankincense, is a symbol, a prayer conveyed by sight and scent instead of words. It speaks of two things: purification and prayer.

As a symbol of prayer, incense is mentioned more than once in the New Testament. St. John in the Apocalypse refers to an angel "having a golden censer; and there was given to him much incense, so that he might offer with it . . . prayers. . . . And with the prayers . . . there went up before God from the angel's hand the smoke of the incense" (8:2–4). St. Paul took up the same theme when he referred to Christ's sacrifice in the Epistle to the Ephesians (5:2): ". . . walk in love, as Christ also loved us and delivered himself up for us . . . a sacrifice to God to ascend in fragrant odor." Later, in the second century after Christ, Clement of Alexandria put the matter directly, saying, "the true Altar of Incense is the just soul, and the perfume from it is holy prayer."

Christian liturgy has used incense as a sign of purification since earliest times. The oldest surviving *Ordo Romanus*, which lists the prayers to be said at Mass, requires a deacon carrying a golden censer to precede the bishop as he enters the sanctuary, as a sign of purification of the church before the liturgy begins. For this reason, too, incense used to be burned, before the liturgical modifications of the Second Vatican Council, at every High Mass, as well as at Benediction and other ceremonies; that's optional now.

It's still required when an altar is dedicated—again, as a sign of purification. And, when the relic of a saint is encased in an altar stone, unburned incense is placed in the tiny crypt, just as aromatics were buried with Christ (Jn 19:39). Today, you still see five grains of unburned incense arranged in the shape of a cross on the Easter candle. And you'll still see a clergyman being censed during certain ceremonies, as well as the congregation itself. A deacon or other minister will take the *thurible*—a censer suspended from chains—bow, and swing it three times toward the priest, who bows in acknowledgement. The congregation usually stands when it's censed, and it likewise acknowledges the deacon's bow with another.

Here, too, the symbolism is of purification, and this practice is as old as incense. As they have for thousands of years, natives of the lands of frankincense still customarily light crystals of frankincense for honored guests, who pass the simple clay censer around and fan the smoke into their clothes.

There's one other ancient use of incense, though, that bears thinking about. Plutarch, in the first century, noted that the Egyptians called it *bal*, "and in translation this comes pretty near to meaning 'the dispersion of silly talk'," he wrote. Today as always, incense in a religious setting is a suitable preparation for prayer, and in fact it's a kind of prayer itself, a prayer expressed in actions rather than in words. "May you be purified in the sight of God," it says; "May your prayers ascend pleasingly to Heaven."

CHAPTER 30

LET THERE
BE LIGHT

Candles in Prayer and Liturgy

ADVENT WREATHS, Easter candles, the candles that signal the presence of the body at funerals and of the Body at the Eucharist, are all examples of the Church's use of lights in and around the liturgy. We've taken this practice over into secular ceremonials, too—imagine Christmas without strings of colored lights, or think of Halloween with no jack-o'-lanterns.

And, like most of the things we do all the time, the ceremonial use of lights has a history that's older than history, really. It's also universal; just as they occur everywhere in the world's folklore, light and its symbolism play an important part in the high culture of every major civilization and every major religion.

The Greeks and Romans, for example, burned sanctuary lamps before their temples. Alexander the Great took a famous lamp-stand from a temple in Thebes that was shaped like a tree hung with fruit-shaped lamps, almost like a Christmas tree; it ended up in the Temple of Apollo in Rome. Everlasting flames were kept on the menorah in the sanctuary and on the altar in the forecourt of the Temple in Jerusalem, as a symbol of the Presence of God in the Ark of the Covenant. In fact, light is more than symbolic in the Old Testament. God himself inhabited the Holy of Holies as a cloud of light, the *shekinah*.

Naturally, Christ and the Holy Spirit expressed their divine presence in the same way. Christ calls himself the Light of the World (Jn 8:12, 9:5, 12:46) and, at the Transfiguration, his face "shone as the Sun" (Mt 17:2) while the Father spoke from a bright cloud, similar to the *shekinah* from the Holy of Holies. At Pentecost, of course, the Holy Spirit appeared as tongues of fire (Acts 2:3). These events, and the prophecies of Revelation (1:14–15), reinforce the idea that light indicates the presence of God.

With all of this behind the symbolism of light, you'd think that there would be all kinds of references to the use of ceremonial lights in early Christian times. Surprisingly enough, there aren't. In fact, all evidence indicates that early Christians didn't use lights, precisely because their symbolism was so strong and so important to ancient pagan religions. Tertullian, writing around the turn of the third century, says with pride that "on days of rejoicing, we do not . . . encroach upon the daylight with lamps." At that time, the Egyptian cult of the mother-god Isis was still giving the Church a run for her money, and they kept lamps lighted day and night, a symbol of the constant hope of the religion's adherents. This Isis cult, like Christianity itself, was a salvation religion—others in the Roman Empire weren't—so it was as well to emphasize the difference, in those days, by any means available.

But the symbolism of fire and light is so strong that people just kept on lighting lights in association with Christian ceremonies. The hierarchy didn't like it, but there were lights everywhere they looked. It got so that the Synod of Elvira in the year 305 closely regulated the use of lights, and Lactanius, the "Christian Cicero" who wrote at about the same time, scoffed at the whole business. "They kindle lights," he said of the pagans, "as though to one who is in darkness. Can he be thought sane who offers the light of lamps and candles to the Author and Giver of all light?"

Well, with attitudes like that in the Church, it's a wonder that the custom didn't get completely obliterated. But, even while Lactantius was sneering, people in the streets were still lighting candles at funerals and lamps in the catacombs, as symbols of everlasting life, of hope, of rejoicing in the new life that had begun, and, as always, as symbols of the presence of God. So it was, to an extent, a case of the educated elite disagreeing with the people in the pews, and because this was not a matter of doctrine but merely a matter of folk custom, there was plenty of room for discussion and compromise.

St. Jerome, with great common sense, sorted things out and laid the groundwork for the customs that continue to this day. There's no harm, he said, if people light candles in honor of the martyrs and saints; there's nothing wrong with lighting a candle or a lamp if you feel like it. Of course, he cautioned, it was wrong of the pagans to do it for idols, but we're doing it as Christians, not as if the act itself will do us any good but only as a symbol, and we know the difference. As for the liturgical use of lights, Jerome pointed out that "in the churches of the East, whenever the Gospel is to be read, lights are lit, even though the Sun be rising, not in order to dispel the darkness, but as a visible sign of gladness." Liturgical candles, in other words, are not practical but symbolic, and as symbols they have a proper and valuable function.

After about the fourth century, testimony abounds to the Church's liturgical use of lights. Patristic writings record their use at funerals, baptisms, ordinations, and, of course, at the Eucharist. The emperor Constantine, and his Christian successors, gave hundreds and hundreds of lamps to various churches in the empire, all of precious metal or glass, worked into fabulous shapes by the craftsmen of the imperial palace. And they gave precious oils, like the aromatic oils pressed from flowers, by the gallon to fuel them. They even gave whole farms specifically to support the purchase of ample supplies of oil, in perpetuity. But gradually, over the centuries, the use of oil lamps declined in favor of the wax candles we see in liturgies today. By the twelfth century, candles were the norm, and it was already customary to place them on the altar itself to underscore Christ's presence in the Eucharist.

Protestants, interestingly enough, rejected Jerome's guidelines and the ancient customs of the Church with regard to candles. In Britain and the northern countries of Europe, they abolished the use of ceremonial lights completely—officially, anyway. English Protestant authorities, for instance, were scandalized by the presence of two lighted candles in the chapel of Elizabeth I, saying that "Candle Religion" was nothing more than "Idolatry". Later, some gentlemen were actually arrested and tried for the "use of wax lights and tapers", which they allegedly used in "superstitious ceremonies" in the cathedral at Durham "contrary to the Act of Uniformity", the legislation that governs the Protestant Church of England.

However, the symbolism of light, though not so strong in northern cultures as it is around the Mediterranean, was so ingrained that no political pressure was ever able to stamp out ceremonial lights completely. Still, some people even today may be a little ambivalent about the votive candles available in every church. A vigil light is nothing more than an ancient and venerable signal of watchful waiting, as when you keep a light in the window waiting for someone's return. But not everyone cares to light them—it's not part of their culture—and some people wouldn't be caught dead near them (a vain hope, considering the way funerals are run).

In fact, candles are indispensable to any ceremony you can think of. Well, the very word *ceremony* comes from the Latin word *cæremonius*, meaning "the person who carries a wax candle at public rituals". By the fifth century, in fact, Pope Gelasius I had already established the feast of Candlemas—the Feast of the Purification of the Virgin, when a church's candles for the whole year were blessed. And, typically, the symbolism ascribed to candles got more and more elaborate as the Middle Ages rolled on.

A sixth-century bishop, Ennodius of Pavia, figured that candles were made of three parts (in numerical harmony with the Trinity) and that each part had a nature that made it an acceptable offering to God. The flame is sent from Heaven, he said, and needs no further explanation. Wicks in those days were made of rushes, and to Ennodius this natural product of fresh water was an apt symbol of purity.

To Ennodius and his contemporaries, the wax symbolized the holy humanity of Christ. Worker bees, however social their existence, lead lives uncomplicated by gender, and wax could be seen as a perfect metaphor for the Virgin's offspring. Later commentators took up the idea about the wax as symbolizing Christ's flesh but used the wick to recall his soul and the flame his divine nature. That way, the candle's consumption symbolized Christ's sacrifice on the Cross. (Bear in mind that this kind of medieval symbol-story doesn't record the reasons for anything. The object or practice existed first, and then the allegory was spun around it. They enjoyed thinking that way, then, but we've lost the habit.)

Soon the ritual use of candles fell into three major divisions, which still pertain today. They may symbolize God's presence, particularly the presence of Christ as the Light of the World, and our rejoicing in that presence. They may be offered as an act of devotion, as in votive lights. Or, if blessed, they become sacramentals, objects useful for the good of the soul and to dispel—symbolically and actually, like any other sacramental properly used—the powers of darkness.

CHAPTER 31

A STAR
OUT OF JACOB
Why Nativity Sets Look That Way

And she brought forth her first-born son, and wrapped him in swaddling clothes, and laid him in a manger, for there was no room for them in the inn.

A YOUNG GIRL, far from home, delivering her own baby in a barn in the middle of the night after an exhausting trek across rough country. But she has the intelligence—the wit—to see that a manger full of hay looks exactly like a cradle. Such a girl is a wonder in any age.

Whatever happened to that manger? If you visit the Church of the Nativity in Bethlehem, you'll see a grotto with a marble floor and a silver star to mark the spot of the birth of Jesus (history holds that the original stable was in a cave, which makes sense, with the Babe in swaddling clothes parallel to the linen-wrapped Savior in the rock-cut tomb). There's no manger in sight.

But in the Church of St. Mary Major in Rome, there are five small boards of sycamore wood from the Middle East that have been traditionally referred to as the crib of Bethlehem. This isn't one of those improbable relics from the Middle Ages that showed up out of nowhere; since at least the fifth century, there's been a chapel at St. Mary Major fitted up to represent the cave at Bethlehem, and the evidence is that the chapel was built specifically to house those boards.

Since the sixth century, St. Mary Major has had the secondary title of *S. Maria ad Præsepe*, St. Mary of the Manger. Today, in the Nativity Chapel there is the oldest existing devotional reconstruction of the stable of Bethlehem. It's been the site of the first papal Mass at Christmas since the seventh century.

But it took six hundred years for anyone to think of setting up a manger scene in any other church at Christmas. It was St. Francis of Assisi—most imaginative of saints—who set up the first one outside of Rome, in the church of Greccio in Italy in 1223. The Franciscans popularized such scenes in churches, and after about a hundred years everybody expected a church to have a Nativity scene at Christmastime.

These parochial manger scenes, in fact, became matters of local pride, and by about 1550 they had grown fabulously elaborate, with dozens of richly gowned figures in an intricate landscape setting. By the eighteenth century, making manger scenes had become an important folk art in Portugal and Austria, and particularly in southern Italy—most particularly of all in Naples. That was where Charles III, King of the Two Sicilies, made manger scenes fashionable by buying them right and left, and soon everybody who was anybody had to have a collection of them, too. This fad reinforced the Franciscans' efforts to encourage Nativity scenes in private homes as well as in churches, and the Nativity scene industry boomed. Then as now, the figures were made of every kind of material: ivory and silk, wood, wax, porcelain, or pottery. Or pastry.

Every English family used to bake a mince pie in the shape of a manger to hold a figure of the Child until Christmas dinner, when the pie was eaten. But this came to a screeching halt when the Puritans outlawed Christmas in the seventeenth century. Frowning on any religious imagery, the black-robed Puritans passed specific legislation prohibiting mince pie. "Idolatrie in crust", they called it.

Well, the Puritans were certainly enthusiastic, but they were never much fun. A Nativity scene, no matter how elaborate, no matter how simple, probably focuses the holiday on the miracle of the Incarnation better than anything else outside the Mass. It just wouldn't be Christmas without a Nativity scene.

The basic elements of our Nativity scenes haven't varied in centuries, but they aren't all there as part of a simple visual representation of something mentioned in the Gospels. The Child in the manger, Mary and Joseph in vigilant adoration, the shepherds and the angel who told them of Christ's birth, are right out of St. Luke's account, but the special star leading the Wise Men to Bethlehem, and the ox and the ass, have their own reasons for being there.

All of these elements mean the same thing: recognition of Jesus as the Son of God. As the Wise Men said, "We have seen his star in the East and have come to worship him." Nowadays, some astronomers spend their spare time trying to determine which stars or planets could have coincided to make a bright new light in the sky at the time of Christ's birth. Others try to prove that it was some star exploding, or a new star being formed.

But the Gospels tell a different story. "Then Herod summoned the Wise Men secretly, and carefully ascertained from them the time when the star had appeared to them" (Mt 2:7). If the Star of Bethlehem had been a spectacular new light, no one could have missed it. It must have been something else.

In fact, the Wise Men are called, in the Latin Vulgate, "Magi", which word is the root of our words *magic* and *magicians*. They were skilled in the high art of reading the stars. They were astrologers.

Astrology may have fallen into disrepute in recent centuries, but it used to be an altogether different discipline, high-minded and generally accepted as legitimate. After all, Genesis says that the stars were created to "serve as signs" (1:14), and Solomon, at least, knew all about "cycles of years and positions of the stars" (Wis 7:19).

And when these astrologers said, "we have seen his star", they simply meant that they had foreseen the Nativity through their erudite observations of the heavens and had set out to find the Savior. Your "star" is just the configuration of the heavenly bodies at the moment of your birth, a meaning that survives today when you say that somebody was born under a lucky star or an unlucky star. The Magi didn't need any spectacular cosmic light. The star that we put atop our Nativity scenes doesn't represent any particular star. It's a symbol telling us that the time was right for Christ's birth.

These highly educated Wise Men must have been surprised, though, to find the Son of God among farm animals. But, like the shepherds, we shouldn't be, if we've read the Bible. Have a look at Isaiah 1:3: "An ox knows its owner, and an ass, its master's manger; but Israel does not know, my people has not understood." So the ox and ass, like all of the other figures at the Nativity, emphasize recognition of Christ as the Messiah.

And, if you listen carefully, the animals will tell you all about it themselves. On Christmas, farm animals receive the gift of speech, as a special favor. The only catch is that the animals, like all civilized creatures, speak Latin. If you can listen to a rooster at dawn on Christmas morning, for instance, you'll hear him shout, *Christus natus est!* "Christ is born!"

The ox, of course, wakes sleepily at this news. He squints at the rooster and asks, *Ubi? Uuuuubi?* "Where? Where?"

It's the sheep that answers: *Bethlehem! Baaa-ethlehem!*

Well, that's the story, anyway.

CHAPTER 32

OUR LADY'S
CLOAK

The Color of the Sky in Christian Art

W HEN YOU HEAR an astonished Frenchman say, *"Sacre bleu!"*, what on Earth is he talking about? "Holy Blue"?

He's talking about the mantle that the Blessed Virgin wears. If you look at very much pictorial art, you've noticed that Our Lady's mantle isn't always represented as sky-blue. Sometimes it's gold, if she's represented as Queen of Heaven, or maybe it's black in a picture of Our Lady of Sorrows. But after the Middle Ages, the color of her mantle came to be, most usually, celestial blue. Today, we see her most often as Our Lady of Graces or as The Immaculate Conception, and in these titles, at least, she will be veiled in the blue of the sky. It's a lovely idea, because it shows Mary to be the mother and protectress of us all. And like most of the significant images you see in the Church's art, the symbolism of this color is universal and very, very old.

In antiquity, among the Jews and other Mediterranean nations, you put a baby (or anyone else) under your mantle as part of the ceremony of adoption, just as it says in 3 Kings 19:19. At weddings during the Middle Ages, the groom took his bride under his cloak as a sign of protection; anyone who sought the protection of a nobleman or bishop had only to take refuge under his mantle. It's a charming custom, and one that must have added a touch of excitement to many an otherwise staid procession.

By the early thirteenth century, this universal symbol of protection sharpened in focus and came to characterize a distinct type of image of the Blessed Mother in the West. At that time, a Cistercian monk was transported into Heaven in a dream. He saw a good many monks, but none of his own order, and he asked the Blessed Mother why the Cistercians, her devoted servants, were excluded from Heaven. "I love my Cistercians so much," she answered, "that I keep them covered with my arms." And opening her mantle—"which", according to the most popular account, "was extraordinarily wide"—she revealed a multitude of Cistercians.

The story became popular all over Europe, and pictures of Our Lady sheltering people with her mantle multiplied. That was only logical—as Mary is the mother of us all, her maternal protection is for everybody. But visually representing the whole world under her mantle is a major compositional problem. Well, it didn't take artists long to figure out how to do it: there's only one "mantle" that covers us all—and we know what color it is. Next time you step outside under a cloudless summer sky, look at it as the cloak of our Blessed Mother, sheltering and protecting all six billion of us, from horizon to horizon, a bright-blue sign of her perpetual care.

But if Our Lady's mantle is blue, why is Our Lord's red? Christ's love and solicitude for us are certainly no less than Our Lady's, and all Christians seek his protection and want to be adopted by him—why is his cloak a different color? Well, one cloak is blue and one is red, but, believe it or not, they're the same color: sky-colored.

That's going to take some explaining, and before we get to the explanation we're going to have to define some terms. Our Lord's dark-red mantle is *purple*—that is, it's the imperial purple of ancient times. What we've come to call purple, the dark mixture of red and blue, is more properly called violet. The dark-red purple of ancient times came, supposedly, from a little shellfish that lived in the Mediterranean near the island city of Tyre. The Tyrians extracted from them a rich, deep-red, permanent, and incredibly expensive dye. Because of its cost, Tyrian purple became a precious mark of rank. You had to be a king to afford much of it, and throughout the Middle East purple was reserved to royalty. Roman senators got to have a stripe of *purpureus* on their white togas, and the higher you got, the wider your stripe.

The emperors, of course, carried this to its logical limit and wore togas that were completely purple, to show that they outranked everybody else. So the rich dark-red of Tyrian purple became the imperial color, the color of authority. Since the emperor was commander-in-chief, army officers got to wear some purple, too, as a sign of their imperial commission. A centurion, like the one in charge of Pilate's troops, would be issued a short cloak of dark red, which was the principal sign of his rank because it recalled the purple robes of the emperor. "And the soldiers, plaiting him a crown of thorns, put it upon his head, and arrayed him in a centurion's purple cloak. And they kept coming to him and saying, 'Hail, King of the Jews!' " (Jn 19:2,3). To the Romans, the purple cloak was a sign of imperial status as familiar as the crown, and even the soldiers assigned to a task like flogging a condemned man knew what the color meant.

But that isn't the whole story of why Our Lord's cloak is customarily the dark red of imperial purple. The Roman emperors used the color not just as a sign of military authority but also as a symbol of their dominion over the whole world, and this brings us back at last to the color of the sky. It's basically the same idea as before, the sky-mantle representing the worldwide extent of the ruler's protection and care. The Roman emperors, as rulers of the whole world, naturally wanted to associate themselves with such a powerful symbol. But the imperial color was purple, not sky-blue, and no emperor could change the color of the sky (although some of them probably figured that they could).

So they did the next best thing. They built their own sky, and they made it the right color: purple. How do you build a sky? Well, have a look at the Colosseum. When it was the primary scene of sporting events in Rome, the Colosseum wasn't open to the natural sky. There were big masts placed around its rim, like candles on a cake. From these masts ropes were stretched out to a big metal load ring hanging over the center of the arena. This rigging supported a canvas awning, a sort of temporary roof over the whole Colosseum, to keep the heat off the crowd. The emperors, in a show of incomparable wealth, had the immense awning dyed imperial purple. And just to make sure that everybody knew what this glowing purple roof symbolized, they stretched across the central load ring a yellow cloth that had the emperor's portrait on it. The whole thing represented the emperor as the Sun, sole ruler of the heavens and light of the world; when you sat in the Colosseum, you saw his purple robe turned into the sky, extending his protection, symbolically, to everyone in the known world.

The symbolism of this purple awning could hardly have escaped the notice of the early Christians. For thousands of them, it was the last thing they saw as they were martyred under this artificial sky. No wonder that Christian artists soon placed the purple sky-cloak on the shoulders of Jesus—and this time not in mockery, but to assert that Christ is the sole and true ruler of Heaven and Earth.

CHAPTER 33

THE MIRACULOUS MEDAL
The History of an Extraordinary Sacramental

THE CONVENT LAY DARK AND still in the quiet heart of Paris. No hoofbeats broke the silence; all the wagons and carriages had found their stables long before this July midnight.

The dormitory door slowly swung inward. The face of a child, five or maybe six years of age, peered in at the rows of sleeping novices. "Sister, Sister, Sister Catherine!" he cried. "Come at once with me to the oratory! The Blessed Virgin awaits you!"

Catherine Labouré, now wide awake, was afraid that the other novices would be awakened by her passage. The child answered her half-formed thought: "Do not be troubled," he said. "It is half-past eleven, and everyone is asleep. Come! I am waiting!"

Catherine dressed quickly and followed the child—who was radiating beams of light. The passageway itself was ablaze with light. When they reached the oratory door, the child touched it lightly, and it swung open. Inside, the oratory, too, was bright with light. Catherine followed the child to the chaplain's chair on the Gospel side of the altar, where she knelt.

Presently, the child said, "Here is the Blessed Virgin!" There was the rustle of silken robes, and Catherine saw a beautiful lady bowing before the tabernacle. Then the lady sat in the chaplain's chair.

The child had to urge Catherine forward. "It is the Blessed Virgin!" he repeated three times. Catherine ran suddenly toward the lady and knelt before her with her hands on the lady's knees. The lady spoke to the novice for some time. Then she gave Catherine some thrilling news: "My child, God wishes to entrust to you a mission. It will be the cause of great suffering to you, but you will surmount it with the thought that it will work to God's glory. You will know later what this mission is to be." Then, as suddenly as she had come, the Lady left. Her departure, said Catherine, "was like a light going out."

Catherine returned to her bed. "But I did not sleep that night," she reported years later.

A few months later, on November 27, 1830, the novices were at prayer in the oratory. Suddenly, Catherine heard the rustle of silk and looked up. The Lady stood, suspended in the air, to the right of the altar. She wore a robe as bright as the glow of dawn, and a long veil that flowed to her feet. Her hair was in braids held by a bit of lace. "Her face," said Catherine, "was so beautiful that I cannot describe it."

The Lady stood upon a large white sphere, her feet resting on a greenish serpent. She stretched her hands toward the globe. Precious stones ornamented her fingers; from some of them, rays of light streamed toward the Earth, but the rest of the stones stayed dark. Just as Catherine was noticing this, the Lady said, "The rays of light are the graces that I shower on those who ask for them. . . . But there are graces for which I am not asked, and it is for this reason that the stones you see are not sending forth any rays of light."

Then an oval formed around the Lady, and around it Catherine saw the words, "O Mary, Conceived Without Sin, Pray for Us Who Have Recourse to Thee." The Lady said, "Have a medal made after this pattern. Those who wear it, blessed, around their necks, and who confidently say this prayer, will receive great graces and will enjoy the special protection of the Mother of God." Then the Lady showed Catherine the other side of the medal—Mary's monogram with the holy hearts of Jesus and Mary.

The Lady told her to have the medals struck, to encourage their use, and to promise great favors to those who undertook devotion to the Blessed Mother through this medal and its prayer. Catherine obeyed. And the story of her obedience is one of the most inspiring in modern Christianity.

After a while, everyone knew that the Blessed Mother had appeared to one of the novices at the convent in the Rue du Bac in Paris—word about these things leaks out, even if no one violates any confidences, directly. Yet no one knew which of the novices it was. Catherine spoke of the visions only to her confessor, and only in the confessional. This priest, Father Aladel, was not easily convinced. The day after her first vision, Catherine had told him of her mission, but the priest, sensibly, told her it was only her imagination and sent her away. When the Lady returned to her, she went to the confessional again to tell the priest, and again she was sent away—a working confessor probably hears hundreds of such stories in his career.

A few months later, though, Catherine reported to her confessor that the Lady was not pleased with Father Aladel because the medals had not been struck. "This time," he wrote, "fearing the displeasure of . . . the Refuge of Sinners, I could not avoid attaching some significance to the words of the sister, although I did not let her know this." But, he added, "I failed to do anything about it."

A few weeks later, Father Aladel happened to see the Archbishop of Paris, and he spoke to him about his persistent novice. The priest was surprised when the Archbishop said that there wasn't anything in the novice's words that was contrary to the Faith, and that he "wished to be the first to be given such a medal".

Well, Father Aladel commissioned an engraver, Monsieur Vachette, to strike fifteen hundred of the medals in silver. Through the confessional's grille, he slipped one of them to Catherine—still unaware of her identity—and he was happy to hear that it was in line with the Lady's design. "The important thing now," said the determined young voice, "is to make it widely known."

How could an unknown young novice keep her anonymity and yet popularize the medal around the world! Impossible, without the help of Heaven. As it happened, the fifteen hundred medals sold out immediately. Vachette couldn't turn them out fast enough. Two other engravers in Paris, and the French Mint, helped him out by striking two million more. And it still wasn't enough. Eleven more engravers each struck two hundred thousand—and sold out in a few days. Engravers in the city of Lyons put out over six million of the medals, and the demand grew. Soon tens of millions of the medals were being struck all over Europe.

Years later, during the official inquiry into the validity of the visions, the investigator asked Vachette if the medals were still popular. The engraver answered, "I still sell at least three thousand a day."

The devotion to Mary through this medal grew so fast because Our Lady is as good as her word. Great and unmistakable graces showered down on those who wore the blessed medal and prayed as she had asked. A young girl was cured in a few minutes of violent and surely fatal cholera during the epidemic that swept Paris soon after the first medals were struck; a child crippled since birth walked after his mother had recourse to Mary through the medal. Within five months, there were over two hundred reported miraculous cures granted through the medal Catherine had made for Our Lady.

Besides all this, all sorts of unbelievers—Jews, Protestants, and even atheists—were all brought into the fold of the Church through devotions centered on the medal. Criminals, too, and others long separated from God. An old soldier, sick unto death in body, tormented in spirit, was sent to a hospital run by Catherine's sisters. He blew up at any mention of God, and his constant, loud blasphemies scandalized the sisters and even terrified his comrades in the ward. One of the sisters hid a medal under his mattress, but he kept up his cursing for six whole days.

Then, on the seventh night, the sister squared her shoulders and pulled the medal out from under the bed. "I have put you under the protection of the Blessed Mother," she announced, holding up the medal. The soldier fell silent and relaxed for the first time. "Look at the little medal," the sister ordered. The soldier said he saw only a candle flame in her hand. The astonished sister turned her eyes to the medal and saw it radiating light. It shone for fifteen minutes, filling the dark ward with light. "I cannot die as I am," the soldier said. He confessed, received the sacraments, and died later in peace.

Before long, the "little medal" came to be called the "Miraculous Medal", and the name has remained just as the graces have.

And what about Catherine? For nearly fifty years, she lived in the convent, unknown. Catherine got up every day at four A.M. and began caring for the derelict and dying old men in the convent hospital, bathing them, dressing their sores, and scrubbing their chamber-pots. Sometimes she took care of the chickens or peeled vegetables. When she got too old for this routine, she was assigned to attend the convent gate. Still, half a century later, no one knew that it was Catherine to whom Our Lady had spoken.

In 1876, Sister Catherine told her sisters that she would not live out the year. Then, unexpectedly, she requested an audience with the Mother Superior—a thing she had never done before in her life. Our Lady had made one other request, asking for a statue and a commemorative altar in the oratory of the convent, and Catherine needed official help to get this done.

The Mother Superior was shocked to learn that Catherine was the favorite of Our Lady! During all of the inquests about the visions, nobody had even considered Catherine because they figured she was too limited in imagination, too much the unlettered peasant girl, to have been entrusted with such a mission. But now, said the Mother Superior, "how often, as she spoke, did I feel like falling at her feet to ask her forgiveness!"

The statue and the altar were set up as Catherine had specified. Catherine then fulfilled her own prophecy of her death and died quietly on December 31, 1876. People flocked to the oratory during her funeral, because word had leaked out that it was Catherine whom the Blessed Mother had spoken to. She was given a triumphal and joyous funeral, with crowds singing hymns in honor of Mary.

In March 1933—fifty-seven years after her death—Catherine's tomb was opened. A committee made up of the Archbishop of Paris, a policeman, two doctors, some undertakers, priests, and nuns, were thrilled by what they saw. Catherine's body was perfect, not at all decayed. Her face was calm, with scarcely a wrinkle. Her clear blue eyes were open and fresh. The nuns who dressed her in a fresh habit reported that Catherine's whole body was as soft and as supple as if she were still alive. She was moved to the oratory where she had spoken with Our Lady, and there she remains today.

CHAPTER 34

UNCEASINGLY CHANT

Music in the Life of the Church

W HEN THE CASUAL OBSERVER looks at the Church, it might seem that the paintings and statues, the stained glass, the vestments and the architecture, and the other arts of the eye take pride of place. But, as a matter of fact, the Church sees music as her "treasure of inestimable value, greater even than that of any other art," in the words of the Second Vatican Council. "The main reason for this preeminence," the Council continued, "is that, as a sacred song united to the words, it forms a necessary or integral part of the solemn liturgy." In other words, the sung parts of the Mass are exactly that: parts of the Mass. They're not just incidental music to listen to until something else happens in the liturgy; they're part of what's happening. So the Church's music has substance. It's entirely different from secular music, and it's entirely different from revival hymns, gospel tunes, and commercial songs with a religious theme, too.

In fact, the main problem that the Church has with music is trying to keep this distinction clear. The Apostles came from a tradition of psalmody as old as Judaism itself—sacred songs written especially for prayer and praise that were adopted by the Church with no problem. But other religions in those days, like the cults of Dionysus or Cybele, consisted largely of using music to whip you into a Bacchic frenzy, and then anything could happen—orgies and incest, flagellation, even self-castration. Who knows what they got up to in Corinth.

Both the early Christians and the people in the mainline pagan denominations agreed that improper music is definitely harmful to decency and good citizenship. Everybody knew how a catchy tune can get into your head and run around in there day after day while you're trying to think, and they knew how easily a lyric can impart values, almost subconsciously. Socrates warned time and again that "education in music is most sovereign, because more than anything else rhythm and harmony find their way to the inmost soul . . . bringing with them and imparting grace . . . it is here that error is at once most dangerous, as it encourages morally bad dispositions."

So there were laws passed in the Hellenic world about what kinds of music you could play in public and what kinds you couldn't. The Fathers of the Church put down strict legislation about music, too, for exactly the same reasons. They generally agreed on banning all instrumental music from liturgy, as some eastern European churches still do, because the few instruments available (things like rattles, drums, harps, and horns) were too closely tied to the orgiastic cults of the day—you never saw Pan without his pipes or Bacchus without his cymbals.

As to singing, though, the Fathers show a whole range of opinions. Some—St. Jerome, for one—wanted to outlaw singing completely, as contrary to the Christian ideals of sobriety and asceticism. Others were a little more ambivalent, like St. Augustine. "Sometimes," he confessed, "I strongly desire that all the melodies and sweet chants with which David's psalter is accompanied should be banished from my ears and from the Church herself. . . . But again, when . . . I am moved not by the singing but by the things sung, I again recognize the great utility of this institution. . . ."

Still other Fathers, like St. Basil and Cassiodorus, were comfortable with the inherent beauty of music. They knew that it had to be regulated, because of its power, but they also recognized that it can be turned to good use. This side eventually won: they had the ancient custom of Israel on their side, as well as apostolic authority—"teach and admonish one another by psalms, hymns, and spiritual songs, singing in your hearts to God by his grace" (Col 3:16). And they defined for the Church a very elevated view of what sacred music is and why it's sacred.

The holiness that they found in music has to do with their view of the universe, one that already had a long history behind it. The evident orderliness of the Sun, the Moon, and the planets moving along swiftly, silently, in their appointed courses deeply impressed the philosopher Pythagoras, about five hundred years before Christ. Ruminating on the *harmonia* ("fitting together") of the *cosmos* ("order of the universe"), he made some passing remark one night, something about the "music" of the movements of the planets, which he alone could "hear" because of his understanding of geometry.

He probably meant that the distances of the heavenly bodies correspond somehow to the musical intervals, the simple geometric relationships that govern the chords of stringed instruments, because those ratios seem to govern the design of everything else in nature. But his disciples took him literally, and for the next twenty-three centuries everybody figured that the stars and planets were set in crystalline spheres that actually made inaudible music as they rotated around the Earth.*

Even the Book of Job, written in or about Pythagoras's day, recalls the moment of creation, when God laid the cornerstone of the Earth "while the morning stars sang in chorus". Music, in this view of things, was the essence of the divine order of creation, and human apprehension of it brought man closer to the mind of God: "Do you know the ordinances of the heavens?" God asked Job and his friends. "Can you put them into effect on the Earth?" (Jb 38:7, 33).

---

*The harmony part happens to be true, by the way. In 1772, when people didn't much believe in the actual spheres any more, an astronomer named Johann Eiler Bode published a principle that lets you predict the mean distances of the planets from the Sun by a simple harmonic series of numbers. Since its publication, Bode's Law has led to the discovery of more than one planet. Make of that what you will.

After that time, people figured that they did know the ordinances, and that they could make them work on Earth. In fact, right up until our own century, not only music, but pictures and statues, even literature and architecture—whole cities, sometimes—were designed according to proportional schemes of simple Pythagorean geometry. That's why traditional music sounds so good in Romanesque or Gothic buildings; both structures are composed of the same simple ratios, so the building and the music resonate together. They really do. That's what the science of acoustics used to be all about, before microphones.

This harmonic view of the universe lets you make music as an image of the heavens, or maybe it lets you see the heavens as an image of your music. Either way, it has a symbolic value; it makes your music speak of harmony beyond hearing, and it elevates your compositions to reflect the overarching Wisdom of God, which reaches from end to end mightily and governs all things well.

The Church fostered this reflection of heavenly harmony, and she fosters it still, by supporting the composers who bring us this great symbol of the mind of God. Palestrina in Rome, Gabrieli at St. Mark's in Venice, Mozart in Austria, Josquin Desprez all over Europe, and countless lesser voices all found steady employment in the Church. Today, American congregations can patronize music on a much broader scale, using harmonies as diverse as those from African music (like the great *Missa Luba*) or the lilting chant of Vietnamese Masses.

This ever-broadening scope is also part of the Church's heritage, of course. Little by little, the Church has embraced all of the great advances in the engineering of instruments and the science of composition—counterpoint, polyphony, and the other mechanisms that shape modern music. But still, the old ideas of propriety hold firm against unbridled innovation, and they've always been expressed in legislation.

The basic vocal music of the Church has been Gregorian Chant since at least the seventh century. (It's named in honor of Pope St. Gregory the Great, who reigned from 590 to 604. He was once supposed to have invented it, but he probably really only insisted on it as a standard, pure form of ancient Roman music, which is otherwise lost.) Classic Gregorian Chant, though, sprouted all kinds of variations and additions that strayed rather too far from accepted norms and were clearly unsuitable to divine worship. In the early twelfth century, St. Ælred of Rievaulx noted again the celestial nature of Gregorian chant—it "transports the soul to the society of the angels," he wrote—but he compared the recent innovations to the whinnying of a horse.

When things got to that point, episcopal and papal regulation took these innovations out of the liturgy, but, characteristically, didn't try to stamp them out entirely. On the contrary, the Church continued to patronize "new" music in the form of liturgical dramas, processional songs, and the like, giving a tremendous boost to the development of secular music.

This strategy kept things in tune for about two hundred years, but musicians are an irrepressible lot. And, by the fourteenth century, the complicated rhythms and other innovations of *Ars Nova* ("New Art") music upset lots of people. Jacob of Liège complained that choristers, "howling like dogs, bay like madmen and . . . use a harmony contrary to nature herself"—that is, not in a Pythagorean mode. Actually, Jacob notwithstanding, people thought that the music sounded great, but it couldn't be used in the Mass because it included the trick of introducing vernacular lyrics into chants, two or three languages at a time. It got so complicated that you couldn't understand a word of it.

So the abuses of Ars Nova were roundly condemned by John XXII d'Euse in 1322: strict adherence to counterpoint in the Pythagorean fourth, fifth, or octave, he said, and that was it. Well, three centuries later, people weren't overly excited by the techniques of Ars Nova any more (a diminished third wasn't likely to take people's minds off the Sacrament by then), but opera had taken the music world by storm. People tend to confuse opera and liturgy —both involve words set to music—but opera stresses fancy technique and emotionality at the expense of clarity. "They do not have thoughts as to whether their efforts of singing may be a shout or a love-cry," said the Council of Trent. So the Council had to ban a number of new abuses that had crept into churches from opera houses: all seductive or impure melodies (whatever that means), all vain and worldly texts, all outcries and uproars.*

As before, the Church didn't try to stamp out the innovations. The great seventeenth-century motets that Jean-Baptiste Lully wrote for Louis XIV are as gorgeous as anything in opera, but they hold their texts sacred, staying well within the bounds of suitability. The point was just to keep things fitting and proper. "We . . . condemn theatrical chant in churches," said Benedict XIV Lambertini in the middle of the eighteenth century, "and want a distinction made between the sacred chant of the Church and the profane chant of the theater."

Today, as always, the Church's judgement on music follows a fine line. You can't have really *avant-garde* art music as part of the Mass, because it's too unrelated to people's expectations; it would be a material distraction from the Mass itself. But on the other hand, you can't just take in music off the street, because you have to have music that's got some dignity, some stateliness about it, owing to the unsurpassed sanctity of the Sacrament.**

Paul VI set the tone here, as in so many other things. "New roads are already open for the future of sacred music," he noted in 1968 to an audience of church musicians.

> This does not mean a renunciation of the great musical tradition of the Church. . . . The Church expects from you . . . the creation of new artistic expressions, [and] that the search for new musical forms be not unworthy of those of the past. Yours is a great responsibility. . . . Simple and accessible compositions have been introduced, yet they lack inspiration and nobility of expression. . . . It

*The Council insisted that the words be clearly understandable, too. And while we're on that point, note that the syllables in Latin are usually a single consonant followed by a single vowel, or *vice versa*, so it stays clear in chanting or singing: *Cré-do in ú-num Dé-um*. English, with its more complicated sounds, tends to get mushy when sung, especially in chorus: *I be-lieve in one God*. When was the last time you understood *anything* sung in chorus in English?

**The music therefore has to be "real", not imitation, just as the bread and wine have to be real; a 1958 regulation, for instance, specifically prohibited electronic organs (thanks be to God), and Vatican II specified the *organum tubulatum*—the pipe organ—thereby again excluding artificial alternatives.

is up to you, then, to contribute to this difficult and urgent task of reasoning and judging, encouraging or checking, as need be. . . .

We are not able to end . . . without recalling to your attention an old saying . . . "He prays twice who sings well." Sing, therefore. Sing with the voice, sing with the heart. . . . Be messengers of joy, of goodness. May your lips be always worthy to celebrate the praises of the Lord, in whose honor you sing.

CHAPTER 35

THE NUMBERS
GAME

Symbols You Can Always Count On

T HE MORE YOU READ the Bible, the more you notice that certain numbers keep showing up again and again. Israel was divided into twelve tribes, and there were twelve Apostles; Noah's Ark had to wait out forty days of rain, Moses took the tribes out of Egypt by wandering for forty years in the desert, and he, like Elias and Christ, fasted for forty days. Carry this over into modern life, and you find that the Church, too, fasts for forty days during Lent and, in many countries, a special commemoration Mass is celebrated for the dead forty days after the funeral.

And look at the other significant numbers in our prayer and liturgy: we repeat the word *holy* three times at the Sanctus of the Mass, we group candles three by three at the altar, and we swing the censer three times when using incense. What do all of these numbers mean?

It all adds up once you know the system. People everywhere have always ascribed significance to numbers, counting things very carefully and making sure that the "right" number of things happen the right number of times. It's the same everywhere you look: in China, ancient Egypt, Greece, Babylon, Rome, and ancient Israel. Every culture has its own distinctive set of "lucky" numbers, but the meanings ascribed to certain numbers seem to show up everywhere. The number of something is an easily grasped symbol, even to people who can't read, as immediate as colors or basic shapes. And the Church has always used this widespread system of number-meanings as an extra way of conveying information about God and the plan of salvation.

Basically, these traditions started in the Middle East, just after people first began writing things down. The Egyptians understood a great deal about geometry, apparently, but they didn't get carried away with it. They just used it to measure everyday things like land, beer, and pyramids, and then they let it go at that.

But the early Greeks, with their penchant for abstract thinking, thought that numbers were the key to all knowledge. They couldn't get enough. The first one who thought it all out was Pythagoras, who used the ratios and relationships of simple geometry to outline the structure of the universe, the way we use atomic theory today. He calculated the beautiful ways of harmony, how the notes sounded by chords make harmonic tones if the lengths of the chords are all interrelated in simple numerical ratios. We still use his musical principles today, because he was right.

And his name still rings through grade schools all over the country because he was the one who came up with the Pythagorean Theorem ("the square of the hypotenuse of a right triangle is equal to the sum of the squares of the other two sides", in case you'd forgotten). That theorem is about the extent of his claim to fame today, that and the musical theories. But in antiquity, Pythagoras was seen as a combination Einstein and Mahatma Gandhi. He gave numbers a religious function; he apparently concluded that things weren't just *measured* by number but somehow *caused* by number, and that you could see the mind of God at work by looking at the ways that numbers work. He developed a whole philosophy of life from these ideas and invented the term *philosopher*—"lover of wisdom"—to refer to those who followed it. His sayings and the writings of his disciples had an immense influence on philosophy for centuries. Even Plato's *Republic* records a lot about the Pythagorean ways of thought and life.

It was largely through Pythagoras that the idea of numbers as divinely meaningful took root in the Mediterranean world and served as the basic structure of physics, chemistry, and natural science (such as they were), as well as philosophy, in Greece, Syria, Asia Minor, Italy, Egypt, and North Africa.

Most of the people in these regions didn't develop any system of numerical notation. There are no Greek equivalents of our figures 1, 2, 3, 4, 5, and so on, which we got from the Arabs much later. Instead, the Greeks, the Babylonians, and other ancient peoples just used the letters of their alphabets to signify numbers. Basically, their letter *A* meant 1, *B* was 2, and so on. This idea was taken up later by the Romans, for whom letters like *X, I, V, M*, and *C* served as numbers.

The most interesting effect of this kind of alphanumeric notation is that sooner or later you get to thinking that words have a numerical value as well as a literal value—you can compare texts not just for what they say, but also for what they add up to. The Pythagoreans did a little of this, but not much; the classical Romans played with it in inscriptions, capitalizing certain letters so that they'd spell out the date or something else of interest. But the study of number-letter correspondences became a serious discipline about three hundred years before Christ, when Alexander the Great conquered Babylon. After this ancient center of mathematical study opened its gates to the lively number-games of the Greeks, the study of letters as numbers took on a whole new vitality, spreading quickly from one end of Alexander's empire to the other. Before long, the Hebrews combined this new hybrid science with their own ancient traditions of this kind and came up with something more systematic and more mystical than anyone had ever known before.

Because the Hebrews also used letters as numbers, they could add up the numerical values of the letters of any word or subtract one word from another, just as you would subtract one string of numbers from another. A numerical relationship between words or phrases in the Old Testament made scholars think about possible mystical connections between them, which stimulated a great deal of meditation on the sacred texts. Admittedly, this can become complicated beyond telling, and it's often about as profound as a crossword puzzle, but sometimes it really does spark some spiritual insight. The rabbi Simon the Just (about 250 B.C.) noted that the word *Torah* and the Hebrew phrase for *deeds of loving kindness* both add up to 611—which he took as a sign of the parallel importance of faith and works, an idea that the Church would agree with, however you figure it.

By the second century after Christ, this branch of learning came to be known as *gematria*, a Hebrew equivalent of the Greek *geometry*. But, gematria or geometry, the principles of number-letter equivalences had been active in Hebrew literature for perhaps a thousand years before that. The writers of the Old Testament purposefully encoded significant numbers in the words that they used, which is why gematria can sometimes actually clarify things.

For example, look at Genesis 14:14. "When Abram heard that his kinsman had been taken prisoner, he called out trained men born in his house, 318, and went in pursuit . . ." Why 318? Were there really so many men born in Abram's house? Maybe; but the number really refers to Eliezar, the only servant of Abram's that we know by name—the letters of that name, in Hebrew, add up to exactly 318. Similarly, when Abram became Abraham and Sarai became Sara, their "numbers" changed, associating them with an entirely different set of phrases in scripture that, to the initiate, "explain" the new roles they have to play in God's plan. Whole books have been filled with such correspondences. Whole libraries have been filled with such books.

After the New Covenant was established, those who remained Jews really didn't have all that much to do for devotions. With the Temple gone, there was no way to fulfill the commandments of the Torah of Moses about sacrifices and holocausts and ceremonies. So the pious Jews turned to intensive numerical study of scripture, digging out all kinds of correspondences between words and sums of words. After the first century, there was truly no end to the making of books of gematria.

Because all educated people in the Mediterranean world knew the language of numbers, any time people got shy about saying something outright, they'd just use the equivalent numbers. There's a coy little Latin graffito in Pompeii, for instance, that does this. "I love her whose number is 545," it runs. One of the Sibylline oracles (predictions written in early Christian times but purported to be by the female prophets of antiquity) announces the coming "child of the Great God" this way:

> . . . *The whole sum I will name:*
> *For eight ones, and as many tens on these,*
> *And yet eight hundred will reveal the Name . . .*

Everybody in the audience would have understood the reference, because the name *Jesus* in Greek adds up to 888.

And, in fact, the Christian writers of the New Testament used the same kind of number code to carry meanings to members, sometimes with the added advantage of not letting unbelievers in on the story. Of course, a little classical education goes a long way toward keeping a sensible perspective on this, but some of these passages still confuse people who don't know how the number-code strategy works. Take Revelation 13:18—the "number of the beast". That number, 666, is a reference to Nero, and you can prove it by the mistakes that were made in translating it.

Of course, St. John wrote Revelation in Greek, not in Latin or Hebrew, but his use of numbers as names shows that they should be understood as collections of Hebrew letters. The Greek form of Nero's name, written in Hebrew letters, works out to be *nrwn qsr*. Numerically, that gives you the "six hundred threescore and six" that St. John mentioned. But by the second century, right after Revelation was written, translations of the book into Latin give the number of the beast as 616. That's because the *Latin* form of Nero's name in Hebrew letters is *nrw qsr*, without the extra *n*, and that adds up to 616. The early Christian Latinists knew that the reference was to Nero, and they translated the numbers accordingly. So that number, whatever its fascination for supermarket tabloids and makers of horror movies, is fairly cut and dried. It means Nero, and that's that.*

---

*The secular world still seems fascinated by it, though, proposing, among other candidates, George III, *L'Empereur Napoléon* (if you write it in Arabic with two letters left out), Parliament (if you include the janitors), John F. Kennedy, Juan Carlos of Spain, Henry Kissinger, the Reverend Sun Myung Moon, Ronald Wilson Reagan (three names of six letters each), New York City, Zip Codes, Social Security numbers, a certain prominent publisher with an unfortunate

A couple of centuries after the Gospels were written, Christianity was pretty much in the ascendant, and it wasn't necessary to put things in secret code any more. But with heresies springing up right and left, you needed to get the message across clearly, in terms that everybody could understand. Everybody in the civilized world still knew and used some kind of number symbolism, so the Fathers of the Church used those means themselves. St. Clement of Alexandria, for instance, devoted a whole chapter of his *Stromateis* to "The Mystical Meanings in the Proportions of Numbers, Geometrical Ratios, and Music", which he applies to the understanding of the Bible.

And St. Augustine—the Christian Pythagoras who brought together all ancient knowledge—systematized the old science of numbers further. "An ignorance of numbers," he said, "is the reason why many things expressed figuratively and mystically in the Scriptures are not understood." And he used number symbols himself—you can't understand his treatise *Christian Instruction* without it, but fortunately he explains it all right there. He also used number symbols in sermons addressed to ordinary congregations, not to hide things as St. John had to do, but as a way of giving ordinary people some easy way to take hold of Scripture's fuller meaning.

For instance, Augustine himself lectured more than once on the symbolism of the number of fish caught in the Sea of Tiberias (Jn 21:1–14), which is given quite specifically as a hundred and fifty-three. The number, Augustine says, obviously carries some signification because it is so specific, and because Christ told the Apostles to cast their nets on the right side. He didn't say anything like that the previous time he directed their fishing (Lk 5:4); he had already told them that he intended for them to be fishers of men (Mt 4:19), and he described the Last Judgement in terms of taking the creatures on his right (Mt 25:31–46). So, the fish in John 21 refer to people, and, says Augustine, "the number signifies thousands and thousands . . . to be admitted into the Kingdom of Heaven."

---

street address, and universal bar-code price tags (any and all of them). And the computer, if you figure *A* as 6, *B* as 12, *C* as 18, and so forth.

The reason he gives is this: there are ten Commandments; you have to follow them to get into Heaven. But no one keeps the Commandments by his own power; we all need the grace of God. This comes in terms of the sevenfold Gifts of the Holy Spirit. So, he says, you see that there is need of the Spirit so that the Law can be fulfilled, so you add 7 to 10. You get 17, but you can't take it as a lump; you need to account for every detail included in the Seven Gifts and the Ten Commandments and all of their implications, so—stay with him here—you add all of the numbers from 1 to 17, and you get 153. "There's no need of mentioning all of the numbers now," Augustine told his congregation early that Easter morning. "Add them up at home."

So, according to St. Augustine, that was why St. John was so specific about the number of fish caught: it lets you derive a general principle of salvation from a specific detail of Scripture. And you probably thought that it was going to be something obscure. But, really, this is a relatively simple example of the geometric gymnastics that people got up to in those days. After all, Augustine was trying to make his point to an ordinary congregation. You should read what the scholars tossed back and forth.

It seems hard to believe nowadays, but people were actually converted by this kind of thing. It was simply the way that most educated people thought, and if you could make a good sound argument by this method, they'd buy it. There are any number of recorded cases of people who got their start in Christianity this way, sometimes tens of thousands of them at a time.

Nowadays, the serious study of gematria has virtually disappeared. Nobody really puts much stock in the interrelationships among numbers in the Bible any more, but those numbers still carry their traditional meanings, which also date from the time of Pythagoras, and each number has a definite symbolic value that carries over into the visual arts.

First, 1 is the number of God, because there's only one God. And when you think about it, 1 isn't really a number; it doesn't multiply into anything, it cannot be divided, it cannot change. It just *is*. So it's appropriate to God, the One Who Is. The Apocalypse simply says, "upon the throne One was sitting," as if it were a proper name. But you can't do much with it in art, because nobody will notice the number of a single thing.

But 2 sets up a kind of tension, because it contains a double unity. In art as in Scripture, opposites run in pairs: day and night, Sun and Moon, good and evil.

And 3 stands for everything that is perfect. The third unit, in Hebrew, Greek, and Christian thought, unites the halves of 2 and reconciles any tension implied; it brings things to a finish, to completion, to perfection. Referring to the number 3 is a way of expressing, for example, the truth that the Holy Spirit "proceeds from the Father and the Son", completing the Trinity.

So when you have three of anything, you have all there is, or at least enough: that's why we say, "Holy, holy, holy"—thrice holy is as holy as anything can be. That's why we always put three Wise Men in manger scenes—the Bible doesn't say how many there really were, but if you show three, then all civilized persons will understand that enough Magi came, and by extension that all Wise Men, all Gentiles who seek him, will recognize Christ.

The significance of the number 3 is why Christ was three days in the tomb: he was there enough time. In the early Church, they used to submerge you in the baptismal water three times—you'd been washed enough, you see. And the significance of 3, more than any other number's, is all around us in our culture. That's why people are forever getting three wishes in fairy stories; that's enough. And it's why we give people three cheers—we've given them all possible cheers, or, at least, enough cheers. This meaning of 3 is even fossilized in some languages: in French and in Latin, the very word for "three" means "very" or "superlatively"—as in *très bon*, "very good," or *ter felix*, "very happy."

The number 3, with all its symbolism, pervades Christian literature and thought just as it pervades our languages. Early Christian and medieval philosophers were forever finding groups of three things: faith, hope, and charity; reason, will, and memory; body, mind, and spirit; the law of Moses, of the prophets, and of the Gospels; and on and on and on. St. Bonaventure's great work on the spiritual life, significantly titled *The Threefold Path*, takes its whole structure from 3. Bonaventure starts out by saying that the teachings of the Bible reflect the Trinity because they have a three-fold meaning, and you have to understand each of them in a certain way: morally, allegorically, or anagogically.*

"But this triple understanding is the counterpart of a threefold hierarchical act," by which, Bonaventure says, you reach spiritual perfection, "to wit: purgation, illumination, and perfection." This triple nature of Scripture and of the attributes of a well-ordered soul also correspond, in his view of things, with the three basic aspects of beatitude: peace, truth, and charity.

So, he concludes, "there is a threefold manner of exercising oneself in this triple way, namely by reading, by praying, and by contemplating." The rest of his book has three main divisions, one for each of these activities, and each part is subdivided into three again, one part for purgation, another for illumination, and a third for perfection. (Note that he works this out so that it adds up to nine sections, which we'll get to in a minute.)

Another number of completeness is 4, but it carries the connotation of more stability than the rather enthusiastic "enough-ness" of 3. There are four seasons to a year and, in classical thought, four elements that make up the material universe (fire, water, earth, and air). Four evangelists told the whole story of Christ and everything we need for salvation. The Church divides Advent into four weeks, marked with four candles, because with the coming of Christ the cycle of times is brought to completeness. Sometimes the halo shown on Christ's head contains a four-armed cross, but that's not a reference to the Passion. It means that Christ, uniquely, is a complete being, God as well as a man.

You don't see many references to the number 5 in Scripture or in Christian art. It's a naughty number, believe it or not. We have five senses, and it's through our senses that we're led to temptation. Hugh of St. Victor said it best in the twelfth century; he noted that, because of this, "the number 5 naturally represents natural men, who . . . pursue and love things that minister to the delight of their outward senses, since they do not know what spiritual delight means." And in fact it has a more explicit symbolism that

---

*Which incidentally makes this a great book to read in case you ever start taking the Bible too literally.

you can't put in a general-readership book like this.* So much for 5.

By contrast, 6 is another perfect number—twice as perfect, some philosophers said, as 3. Six can be divided only by 1, 2, and 3, and the sum of these divisors is—6! Gematrists and ancient geometers found this very impressive. They used to meditate for hours on 6. Mathematically, no other number is so self-contained as 6 until you reach 33,550,336, and nobody can sit around contemplating the perfection of 33,550,336. But everybody admired the perfection of 6, its symmetry within itself, which is probably why Genesis tells us that all of creation was accomplished in six days. "Six days shalt thou labor"—time enough to bring your work to perfection.

In art, you often find 6 where the idea of perfection comes through. For most of the Middle Ages, for example, chalices were made with six sides, to reflect the perfection of the Sacrament within. And the little canopy over the tomb in the Church of the Holy Sepulchre stands on six marble columns.

Seven of anything makes a complete series: days in a week, for instance; the Seven Gifts of the Holy Spirit—often represented by seven tongues of fire on Pentecost banners and vestments—the seven sacraments; the Seven Virtues; or the Seven Deadly Sins. There are seven petitions in the Lord's Prayer—a complete series of petitions. There were seven liberal arts (Grammar, Rhetoric, Logic, Arithmetic, Geometry, Astronomy, and Music) that, then as now, made up a complete course of gentlefolk's education. While western Christians were producing most of our traditional art, there were seven known planets (Mercury, Venus, Mars, Jupiter, Saturn, the Sun, and the Moon) and seven colors in the spectrum, which reinforced the idea of seven as a complete series, as every possible option. "The just man," says Sirach, "stumbles seven times a day"— that is, in every way possible, you're tempted. This is why people always feel compelled to make a list of exactly seven Wonders of the World. And it's why, under civil law, you can be declared dead if no one has seen or heard from you for seven years; the seventh

---

*Well, all right—it has (if you show it as four dots in a square and one in the middle) four extremities, like a man, and a "generative middle part".

year closes the complete set, and your time can be considered finished.

The number 8, as 7 plus 1, represents the beginning of a new series or a new phase. The moon's phases last seven days, and a new one begins on the eighth day. That's why Jewish babies are named on the eighth day after birth, to mark the beginning of their new identity, and why, customarily, we put eight sides on a baptismal font—to refer to the new life we get from baptism.

The number 9 is 3 times 3, so 9 is symbolic of perfection multiplied by perfection. Nine doesn't show up much in the arts or in Scripture, but it was of the utmost importance during the three or four thousand years that number games were a serious branch of philosophy. That's why St. Bonaventure structured his treatise on the perfection of the soul in nine parts. St. Thomas Aquinas, sifting through the Bible and patristic writings, said that "in the hierarchy of angels, orders can be distinguished according to their acts and offices; and all of this diversity reduces to three, to wit: highest, medium, and lower. And, in this hierarchy, Dionysus in his *Celestial Hierarchy* puts three orders, thus: Seraphim, Cherubim, and Thrones in the first, Dominations, Virtues, and Powers in the second, and Principalities, Archangels, and Angels in the third"—so it comes out to 3 times 3 again. Most astronomers took it for granted that there were nine crystalline spheres above the sky that made up the universe—one for each of the seven planets, one for the stars, and the last and largest spun around by the angels to keep the others moving.

Sometimes you'll encounter 9 used as a numerical symbol of completeness because it marks the term of pregnancy, but most ancient cultures used lunar calendars and therefore reckoned the time as ten months, as in Wisdom 7:2. The number of the Commandments, 10, and 11 are other numbers you probably won't encounter too much in the arts, but when we reach 12 things get interesting again.

The number 12 indicates a complete cycle, as distinct from a complete series like 7. It doubles the perfection of 6, and it occurs importantly in nature. The signs of the Zodiac, perfectly proper symbols for Christian art, mark the twelve months, the twelve moons that make up a solar year. Because of this, 12 signifies a universal completeness: if you have twelve of anything, you have all of it that there is in the world bounded by the band of the Zodiac. All Israel was composed of twelve tribes; Solomon appointed twelve governors over his empire; and Christ covered the Earth with twelve Apostles. Their number, in fact, has been taken as evidence that Christ meant for all humanity to be included in his Church.

After 12, numbers tend to get complicated, because they are all written in more than one digit, and if you're going to add up letters for meanings you generally take them one at a time. But 22 is a special number because it's the number of letters in the Hebrew alphabet, and, since the Old Testament conveys all that God revealed to the Jews by variously combining those letters, 22 signifies the whole story, everything that exists. Isidore of Seville, a Christian patriarch of the seventh century, classified all of creation into twenty-two sorts of things, and he worked out a schedule fitting them into the six days of creation.

Naturally, it's hard to use a large number like 22 meaningfully in visual art, but note that Revelation is divided into twenty-two chapters, and that there are twenty-two books in Augustine's *Confessions*. So intent were some Jews to make all Scripture fit this pattern that some combined Ruth with Judges and Lamentations with Jeremiah, to reduce the twenty-four books of the Old Testament to a more symbolic twenty-two.

The best number of all, really, is 40. It means eternity. Or, sometimes, everlasting time, or all the time that there is. Many eastern churches have forty little windows in the circumference of their domes, to show that the domes represent the everlasting heavens. The Jews reckoned that if you fast forty days, you've fasted long enough to atone for all your sins; forty days of rain is enough to wipe out everything on Earth. This is distinct from 3, and from 6, which also mean enough time, but in different ways; 40 bears the connotation of forever, of permanence, of completeness. If Christ had been in the tomb forty days, that would have meant that he'd be gone until all possible time was gone. But staying dead three days is staying dead enough days; by staying with us in his human body for forty days after the Resurrection, he showed us that he'd be with us forever.

The ways that you manipulate numbers bear symbolism, too. For instance, St. Augustine points out that multiplying a number by itself is intended to expand its meaning, to emphasize it, which is why 9 is seen mostly not as an entity in itself but as 3 times 3, enough times enough. By this line of reasoning, if 12 is the totality of a thing, 12 times 12 is the total total—everything or everybody. Multiplying a number by 10, or by 100, or by 1,000 stresses its primary meaning all that much more. That's why, as Augustine says, the hundred and forty-four thousand saints mentioned in Revelation 7:4 signify the complete totality of saints, an innumerable host of totality times totality times a thousand. Nobody was ever supposed to take the tally literally, as if only that many people out of all the billions who have ever lived will get to Heaven.

It's through this kind of number-play that our ancestors took intellectual hold of the world and broke it down conceptually into meaningful patterns. And remember that, in Scripture, God himself speaks in these terms, to help us catch on. The next time you read through the Bible, take careful note of the numbers you find. Remember that most of them are lost when Greek and Hebrew are translated into English or even Latin, but Exodus, Leviticus, Daniel, and Revelation still contain lots of very intriguing number-puzzles.

IF YOU'D LIKE
TO KNOW MORE

E VEN IF YOU'RE NOT particularly interested in religion, all of
our philosophy, music, architecture, sculpture, painting, literature, and everything else that makes this life livable is,
basically, a by-product of the Church's activity. In fact, the only
constant in western culture is that we have a Church that is indefectible and that happens to cultivate the arts of civilization. Wherever you start looking, you end up at the Church, so it's really
easier to just start there in the first place, whatever your interest.

The best place to get good, reliable information about the
Church is at your local parish. To find it, you can call the bishop's
office, which is probably listed in the phone book under "Diocese
of" whatever big city you're near, or maybe "Archdiocese of";
sometimes it's under "*Catholic* Diocese of". Or you can look
under "Saint", which is how most parish churches' names begin.

Ask about R.C.I.A. That stands for *Rite of Christian Initiation of
Adults*. It's a program that runs classes for those who are seeking to
enter the Church, or who just want to know more about it—
there's no pressure to join if you take the classes. Usually, classes
are somewhat informal; you can ask whatever you want to know,
and, within the bounds of common courtesy and limited sched-

ules, debate opinions. But chiefly, the classes are in business to help you get the information you want.

If you want to do some more reading, every major city has a catholic university, and every university has at least one bookstore; mail order is available across the country. But you have to be careful in selecting your books. Some authors outside the Church—and some few inside—may write books that claim to give accurate information about the Church but don't. Check for the following notations on the copyright page.

Nihil Obstat is the Latin for "nothing obstructs [publication]". It's an official certification given by the diocese's *Censor Librorum* ("Reviewer of Books") that means that he's found no statement contrary to the Church's teachings. After that review, the manuscript goes to the competent ecclesiastical authority, usually the local bishop, for permission to be printed. If he approves publication, the book gets an additional notation: *Imprimatur*, which means "Let it be printed".

The *nihil obstat* and *imprimatur* are official declarations that a book or pamphlet is free from doctrinal error, but the officials who review it and permit publication may still disagree with its contents. This qualification means that even books of speculative theology can be published, but it also means that approved books can contradict each other flatly, on matters other than faith and morals. On matters outside the deposit of faith, there's always room for opinion and debate.

If the book is written by a member of the regular clergy, the order might require, as part of their regular vow of obedience, the extra certification *Imprimi Potest*. This means "It can be printed". It shows that the order's authorities gave permission for the author to write the book.

So, when you read books about things related to the Church, tread very, very carefully; you can pick up false or worthless ideas, or even harmful ones, if you're not well grounded in the theology of such matters. Don't go by only one book on this kind of subject. Read enough, and ask questions of competent authorities, so that you can approach each case with some degree of informed judgement.

The following publications are good general reading. They give wider information about lots of subjects that couldn't be addressed fully here. You should be able to find them all at religious bookstores (or even at regular ones) or at your local library.

Abbott, Walter M., S.J., editor. *The Documents of Vatican II.* Chicago, 1966. A real eye-opener.

Aladel, Rev. Jean-Marie. *The Miraculous Medal: Its Origin, History, Circulation, and Results.* Baltimore, 1881 (still in print). By St. Catherine Labouré's confessor, the man who brought the devotion out of the convent into the world.

St. Alphonsus de Liguori. *The Passion and Death of Jesus Christ.* A powerful meditational text for the devotion of the Stations of the Cross.

Annuario Pontificio. Libreria Editrice Vaticana, yearly. If you want to know every detail of how the Church is organized, complete with names and addresses, this chunky little two-thousand-page tome is full of information. It's in Italian, but it's full of information.

Association of the Miraculous Medal, Saint Mary's Seminary, 1811 West Saint Joseph Street, Perryville, Missouri 63775, maintains a mailing list of persons enrolled in, or interested in, the Medal and associated devotions, and they can supply books and pamphlets, as well as regulation medals.

Belloc, Hilaire. *The Crisis of Civilization.* Shows the formative role of the Church in the history of western culture. You might also want to look at his *How the Reformation Happened, Characters of the Reformation,* and *The Great Heresies.* A liberal member of Parliament, Belloc (1870–1953) was a brilliant advocate of social justice, long before it was fashionable. He wrote more than one hundred books—political tracts, biographies, histories, travel books, comic verse, novels, and horribly clever children's books—all of them worth reading; they were published in the 1920s and 30s, mostly, but many of them are still in print.

St. Benedict of Nursia. *The Rule of St. Benedict.* Monte Cassino, c. 520 (still in print). The best book ever written on the management of a family, or of a business, proven by more than fourteen centuries of worldwide success.

St. Charles (Carlo) Borromeo. *Instructions for the Building of*

Churches (Instructiones Fabricæ Ecclesiasticæ). This is an excerpt from the *Acta Ecclesiæ Medialanensis*—the ordinary administrative archive of his Archdiocese of Milan—first published in 1599. It compiles almost all of the scattered regulations on church building that were in effect from the Council of Trent until the Second Vatican Council. The book itself never had the force of law, but no other had such a strong influence on church architecture. It's available in many editions and in at least one good English translation: Wigley, George J., M.R.I.B.A., *St. Charles Borromeo's Instructions on Ecclesiastical Building* (London, 1857).

Boyer, Paul. *When Time Shall Be No More: Prophecy Belief in Modern American Culture.* New York, 1992. This book doesn't address the Church directly, but it's one of the best available maps of the culture in which she is so often misunderstood.

Butler, Rev. Alban. *The Lives of the Fathers, Martyrs, and other Principal Saints.* 12 vols. Dublin, 1779 (still in print). "You lay down Butler with a sweet and tranquil devotion, and with a profound admiration for the Christian heroes whose lives he records," said Cardinal Gibbons. But then he apparently had enough willpower to lay it down.

Cassiodorus Senator. *Institutes.* This contains the complete course of study that he distilled from classical Rome to hand on to us through the monks. Every time schools listen to him, we have a Renaissance.

Catechism of the Catholic Church. This was officially promulgated in Rome, in December 1992, as the first universal catechism in four hundred years. It covers what the Church teaches and celebrates, as well as how she lives and how she prays.

Code of Canon Law: A Text and Commentary (English translation of the *Codex Iuris Canonici auctoritate Ioannis Pauli PP. II promulgatus,* 1983, which is published in Latin by the Libreria Editrice Vaticana; this study edition, commissioned by the Canon Law Society of America, is edited by Coriden, Green, and Heintschel; Mahwah, N.J., 1985). You'll learn a lot from this, but don't interpret the regulations without expert consultation here, any more than you'd start a civil lawsuit without a lawyer.

St. Claude de la Colombière. *The Devotion to the Sacred Heart.* 1691 (still in print). This is a good introduction to the ways these devotions get started, their rationale and practices, obstacles to their approbation, and so on. It was written by the spiritual director of St. Margaret Mary Alacoque, the nun who had the visions that initiated the devotion.

Coriden, James A. *An Introduction to Canon Law*. Mahwah, N.J., 1991. This little book opens the subtlety of canon law to the lay reader and brings the deep and ancient treasure of its thought into focus. Certainly one of the best on the subject.

Dawson, Christopher. *Religion and the Rise of Western Culture*. New York, 1957. "Unless we read this," said one reviewer, "we are uninformed." He was right.

Englebert, Omer. *Catherine Labouré and the Modern Apparitions of the Virgin*. New York, 1959. Includes accounts of several apparitions that you don't hear enough about these days, like the one at Pontmain.

St. François de Sales. *The Catholic Controversy*. St. François was sent down to the Chablais region of France, where 72,000 people had converted to Calvinism some sixty years before. In four years, he converted them all back, and this book shows how he did it.

Gibbons, James Cardinal. *The Faith of Our Fathers*. Baltimore, 1876 (still in print). Old but good. Very, very good.

Hardon, John A., S.J. *The Catholic Catechism*. Des Plaines, Ill., 1981. This is a great book for looking things up. Quoting the Bible, early Christian writings, and modern documents, it gives detailed accounts of the histories of the Church's rulings and teachings on matters as diverse as contraception, superstition, sacraments, and devotion to the saints, all packed into six hundred pages of prose that makes you understand what they say about the quality of Jesuit education. If you don't want to know quite that much about things, there's his *The Pocket Catholic Catechism*, 1988, a much briefer version of the above; a handy reference, and still full of insight.

St. Ignatius of Loyola. *The Spiritual Exercises of St. Ignatius: A Literal Translation and a Contemporary Reading*. The edition by David L. Fleming, S.J., from the Institute of Jesuit Sources, 3700 West Pine Boulevard, St. Louis, Missouri 63108, presents this great classic of meditational literature in a form that lets you get the fullest meaning out of it.

Jacobus da Voragine. *The Golden Legend.* The excerpts from the *Legend* used here—the story of St. Christopher in chapter 5—were compounded from some French and Latin editions more than a hundred and fifty years old, thereby cleverly sidestepping all of those tiresome copyright restrictions. But there are plenty of more recent editions in English, and you should have one. This is the source for all of the standard stories about familiar saints like Valentine and Patrick, and it tells you about more obscure luminaries, too, like St. Wolfgang and St. Arsenio. The poem by Longfellow that goes by the same title, which was set to music by Sir Arthur Sullivan, has nothing to do with this book, by the way.

Jungmann, Josef Andreas. *The Mass: An Historical, Theological, and Pastoral Survey.* Collegeville, Minn., 1976. The last work of a true giant among scholars, the man who advised Vatican II on liturgical matters. If you're ready to dive into deeper waters, check out his *The Mass of the Roman Rite: Its Origins and Development* (New York, 1951).

Jurgens, William A. *The Faith of the Early Fathers.* Collegeville, Minn., 1970. This is another highly addictive work. It's made up of excerpts of Christian teachings, starting with the first century. All of the great lights are well represented, but it's much more entertaining than you'd expect—you'll enjoy rummaging through the *Medicine Chest Against Heresies*, written by Epiphanius of Salamis, and browsing in the *Wisdom of the Elders of Ethiopia.* And you can find out all about the early Christian writer whose habit of grunting and snorting during sermons made Jerome nickname him Piggy. But it's scholarly and accurate throughout, and it has a topical index so that you can easily trace the continuity of teachings through time, which makes it a dynamite gift for any fervent adherent of a separated sect that you might know.

Deferrari, Roy Joseph, ed. *The Fathers of the Church.* Washington, D.C., Catholic University Press. This comprehensive series gives new and highly readable translations of more patristic writing than you'd think existed.

Hoffman, Elizabeth, ed. *The Liturgy Documents: A Parish Resource.* Chicago, Ill., 1991. A fascinating collection of excerpts from official rubrics, with guides and explanations. It's full of elusive information like what the guidelines are for women's liturgical ministry, what direction you can give an architect designing a new church, and how to manage a Mass for children. It also puts you in the know on some of the finer points of liturgical etiquette, like what the two kinds of bow are, when to bow, and to what, and it settles burning questions like exactly how you're supposed to hold a censer.

St. John of the Cross. *The Collected Works of St. John of the Cross.* Translated by Kavanaugh and Rodriguez. Washington, D.C., 1979. If any one person epitomizes the Church's attitudes about texts and images, signs and wonders, it's San Juan de la Cruz (1542–1591). When he saw a particularly beautiful statue of the Virgin, he exclaimed how happy he would be to live in a desert with only that to look at. But he also spent every possible hour closeted with his Bible, and he just stayed there with it when all of the other monks ran off to town to see a reported stigmatic. He and his friend St. Teresa of Avila (see below, under "Teresa") made the techniques of prayer—which is, after all, a skill— accessible through their books, down-to-Earth manuals about how a soul can ascend to God.

Keating, Karl. *Catholicism and Fundamentalism.* San Francisco, 1988. A useful resource if you want to sort out culture and religion in America.

Knox, Ronald. *Enthusiasm.* Oxford, 1961. Required reading for anyone who has a religion or is thinking of getting one.

Le Bec, E. *Medical Proofs of the Miraculous: A Clinical Study.* London, n.d. This is apparently from the early years of this century. A little dated, maybe, but nobody would let you publish photos like those nowadays.

Migne, Jacques-Paul. *Patrologiæ cursus completus, Series græca.* 161 vols. Paris, 1857–1866; and *Patrologiæ cursus completus, Series latina.* 221 vols. Paris, 1844–1855. Migne was a little French priest who got fed up trying to track down some quote or other from one of the Fathers of the Church. So he founded a publishing company to put out standard, complete editions of all known patristic writings. Over the next thirty years, his Imprimerie Catholique published nearly eight hundred huge volumes of early Christian texts—more than two a month, on average, each bristling with scholarly footnotes and indexed every which way. There were some misprints, of course, but, considering how quickly he produced everything, the achievement is astounding. And we certainly wouldn't have so many really good editions now without Migne's as a starting place; he boosted scholarship into a quantum leap. Everybody assumes that you're familiar with these two major series of Greek and Latin patrology; in scholarly works they're usually referenced simply as *PG* and *PL*, or just as "Migne". You can find them in any large public or university library, and on microfiche, too. It's worth learning Latin (and probably even Greek) just to browse through them, but if you'd rather not, see Jurgens, *The Faith of the Early Fathers*, listed above, which is in English. (There's also the *Enchiridion patristicum* by M. J. Rouët de Journel, which is simple in arrangement but kept in Greek and Latin.)

Mitford, Jessica. *The American Way of Death*. New York, 1963. Examines the history and practices of the American funeral industry. Read it anyway.

Nardone, Richard. *The Story of the Christian Year*. Paulist Press, 1991. A comprehensible account of that most ornate of sciences, calendrics.

Nevins, Albert J., M.M. *Answering a Fundamentalist*. Huntington, Ind., 1990. Clears up a lot of common misunderstandings about the Church's teachings and practices in an easy and very readable style.

Pastor, Ludwig Friedrich August, Freiherr von Camperfelden. *Geschichte der päpste seit dem Ausgang des Mittelalters*. 16 vols. Freiburg in Breisgau, 1901. Only kidding. Look for this under the listing Pastor, Ludwig, *The History of the Popes*, which is a translation of this monument of German scholarship.

St. Teresa of Avila. *Collected Works* Translated by Kavanaugh and Rodriguez. Washington, D.C., 1987. Like her friend St. John of the Cross (see above), St. Teresa was austere in personal habits and strict in administration, but brilliantly funny and immensely kind, too. Both had really spectacular spiritual gifts (documented ecstasies, visions, levitation) that made it through the constraints of their superiors and the Inquisition at its worst, to say nothing of their own modesty, and they articulated the goals and mechanisms of Christian mysticism with unsurpassed clarity. St. Teresa wrote exactly as she spoke, and reading her books makes you sorry that you missed her conversation. Most important, though, you can see in her works how a soul can draw nearer to God in a particularly personal, intimate way. If you've ever been beguiled by reports of oriental mysticism, you owe it to yourself to read the works of these two Doctors of the Church.

Thomas à Kempis. *The Imitation of Christ.* A steady best-seller since it appeared in 1471, it stands second only to the Bible in its universal appeal, some say. Even John Wesley, the founder of Methodism, liked it. ("A person will never be satisfied with *The Imitation*, though it were read a thousand times over; for those general principles are the seeds of meditation, and the stores they contain are never exhausted," he said.) But he only used one of the many Protestant editions that carefully cut out any and all allusions to the Church's doctrine. So accept no *Imitation* until you're sure it's the real thing.

St. Thomas Aquinas. *Summa Theologia.* St. Thomas was the one who figured out a lot of things about grace and angels, humanity, and everything else that's still taught (and still debated). The original comes in Latin, but there are plenty of translations, abridgements, digests, abstracts, and summaries of the *Summa* available.

Your Rosary Booklet. Franciscan Mission Associates, Box 598, Mount Vernon, New York 10551. An excellent guide to this devotion. You can send for it, and you can enclose a little donation to feed and educate people who urgently need help.

Periodicals

There are countless newspapers and magazines about the Church and Church-related matters. Almost every diocese runs its own newspaper, and if you're registered in your parish you should be getting one, free or at a nominal cost. Probably the largest

Church-related magazine in circulation is *Catholic Digest* (Box 64090, St. Paul, Minnesota 55164). The oldest in continuous publication is *The Josephite Harvest* (1130 North Calvert Street, Baltimore, Maryland 21202), which is the publication of the only American congregation of priests exclusively devoted to the evangelization of blacks. *The Catholic Answer* (200 Noll Plaza, Huntington, Indiana 46750) is a monthly magazine that examines questions like those addressed in this book. Check your local library for other periodicals that might target your exact area of interest.

INDEX

death (cont)
  Christian practices surrounding, 87–90,
    172, 182
  grief and, 87
  secular attitudes toward, 85–87
debt, interest on, 12–13
Decree on Ecumenism, 131
Decree on the Apostolate of the Laity, 131
Decree on the Catholic Eastern Churches, 82
Decree on the Missionary Activity of the Church,
  83
"Decretal of Gelasius," 23
decretals, 17–18, 23, 114
Dedication of a Church and an Altar, 168n
della Porta, Giacomo, 198
Denis, Saint, 106, 264
Desprez, Josquin, 250
Deuteronomy, Book of, 29
devil, 40, 44, 48–49, 151
devil's advocate, 146–47
Diego, Juan, 153, 163
dioceses, 123–24, 136, 169
Diocletian, Emperor of Rome, 23, 123, 188
Dionysius the Areopagite, 106, 264
Dionysus, cult of, 247–48
Dismas, Saint, 39
Divine Office, 98
Dominic, Saint, 42, 101
Dominican order, 96
dos Santos, Lucía, 52

Easter, 5, 17, 60, 81–82, 83, 84, 91, 182, 210
ecumenism, 3n, 17, 82, 161–63, 197
Egypt, 6, 30, 79, 106, 138, 186, 218, 223–24,
  229, 254
Eight Books of Miracles (Gregory of Tours), 42
Einstein, Albert, 255
Elias, 144, 154, 254
Elizabeth, Saint, 71, 99
Elizabeth I, Queen of England, 26, 230–31
Enchiridion of Indulgences, 94–95
England, xiv, 46, 97, 111, 112
Ennodius of Pavia, Bishop, 231
Environment and Art in Catholic Worship, 168n
Epiphanius, 9
Epiphany, 80
Episcopal Church, xv
Epistles, 58n, 62
  of James, 23
  of John, 21n, 23
  of Jude, 21n, 23
  of Peter, 21n, 23
Epistles of Paul, 5–6, 16, 17, 20, 22
  to the Corinthians, 23
  to the Ephesians, 21n, 226
  to the Hebrews, 23, 25n, 71, 73
  to Philemon, 21n, 23
  to the Philippians, 21n, 183
  to the Romans, 23, 221
  to Titus, 21n
Ethiopia, 106
Eucharist, 10, 16, 17, 20, 47, 73, 74, 106,
  108, 123, 128, 204
  Christ's presence in, 57–59, 67–68, 71,
    187, 190
  distribution of, 128, 170

establishment of, 57–59, 64, 69–70, 71n,
  74, 190, 214
Liturgy of, 58–59, 60, 64–68
reception of, 67–68, 91, 114, 170, 171,
  189–91, 220
transubstantiation of, 59, 66
vessels for, 181, 187–91
Eucharistic Prayer, 66
Eulalia, Saint, 100
Eutychians, 58n
Evangelists, 4–5, 58n, 183
Eve, see Adam and Eve
excommunication, 52
Exodus, Book of, 29, 71, 266
Exposition of the Blessed Sacrament, 191
Ezekiel, 75–76
Ezra, 29

Faith, 3–54
  basic tenets of, xiv, 111n
  deposit of, 16, 163
  good works and, 48–49
  theological vs. fiducial, 111n
faith and morals, 9, 16, 111
  infallibility and, 112–15
  regulations on, 13, 15, 16, 18, 35, 111–15,
    132
fasting, 16, 41, 50, 67, 139, 216, 254
Fathers of the Church, 8–10, 36, 42, 52, 53,
  58n, 77, 113n, 133, 160, 199, 204, 221,
  248–49
Fátima, 52, 101–2, 154, 156, 21
Feast of the Holy Cross, 212
Feast of the Purification of the Virgin, 231
Felix III, Pope Saint, 125
Firmilian, Bishop of Caesarea, 116
First Communion, 67, 217n
First Rising Mt. Zion Baptist Church, xvn
Four Books of Architecture (Palladio), 175
France, xiv, 15, 59, 106, 142n, 188, 211
Frances Xavier Cabrini, Saint, 146, 203
Franciscan order, xiii-xiv, 93–94, 107, 143,
  178, 234
Francis of Assisi, Saint, xiii, 145, 234
frankincense, 223–27
free will, 44
French Revolution, 107, 191, 192
funerals, 86–90, 123, 134, 169, 182, 222n,
  228
  Christian practices of, 87–90
  preplanning of, 89–90

Gabriel, Saint, 14, 98, 151
Gabrieli, Andrea, 250
Gaguin, Robert, 113n
Gandhi, Mohandas K. "Mahatma," 255
Garden Tomb, 92
Gaudete Sunday, 183–84
gay lifestyle, 132–33
Gelasius I, Pope Saint, 111n, 231
General Instruction of the Roman Missal, 168n
Genesis, Book of, 29, 46, 48, 74, 235, 257,
  263
genuflection, 98, 155, 162, 216
geometry, 249, 250, 255, 257, 263
Germain of Constantinople, Saint, 113n

ABOUT THE AUTHOR

KEVIN ORLIN JOHNSON holds a doctorate in the history of art, with a specialty in seventeenth-century church architecture in France and Italy. His scholarly publications appear in journals in Vienna, Rome, Paris, and elsewhere, and he is currently working on a monograph about the Dome of the Invalides in Paris. For many years he wrote a column, "Signs of Faith," syndicated in diocesan newspapers across the country, on which this book is based in part. Now a resident of Dallas, he frequently speaks to civic and religious groups interested in the meaning and purpose of public art and architecture.